MY
HOME
TEAM

MY HOME TEAM

A Sportswriter's Life and the Redemptive Power of Small-Town Girls Basketball

DAVE KINDRED

PUBLICAFFAIRS

New York

PublicAffairs
Hachette Book Group
1290 Avenue of the Americas, New York, NY 10104
www.publicaffairsbooks.com
@Public_Affairs

Printed in the United States of America

First Edition: September 2023

Published by PublicAffairs, an imprint of Perseus Books, LLC, a subsidiary of Hachette Book Group, Inc. The PublicAffairs name and logo is a trademark of the Hachette Book Group.

The Hachette Speakers Bureau provides a wide range of authors for speaking events. To find out more, go to www.hachettespeakersbureau.com or email HachetteSpeakers@hbgusa.com.

PublicAffairs books may be purchased in bulk for business, educational, or promotional use. For more information, please contact your local bookseller or the Hachette Book Group Special Markets Department at special.markets@hbgusa.com.

The publisher is not responsible for websites (or their content) that are not owned by the publisher.

Print book interior design by Amy Quinn.

Library of Congress Cataloging-in-Publication Data

Names: Kindred, Dave, author.
Title: My home team: a sportswriter's life and the redemptive power of small-town girls basketball / Dave Kindred.
Description: First edition. | New York, NY: PublicAffairs, 2023.
Identifiers: LCCN 2023018297 | ISBN 9781541702202 (hardcover) | ISBN 9781541702226 (ebook)
Subjects: LCSH: Kindred, Dave. | Sportswriters—United States—Biography. | Basketball for girls—Illinois. | High school athletes—Illinois. | Women basketball players—Illinois.
Classification: LCC GV742.42.K553 A3 2023 | DDC 070.4/49796—dc23/eng/20230419
LC record available at https://lccn.loc.gov/2023018297

ISBNs: 9781541702202 (hardcover), 9781541702226 (ebook)

LSC-C

Printing 1, 2023

For Cheryl, forever and a day

If you want to write, if you want to create, you must be the most sublime fool that God ever turned out and sent rambling. You must write every single day of your life. You must read dreadful dumb books and glorious books, and let them wrestle in beautiful fights inside your head, vulgar one moment, brilliant the next. You must lurk in libraries and climb the stacks like ladders to sniff books like perfumes and wear books like hats upon your crazy heads. I wish you a wrestling match with your Creative Muse that will last a lifetime. I wish craziness and foolishness and madness upon you. May you live with hysteria, and out of it make fine stories—science fiction or otherwise. Which finally means, may you be in love every day for the next 20,000 days. And out of that love, remake a world.

—*Ray Bradbury*

If you have any young friends who aspire to become writers, the second greatest favor you can do them is to present them with copies of *The Elements of Style*. The first greatest, of course, is to shoot them now, while they're happy.

—*Dorothy Parker*

INTRODUCTION

● ●

I N A TIME OF MIDLIFE CONFUSION, I IMAGINED BEING THE EDITOR OF A newspaper. Ben Bradlee was the model, once a foreign correspondent, a handsome devil, profane and provocative, the leader of a newspaper uncovering low doings in high places. Other sportswriters had risen to the top. Joe McGuff did it in Kansas City, Bill Millsaps in Richmond. James Reston of the *New York Times* was a sportswriter before he became an oracle in the swampland around the nation's capital.

I whispered my secret ambition to a friend. He was aghast. He said, "Why would you take a demotion?"

I admit, the man had a point. Only a fool would ask for an end to all the fun in a sportswriter's life. They pay you to go to games. Even better, if you like to write, they pay you for that, too. And hot dogs! Press boxes have long kept the hot dog industry in business. Of course, it was also true that no owner of a newspaper ever looked upon my wardrobe of mustard-stained golf shirts and thought I might be a corporate chieftain fit to run his money machine.

So here I am, a sportswriter. I came from small-town America to work for great newspapers and magazines. (Ben Bradlee's, for one.) Then, after five or six decades at it, I closed the circle by returning to

1

Illinois. I thought my typing days were over. Instead, one happy thing led to another, and I found myself having fun again, this time writing about a girls high school basketball team. This takes some explaining.

It is a three-act story. In Act One, Muhammad Ali, the greatest of all time, is a constant presence, our lives moving in tandem from youth to old age. There are Super Bowls, World Series, Olympics, a movie goddess, terrorists, a bomb, a libel suit, and a trip around the world playing golf in twenty-two countries on four continents, last at Pebble Beach and Augusta National. A friend eaten up with envy spoke of that trip as "the mother of all boondoggles." My traveling partner, Tom Callahan, said, "We prefer to think of it as a calling from God."

In Act Two, at an age when most people know better than to start over, I start over. I go back to those small Illinois towns, into those little gyms surrounded by cornfields. I get lucky with Morton High School's Lady Potters. Across a dozen seasons, they win so often with such self-less grace that I call them "the Golden State Warriors, only with pony-tails." Also, when my life turns dark, those girls lead me into light.

Act Three, like all third acts, is a mystery waiting to be solved.

SCENES FROM ACT ONE . . .

- Muhammad Ali was twenty-four; I was twenty-five. He was already a star, known for changing his name from Cassius Clay and beating Sonny Liston. I was new in Louisville, an untested rookie up from the bush leagues and chained to the copy desk. A boss came by and said, "Clay's in town, go find him." For the next fifty years, I hung with Ali in the usual places—at ringsides coast to coast—and in unusual places, including Las Vegas, where he raised the corner of a bedsheet and invited me in to do an interview with, "Louisville, come here." Another time, we went into a forlorn Philadelphia funeral home to see a man who had been shot and killed at an Ali fight. To visit a youth camp in the Pennsylvania mountains, Ali drove, one hand on the wheel, at God only knows what speed, down a skinny, rutted logging road through a forest. I asked, "You ever think of dying?" He said, "You don't ever want to die." I said, "Glad to hear that."

- Terrorists changed the world during the 1972 Olympics in Munich, and I stood below Building 31 watching a killer with a machine gun on patrol outside rooms where Israelis had been murdered. Twenty-four years later, at another Olympics, a bomb exploded in Atlanta. Outside Richard Jewell's apartment, I stood in a parking lot with television crews, staking out the news, Jewell sitting alone in a stairwell, the Olympics security guard first hailed as a hero, then named by the FBI as a suspect, and finally confirmed as a hero.

- On a road trip to do a cover story for a new national sports newspaper, I shadowed Michael Jordan so long he mistook me for an errand boy. "Give these shoes to that kid out there," he told me. I delivered the Air Jordans to a young fan because it was early in the trip and I needed better quotes than that one.

- Martina Navratilova wept when I asked about a grandmother she had left behind in Czechoslovakia. We met the next day to exchange understandings and apologies. She brought along her dog, a Corgi, a tiny beauty she called Killer.

- Speaking of dogs, I hear Ted Williams yet declaiming on a famous pitcher. "And Hoyt Wilhelm's all-time for me.

I'd get up against Hoyt Wilhelm and his first knuckleball, you see it good, but it was moving. The second one, it's moving more and you'd foul it off and you'd say, 'Geez, that's a good knuckleball.' And now he throws you the three-strike knuckleball. It's all over the place, and you're lucky if you don't get hit with it because you don't know where the hell it's going. You could swing at it *AND GET HIT BY IT!*" Seventy-six years old then, his voice that of an enthusiastic, rambunctious kid, Ted Williams heard a dog bark somewhere in the house and called out, "Slugger, where are you? Come here, boy, come here, Slugger." A few things in sports are perfect. Perfect that Ted Williams had a dog named Slugger.

- Secretariat flew down Belmont's back stretch, and the big red colt did what horsemen say the great ones do, only this time this horse was so far beyond great that I swear the trees did sway, or at least bow in admiration.

- That Carlton Fisk home run in the '75 World Series? Past midnight, on deadline, in freezing Fenway Park, on my Smith-Corona portable, I flash-typed a breathless thirty-four words after the baseball crossed over the Green Monster, and I flung the hot copy to a Western Union operator older than my mother.

- I saw the preternatural Tiger Woods win his first Masters in 1997, turning every golfer ever into mere mortals, and twenty-two years later saw him win the Masters a last time, doing it the hard way, as a mortal broken and repaired.

- Pete Rose lied to me. (But then, he lied to everybody.)

From the twentieth century into the twenty-first, Act One played out as a charmed life, as much fun as any sportswriter could hope for.

My wife and I came home after forty-five years gone. We had been high school sweethearts in Atlanta, Illinois, population 1,300, forty miles south of Morton. I had been the nomadic, workaholic sportswriter, and Cheryl, the world champion wife, mother, grandmother, and homemaker. When we returned to Illinois, we found a log cabin in the country and put up a barn for two horses. We had no plans other than to sit on the deck at sunset and watch ducks do splash landings on the pond. It was time to be old marrieds looking forward to winter's snowfalls and spring's flowers.

One day I said, "Want to go to a basketball game?"

"Who's playing?" she said.

"The Lady Potters."

"The lady whos?"

"Potters. Morton used to be big in the pottery world."

We lived a half hour east of Morton, 17,117 people, a small town by most measures, but a metropolis on the rural flatlands of west-central Illinois. It was a cameo brooch of a place that, in a bow to the region's pumpkin farmers, bragged on itself as the Pumpkin Capital of the World. It sat atop a gentle rise east of the Illinois River across from Peoria, the state's second-largest city outside the Chicago landmass.

Three years earlier, I had learned about the Lady Potters in my sister's kitchen. Carly Jean Crocker stood by Sandy's hutch. What a darling Carly was, thirteen years old, blonde and blue-eyed, tall and trim in blue jeans, stylish in a denim jacket and red canvas sneakers. We had known her since she was an infant as cute as she was loud (very). Sandy had been her babysitter from six months on, long enough that Carly called her Grandma.

That day in the kitchen, Sandy, Cheryl, and Carly's mother, Lisa, talked about their school days. Because they all had been cheerleaders, a neighbor said, "Carly, are you going to be a cheerleader, too?"

There was a time in the past—before Title IX mandated equal school facilities for boys and girls in 1972—when that would have been a natural question. But not in the twenty-first century. Carly was an athlete headed for high school and Lady Potters basketball. She rode horses in 4-H competition, played second base in softball, ran cross-country, and went up against neighborhood boys in driveway basketball games.

Hearing the cheerleader question, Carly raised her chin a click.

"No," she said, "I'm going to be the one they cheer for."

She had me at no.

Carly was sixteen when Cheryl and I climbed three rows up in the bleachers at the Morton High School gym, the Potterdome. The game was the first sporting event for which I ever bought a ticket. Though I resisted saying the word, friends counted me as, quote, retired. With newspapers and magazines dying in the Digital Age, there was also the unhappy circumstance of nobody looking to coax geezers out of, quote, retirement. Without a press credential for the first time since I was seventeen, I was an official spectator.

Then this happened. The PA announcer's voice exploded against the Potterdome walls. "AND NOW, YOUR LADY POTTERS!" A dozen girls came streaming onto the court in red-and-white candy-striped warm-ups, wheeling into layup lines that became a kaleidoscope of swirling, dizzying colors. I was not so far removed from a lifetime of sportswriting that I could ignore such a phenomenon. Borrowing a pen that Cheryl found deep in her purse, I scratched a note on a McDonald's bag smeared with ketchup. *Last saw a girls game 1975. Not 1975 anymore.*

The good news, this was fun.

The better news, I wanted to write something. Writers write.

Carly's mother, Lisa, said, "Go talk to Dave Byrne. Over there. He runs the team website."

Byrne was the father of a freshman point guard, Kait Byrne. A big man with the loose-limbed look of an athlete in middle age, he leaned against a stage at one end of the court. I said, "I will be at most games, and I'd write something for your site if you could use it."

Perhaps I had missed my annual haircut. Perhaps my country-farmer blue jeans carried reminders of barn work. Webmaster Byrne later told a WZPN reporter, "This old, disheveled guy came out of the stands and asked if he could help with the website."

He had reason to be amused. He did not know whether I could spell or type, let alone do both. I must have used enough basketball jargon to pass for somebody who knew a back cut when he saw it. He allowed me to keep a measure of dignity by saying, "OK, yeah, sure, but let me run it past the coach first."

The next day, we met the Potters' coach, Bob Becker, at the local Steak 'n Shake. (I had the franchise's famous double steakburger with string fries and a chocolate shake thick enough for a spoon. The straw is mostly decorative.) Becker was forty-one years old and in his tenth season. He had the fresh-faced look of a kid straight out of college. His best team, three years earlier, went 31–3 and finished fourth in the Illinois state tournament.

I knew that much about Becker. He knew nothing about Disheveled Old Guy.

Becker: "Why do you want to do this?"

Me: "It'll be fun."

Becker: "Really?"

Me: "Like, the other night, out of the blue, I wrote a note about how I hadn't seen a girls game in forever."

Becker:

Me: "It would be all new to me, something I've never done."

Becker:

Me: "These fries are good, want some?"

Becker:

Me: "So, you're OK with me doing this?"

Becker: "No second-guessing?"

Me: "I save that for the NFL."

Becker: "OK, I guess, OK for now, we'll see."

For the next Potters game, I slid a Professional Reporter's Notebook into my back pocket and brought along two pens. Big-time publicists delivered play-by-play sheets in the press box. The Potterdome had neither publicists nor a press box. That first time out, I stared at my notebook until ancient muscle memory kicked in and caused me to draw a line down the middle of a page. Morton play-by-play would go on the right, the opponent's on the left. I had done it that way at the Bloomington, Illinois, *Pantagraph*, then a boy reporter eighteen years old, working his way through Illinois Wesleyan University at thirty-five dollars a week.

I was that boy again, now working his way through life.

For a laugh, I reminded Dave Byrne that I had been a professional sportswriter paid for my work. Now I was a senior citizen on a fixed income. He caught my drift. He assessed my talent, experience, good looks, and said, "How about a box of Milk Duds every game?"

I said, "Deal."

Writing for Milk Duds. Perfect.

ACT ONE BEGINS IN ATLANTA, ILLINOIS, AND MOVES TO LOUISVILLE, then Washington, a Virginia farm, Atlanta (the big one in Georgia), and back home.

ACT ONE

1

● ●

I HAD SEEN HER IN FRONT OF THE PALACE, ATLANTA'S LITTLE MOVIE house. Memory is kind if you live long enough, and I remember that night. I was about to put down a quarter for a ticket. Across the street, she stood under a streetlight, the light on her, the light seeming to choose her. I knew her name, Cheryl Liesman, and I knew she was from out of town, from Lincoln, the county seat, and she was someone's steady girl. I went into the movie and never saw her again that night, never thought of her again, never saw her again at all until the second semester of my junior year in high school. There she was in a hallway outside Mrs. Brak's English class, putting her stuff in a locker, suddenly the prettiest girl in school. Cheryl. Her face a doll's, such a smile.

What to say? She didn't know me. I stood at my locker, two down from hers.

"I haven't seen you," I said, "since that night at the movie."

Oh, great. No way that made sense to her.

"You're Dave, aren't you?" she said.

She knew *me*?

We talked and we found seats together in Mrs. Brak's class. She had been a cheerleader at Chester–East Lincoln grade school and had seen my seventh-grade basketball team. Her family had moved to a farm inside Atlanta's school district. I even knew her boyfriend, Teddy, a drummer with his own band. (I knew him as a kid baseball player in Lincoln. Coke-bottle glasses. Could not throw a strike.) She rode to nightclub shows in Teddy's Cadillac. I let time pass before inviting the prettiest girl in school to ride in my '52 Chevy.

She was out of my league and would have remained out of my league except my sister dear, Sandra, noticed all the talking. The junior sock hop was coming up, Sandy said, and I should ask Cheryl to go. I did that brave thing. We danced one dance, maybe two, to a slow Elvis song, maybe Johnny Mathis. I did not die or anything, and one day that next summer she told me she had broken up with Teddy.

"Why?" I said, not caring why that great thing had happened, caring only that we lived in a world where such a great thing could happen.

"He kicked Tuffy," Cheryl said, "and I kicked him out of the house," Tuffy being her Chihuahua, a scrawny, snippy, yapping brat, and you never saw anyone pour more kindness onto a scrawny, snippy, yapping brat than I did on Tuffy that summer we were seventeen.

We must have been news at school, the new girl who became homecoming queen and the shy guy who had been all baseball, basketball, and books. Our senior year we were together in Miss Swinford's English class, Miss Swinford an imperious woman, a classics major in her college days, half-glasses hanging by a shiny ribbon, silver hair gathered in a bun.

As director of our class play, Miss Swinford handed me a script and said, "You'll be Dr. Edward Appleby."

Then she said, "And Cheryl will be Jeannie Peabody."

In Act III, Scene 2 of *It's a Great Life*, the doctor and the beautiful debutante agree to a life together. They bring down the curtain with a kiss. Art as prophecy.

ATLANTA WAS A NO-STOPLIGHT DOT ON THE MAP ALONG US ROUTE 66 midway between Chicago and St. Louis, population 1,300. The business district, what there was of it, was cut into three pieces by 66 and the Illinois Central tracks running parallel through town.

You could have chickens in the yard, pigs in a pen, a cow out back and call yourself a city kid. Mom and Dad did not name the chickens; eggs were delivered anonymously, so no one got too attached to the birds when it came time for Grandma Martha to wring a neck. Mom dipped the remains into boiling water to soften them up for Sunday dinner. She also plucked feathers for pillows. Our three pigs began life as Huey, Dewey, and Louie. The arrival of piglets caused Louie to be renamed Louise. Our cow, Penny, became Atlanta's most famous Guernsey the day she escaped.

My sister was at Deuterman's Café for an after-school Coke when a friend said, "Sandy! Look! Is that your mom chasing that cow?"

Penny had jumped over the pasture fence.

Penny had decided to run away from home.

Penny went clippity-clopping south on First Street along the train tracks, past Schmidt's farm implements office, past the meat locker and city hall, past the fire department, barbershop, and Harris's tavern, about to arrive at the corner drugstore across from the bank next to Paul Ball's hardware store, ker-lumphing past the post office toward Newby's pool hall, where she would have been a sensational interruption of the old boys' card games, mostly poker, sometimes euchre.

Only in Atlanta, Illinois, could there be such a scene, Mom a young woman, thin, strong, and independent, not shy about giving chase to Penny on a downtown street, Mom in her kitchen apron, cursing both the cow and her husband who had been told to make that fence higher because that cow's gonna jump over that fence.

Sandy watched the Penny parade and thought to run from Deuterman's and intercept the Guernsey before it got out of town. She let the thought pass. How Mom corralled Penny, Sandy never knew. She knew only that Mom soon advised Dad to put a rope on that damn cow's neck and attach it to an anvil.

Throwing in a farm animal or two, the Kindreds were a heartland version of America's favorite 1950s family television show, *The Adventures of Ozzie and Harriet*. Our telephone was on a party line (two long rings, one short). Our black-and-white TV came with a roof-top antenna that had to be turned, sometimes by Dad on the roof, toward the transmitting station. In summers, Dad, a carpenter, made $100 a week. In winters, he made nothing, and Mom waited tables at the famous Dixie Truckers Stop, three miles north on 66. She said Louis Armstrong and his jazz band, stopping on trips to and from Chicago, asked for her because no one else would serve African Americans. Our house was a two-story white clapboard built in the early 1900s by a Civil War veteran, a black artillery officer on the Union side, and redone by Dad when he came home from World War II. We were five minutes from every place important—the ball diamond, Newby's, Deuterman's, the Palace movie theater, and the Atlanta school where we did grades 1 through 12, usually with all the same classmates.

Sandy and I walked the half mile to school, first through Faye and Deb's yard (with Sandy snatching onion tops out of the garden for a breakfast snack). We turned left on the dirt street between Grandma Martha's and the Deharts'. The Dehart house used to be a Baptist church led by pastor Daniel Fitch. His daughter, Serena, married Edward Wright, the artillery officer who built our house and left it to a son, Frederick (Buck) Wright, whose estate sold the house in 1945 for $2,400 to his friend and neighbor, Marie Magdalena Maloney Kindred, our mother.

"He was a black man, six feet, six inches tall, a big man," Mom said. "He used to be a policeman in Chicago and then was a Pullman porter on the train to Chicago. He called me 'Miss Marie.' If we had meatloaf, I made meatloaf for him. If we had beans, I fixed him beans. He had nobody at home with him. You were three or four years old, and you took cake up to him, one block up. And you told me, 'Mr. Buck says thank you, Miss Marie, your cake is good.'"

Our route to school took us past Maggie June's, Maggie June a robust woman who wiggled through her front door one body part at a time. Around the corner from Maggie June's, we passed the Christian church and its parsonage, the site of a boy's first heartbreak. We were in the third grade when the pastor's daughter, Luanne, announced that her family was leaving Atlanta for a church in southern Illinois. She promised to write me letters. (I got one.)

Closer to school there was a bad sidewalk with one section that had buckled up over a tree root. Sandy alleged that I ran ahead of her and distracted her from the raised concrete so she would trip and fall and give me reason to laugh. She further alleged that one winter day I rubbed snow on that buckled concrete until it became an off-camber sheet of ice and she would fall in a new and more laughable way. Now, I ask you, would any brother a year older do that to any little sister just for fun?

Next corner up, we could see the school.

Every time, it was thrilling.

Good things happened there. Five days a week for nine months every year from ages six to eighteen, I hurried to get there. Basketball, baseball, books! What more could be better? I first entered that building in 1947, last in 1959, and I can tell you which floorboards squeaked in the big hallway separating classrooms. The school was not only the biggest building in Atlanta; it was one of the wonders of the world.

The big-shouldered brick colossus, 150 feet from north end to south, had sixty-nine windows on three levels across the west side and, visible above the neighborhood's mighty oaks, a clock tower with a bell that tolled five minutes before classes began. We entered through double doors and climbed a staircase to that wide hallway running the length of the building. At the top of the stairs was the fifth-grade classroom. (A second heartbreak, Miss Moore leaving in midyear to get married.) In her seventh-grade room at the north end, Mrs. Pryor read aloud to us every morning.

From that hallway, another set of stairs led up past Mr. Harwood's principal's office to the high school classrooms. At the north end, past Miss Swinford's room, Mr. Efaw taught business. In the fifties that meant girls learning shorthand and typing. (One boy in typing. Me.) Two or three times a year in Mr. Efaw's room we huddled under desks in preparation for an atomic bomb explosion. (The fifties: Elvis, poodle skirts, *American Bandstand*, and A-bomb drills.)

Only one basketball gym gets to be your first. Three flights of stairs down from the high school rooms, past the cafeteria, past a trophy case, along a hallway past the Future Farmers of America meeting room, and through double doors—behold, the Redwings' gym. I first walked onto the shiny hardwood basketball court as a sixth grader who had never touched a basketball. The coach, Mr. Kampf, explained "dee-fense" and "oh-fense." He told us to shoot only set shots. There's a chest pass and a bounce pass. Stay between your man and the basket. Don't look at the ball when you're dribbling. Six years later, Atlanta High School with its one hundred students won its first twenty-nine basketball games. We beat big, scary Lincoln (84–80, hooray for oh-fense) for Atlanta's first and last regional championship. We lost by 25 in the sectional to an even bigger, scarier school.

Out the gym's back doors and down the street a couple blocks, there was the ball diamond. (Always "ball diamond," never "ball-park" or "baseball field.") It was 272 feet down the left field line to a rusting wire fence nailed to twisted tree limbs driven into the ground. That fence separated the outfield from a stinking, muddy pig lot. Rocks multiplied overnight on the bare-dirt infield and caused so many evil bad hops bouncing against a shortstop's shins that an old man forever felt a young boy's pain. The bleachers were four rows high and twenty feet wide. (Mom, Dad, and Cheryl sat up top.) The Redwings' bench was a two-by-ten piece of lumber, ten feet long, weathered, warped, and splintered. The ball diamond was heaven.

I WANTED TO BE A MAJOR LEAGUE BASEBALL PLAYER.

Summers, I played Pony League baseball in Lincoln. Sandy and I were little kids when we caught the Greyhound at Howser's Feed Store in Atlanta, along Route 66, and rode the bumpy ten miles south to Grandma Lena's, counting telephone poles along the way. My sister alleged (she did a lot of alleging) that on arrival in Lincoln, I was, to quote her, "a little snot." She said she waited for the bus driver to open the baggage compartment. Meanwhile, I ran up San-gamon Street to Forehands' West Side Tavern (Grandma's place) and left her alone to lug our suitcase.

I still own the best baseball glove ever, a Wilson A2000. In 1959 it cost thirty-five dollars at Red Ringeisen's sporting goods store in Bloomington, Illinois. A lifetime later, the ancient leather has a golden glow under a patina of dirt carried away from infields all over Illinois. Hold it to the light just so, you can make out in the pocket those magic words, "Pro Model." On the outside of the glove's thumb, printed in inky block letters: KINDRED. It could be the glove of a retired major league shortstop invited back for Old-Timers' games.

All boys must have had that dream. Dwight Eisenhower did. "When I was a small boy in Kansas," he said, "a friend of mine and I went fishing and as we sat there in the warmth of the summer afternoon on a riverbank, we talked about what we wanted to do when we grew up. I told him that I wanted to be a real Major League Baseball player, a genuine professional like Honus Wagner. My friend said that he'd like to be president of the United States. Neither of us got our wish."

I was seventeen when reality interrupted my wishing. Dad said he could outrun me to first base. He was an old man, forty-six years old, a geezer who would be better off whittlin' twigs than challenging his speedburner son. The day of the race, he wore khaki work trousers. He had on his carpenter's cap with the stub of a yellow No. 2 pencil behind one ear. I sneaked a peek at his shoes. They were ankle-high scuffed brown boots that he called "clodhoppers." On my flying feet were Rawlings's best baseball spikes, the Fleetfoot model. I turned the tongue flaps down over the laces. Very cool.

I had worked at being a better player. Because we owned a full block in a neighborhood along the railroad tracks, Dad made half of it our baseball field. He carried away stones, chopped out stumps, and leveled the ground by dragging a chain-link fence behind his '48 Ford pickup. To teach me the strike zone, he hung twine on laths driven into the ground, creating a rectangle seventeen inches wide and set at shoulder and knee heights. When he was not behind the twine catching my hard stuff, he threw batting practice with corncobs. The corncobs were dark red and small and flew in flight so erratic, it was like trying to hit bumblebees. To get quick hands, I threw a golf ball against the concrete steps of our back porch and caught the ricocheting pellet. To get stronger, I went to the railroad tracks and tossed up the big white rocks from the train bed and hit them until my bat was reduced to splinters.

I would be Stan Musial, Stan the Man, the greatest of all Cardinals. A natural right-handed hitter, I tried to hit left-handed from Musial's unorthodox stance, deep in a crouch, his back turned to the pitcher, a stance described by Hall of Fame pitcher Ted Lyons as "a small boy looking around a corner." The experiment failed. Every pitch coming at me hit me. Scientists call it a neuromotor deficiency; the brain receives information from nerves too late to be translated into action. Laymen call it paralysis. Neither neuromotor deficiency nor paralysis fit into a boy's big-league plans.

We staged our race, Dad and I, at the ball diamond. One step away from home plate, I found myself one step behind the old fella. It stayed that way. Past first base, I did what any teenaged aspiring immortal would do. I lied. Without hesitation and with absolute certainty there would be no next time, I said, "I won't let you win next time."

I was twenty-one when Dad died of lung cancer at fifty-one. Mom opened a little wooden box of his stuff. Under his army discharge papers, she found two ribbons, both in shreds, faded blue ribbons dated 1928. Dad had been fifteen that summer. In the Logan County track meet, he won the 220-yard and 440-yard dashes. The kid in Fleetfoots had been hustled by the geezer in clodhoppers.

A KID AT SEVENTEEN SHOULD JUST SHUT UP SOMETIMES.

When we were seventeen, it was a very good year for small-town dreamers on soft winter nights. We brought down the curtain on another rehearsal of *It's a Great Life*. We stopped for a milkshake at Deuterman's. We drove three miles south of Atlanta on 66 and made a hairpin turn through trees into a narrow, dark tunnel under the Illinois Central railroad tracks. The tunnel exited onto a dirt road twisting between snowy, moonlit fields. The road led to her farmhouse on a hill, and we parked near enough the chicken coop to hear a rooster's complaint that he had been awakened before dawn. There we did what boys and girls do in cars late on cold winter nights when they are seventeen.

One night in February, I made more of basketball than a girl wanted to hear.

Cheryl said, "I play basketball, too, you know."

"Really?" This was long before Title IX.

"At church," she said.

I asked, "Is your team good?"

"Not much," she said. "We're mostly beginners."

"How about you?"

"In our last game," she said, "I scored all our points."

Here a boy on a moonlit winter night might have told the prettiest girl in school that she must be a very good player to have scored all her team's points. Done well, the compliment would take the edge off the freezing cold air finding its way through the rusted-out floorboards of a '52 Chevy.

Instead . . .

I asked, "How many did you score?"

"Fourteen."

Hmm. "How many did the other team get?"

A pause. "Seventy-two," she said.

Here, alas, I laughed out loud.

Cheryl scooched away, past the dashboard clock, past the radio knobs, scooching sideways until she bumped against the passenger door, where she quit with the homecoming queen smile and took up an arms-crossed position. Conversation was over. Everything was over. Soon, it was really cold in that Chevy.

MY PARENTS SAW ME CHASING AMBITION.

Dad did the baseball part.

Mom did the typewriter part.

She found the beauty at an auction, five dollars, a Royal, cast iron, its keys concave and rimmed with chrome curled to embrace a typist's fingertips. It was a gift for my fifteenth birthday. I sat at our kitchen table staring at it. I waited. I wanted to remember the first words I ever typed. It took a few minutes. Finally, hunting and pecking . . .

S-t-a-n-l-e-y F-r-a-n-k M-u-s-i-a-l.

I learned stories had beginnings, middles, and ends by listening to our seventh-grade teacher, Mrs. Pryor, who began each morning's class by reading aloud, memorably from Jack London's *Call of the Wild*. I knew nothing about grammar until my freshman year in high school when Mr. Wright's Latin class taught us English grammar. Mostly, I was learning to write by reading. Nights when I should have been asleep, I read anthologies of sportswriting. (W. C. Heinz on Vince Lombardi, Jimmy Cannon on Joe Louis, Grantland Rice on Babe Ruth.) I read newspapers. From Grandma Lena's house on Sixth Street in Lincoln, I rode my bicycle seven-tenths of a mile to the train depot, where, on Sunday mornings, the Chicago papers arrived. Nights in Atlanta, in my bedroom upstairs, listening to the radio, I took notes on basketball games and typed up stories.

At some point, I had decided, if I could not be Stan the Man, maybe I could be a sportswriter.

Reality hurried along that decision. On a summer baseball Sunday, as a teenager on Atlanta's men's team in a raggedy-ass pasture outside the village of Wapella, I stood in against a pitcher named Jack Chick. He was grown up more than most grown-ups. From his spot atop the mound, he cast a shadow that reached halfway to home plate and suggested doom. I later learned Chick's size, six foot five, 240 pounds. He was a mountainous, black-bearded, scowling lumberjack who roared in evil laughter as he threw axes at teenagers. Three strikeouts later, I returned to my safe place in front of a typewriter.

I was seventeen when my byline first made it into a real newspaper. The date was February 19, 1959. On page 3 of the four-page local weekly, the *Atlanta Argus-Lens*, the playmaking guard typed up a story about the high school basketball team, then undefeated in its first twenty-three games.

A fragment of the lede . . .

The Atlanta Redwings, a picture of teamwork, the epitome of determination, and a favorite of Luck . . .

And the kicker . . .

. . . there are those who give this five a better than even chance to capture the regional crown at Lincoln.

I got my first newspaper job in the summer of 1959, the week after graduation, eighty cents an hour. As the only intern at the *Lincoln Daily Courier*, I filled in for staffers on vacation. One week I would be a photographer (Speed Graphic, with flashbulbs), society editor the next. I did sports (Pony League baseball) and obituaries. On Friday afternoons, the managing editor, Bob Liter, came around the tiny newsroom with pay envelopes. Perhaps because my intern's salary was so comically low, he made a show of paying me with a stack of thirty-two $1 bills. They were clean, unwrinkled, and had the sharp edges of a new deck of cards. In years to come, I imagined the bills having been printed and trimmed in the pressroom every Friday morning just to see how long the kid would accept counterfeit money.

I was also the flyboy. Sounds adventurous, "flyboy." The flyboy watched as newspapers came off the press and fell into a stack. Every fiftieth newspaper came out crossways. The flyboy picked up the stack of fifty. Then he waited for the next fifty. And the next fifty. He delivered them to a waiting truck. The flyboy soon realized there was no romance in newspaper flyboy-ing. I preferred being the society editor even if it meant typing words and sentences that I had never read in a story typed by Heinz, Cannon, and Rice. "The lovely bride," for example, "completed her ensemble with a veiled pillbox hat."

Miss Swinford had made a curt dismissal of my English class theme in which I declared my ambition to be a sportswriter. "Maybe, someday, you can be a foreign correspondent." Probably not. There were all those sports stories typed up at night for no one to read, and all the sports reports in the *Spotlight,* our high school's mimeographed "newspaper," and the Redwings' stories in the *Argus-Lens* and the *Courier.*

I became a real newspaper person by winning an essay contest. The contest offered a scholarship that would pay half the tuition at Illinois Wesleyan University in Bloomington, twenty miles north of Atlanta. The winner earned the tuition's other half by working at the Bloomington *Pantagraph,* a distinguished regional newspaper. This was perfect. I was already a published reporter. I was a *Pantagraph* subscriber. I was a good high school baseball player and an Illinois Wesleyan baseball fan. Here came a chance for a small-town kid to attend a good school while working at a good newspaper and playing baseball for Jack Horenberger, the coach who made IWU's baseball program so good that a veteran major league scout, Ellsworth Brown, took me aside one day for a man-to-man talk.

We stood out of the rain in the small entryway to the Ace Novelty shop in Lincoln, across the railroad tracks from Grandma Lena's tavern. Brown had been to Atlanta for games, usually to see a real prospect on the other team. That day in Lincoln he said, "Son, you gotta go to Wesleyan if you can. You've got a big-league arm, and you know how to play, but, I dunno, son, you're not big and the way you run, maybe pick up your knees some would help, but I don't think there's Class D in you, and I know you'll play for Horenberger and get an education."

The theme of my contest essay was curiosity. "Being a reporter," I wrote, "you can be nosy and get paid for it." One day, along Penny the cow's escape route, I stopped at the post office, twirled the dial to open our small mailbox near the back of the room, and there was an envelope with the *Pantagraph* logo on it. I took the envelope home, unopened. At the kitchen table, where I had first typed Musial's name, I read that I had won the scholarship.

At Illinois Wesleyan, I was a three-year regular at second base. I was good enough in the field to be tolerated as a banjo hitter slapping one-hop singles. Horenberger called me a smart baseball man, even a Casey Stengel, he said, before realizing a need to add, "He runs like Casey, too," Casey then being seventy-five years old. And there was a day against Purdue. Oh, God. If only I could forget that day. I lost a pop-up in the sun, down the right field line, two outs, the bases loaded, the ball thudding against the heel of the A2000 and falling to the ground, everyone scoring. Next inning, with the bases loaded,

I slapped a one-hopper that went between the third baseman's legs and drove in two runs. The *Pantagraph*'s veteran sports editor, Fred (Brick) Young, once an IWU athletic star and likely responsible for my scholarship, gave me a base hit on that one-hopper, calling it too hot to handle. Forever after, I scored baseball generously, especially when a kid needed a hit.

At the *Pantagraph*, for four years during school and two years full-time, I wrote features and game stories. I also wrote a weekly bowling column. On Tuesday and Friday basketball nights, I was a one-man band on the copy desk. I carried a Speed Graphic to a local game for first-half photos that I developed and printed. Twenty part-timers spread around the newsroom took box scores by phone from sixty area games. I did the layouts, copyediting, and headlines for all the section's pages and oversaw the printers' work in the composing room (earning pica-stick slashes across the knuckles for touching any piece of metal, a sin against printers' union rules). I loved the frenzy of those desk nights. I also loved the freezing challenge of walking football sidelines and taking notes in snowstorms when you cannot make out the uniform numbers and the yard markers are buried under snow and every punt comes from the other end of the field and then, at game's end, you drive through the snow to the office and figure up the statistics before you write.

I covered Game 7 of the 1964 World Series in St. Louis. The sports editor did not want to go. He asked, "Want my credential?" No question has ever been put to anyone quicker to answer. The game ended on a pop-up to the Cardinals' shortstop, Dal Maxvill, though my account treated that pop-up as the most dramatic pop-up in baseball history. But hey. I might never be at another big-league game, let alone a World Series, let alone a Game 7.

I had been to high school basketball games in small-town gyms all over central Illinois—Chenoa and Hartsburg-Emden and

Maroa-Forsyth (with a ceiling so low it discouraged jump shots). Put a pin in the map, I was there: Beason, Elkhart, Saybrook-Arrowsmith, Fairbury-Cropsey, and Mason City, Middletown, Minonk-Dana-Rutland, San Jose, Delavan, and Heyworth. My biggest assignment was the Pontiac Holiday Tournament. Its basketball tournament was a thirty-two-team event that drew potential state champions. It is likely that veteran Pantagraphers begged off. Pontiac meant sitting at courtside for twelve hours. Twelve hours! A kid could hardly believe his luck. He could go typing into the night, as always, but now he was typing stories to be published, perhaps even read.

I had been out of Illinois only for baseball trips to New Orleans with Illinois Wesleyan. The most famous person I had seen was the broadcaster Chick Hearn, not yet the iconic Chick Hearn of the Los Angeles Lakers but the Chick Hearn of Peoria TV who spoke at our grade school athletic banquet in 1954. I met one big-league baseball player, a Lincoln native, Emil Verban, an all-star with the Phillies in the late forties. He once worked with infielders at our American Legion practice. He said I had good hands, praise that prompted me to recount how I had thrown golf balls against our concrete porch steps to practice my fielding. Emil Verban said, "Mmm."

AND THERE WAS CHERYL.

She had finished nurse's training in 1962. Her class celebrated by putting on a variety show based on *South Pacific*.

She came rocking onto the auditorium stage as a sailor boy in a sailor boy's whites. The uniform was too big for her and just right for the way it shimmied with her every move. She brought down the house singing "Honey Bun" and dancing across the stage to a sailor boy's bawdy lyrics.

She's broad where a broad should be broad.
I call her hips "twirly" and "whirly."

Mitzi Gaynor did it in the movie. Cheryl did it better.
Thank you, Miss Swinford, wherever you are.

CHERYL HAD FORGIVEN ME FOR THE 72–14 NIGHT. SHE EVEN BOUGHT into my idea of a sportswriter's life: "I'll never be a nine-to-five, home-for-dinner guy, OK?" By 1965, Cheryl was a registered nurse. We were young marrieds with a son, Jeff. We rented a three-room house in Lincoln, fifty dollars a month, distinguished by a humongous iron heating grate in the living room that dared us to try to leap across it barefooted. We were ready to get on with life.

Cheryl could get a job anywhere. I searched the help wanted ads in *Editor & Publisher* magazine for a step up from the *Pantagraph*. The Louisville *Courier-Journal*, listed by *Time* magazine among the ten best newspapers in the country, needed both a sports copy editor and a writer. The sports editor, Earl Cox, asked us down for an interview.

Getting hired there would be big. The *Pantagraph* was a good newspaper. I had grown up reading it. It paid my way through college. But the *Courier-Journal* was the real deal, a big-time, top-ten newspaper in a big city. Lincoln to Louisville was three hundred miles. It was a six-hour drive into our future.

2

· ·

CHERYL WAS A FARM GIRL. SHE WOULD HAVE BEEN HAPPY TO STAY where we were. Her father, Glenn, had worked 220 acres east of Route 66 between Lincoln and Atlanta. When he was disabled by Parkinson's disease, Cheryl's mother, Hazel, went to work as a licensed practical nurse. That left Cheryl in charge at home. As a freshman in high school, she did the cooking and cleaning for her parents, grandfather, and two young brothers.

She had been a precocious student in 4-H, the farm girl's version of charm school. She learned to bake cookies at age ten and moved on to dinner rolls, cakes, brownies, and steaks. By thirteen, she was her club's junior leader, teaching preteen girls what she had mastered. At fifteen, given a week and lots of sequins, she could make a prom dress to die for.

Her mother called their 4-H group the "Straight Row Chicks" in honor of all their farmland neighbors who planted corn and beans in straight rows. Hazel wrote a commendation for her little chick: "I feel that the 4-H program has helped Cheryl to be methodical, consistent, self-confident, thoughtful, and understanding of others.

Through necessity she has learned to operate a farm home in my absence."

It was my great good luck that I got to Cheryl before somebody made her a perfect farmer's wife.

Then came our six-hour drive into the unknown. We left Lincoln on two-lane roads through cornfields and on to the nation's new interstate highway system. At Indianapolis we turned south on I-65, and soon we saw Louisville's skyline rising on the far side of the Ohio River flowing between Indiana and Kentucky.

We worked our way to the Courier-Journal & Times Building. Seven stories high, its facade was a graceful curve on the corner of Sixth and Broadway. Its lobby spoke of grandeur. The walls were polished granite covered with murals of Kentucky's mountains and the state's historic characters, among them Daniel Boone and Henry Clay. Suspended by a cable, a giant globe floated below a high, domed ceiling. Above the elevator's doors, etched in marble, there was a quotation from Robert Worth Bingham, who had raised the *Courier-Journal* and *Times* to national prominence.

I HAVE ALWAYS REGARDED THE NEWSPAPERS OWNED BY ME AS A PUB-LIC TRUST AND HAVE ENDEAVORED SO TO CONDUCT THEM AS TO REN-DER THE GREATEST PUBLIC SERVICE.

His successor, Barry Bingham Sr., was a handsome man with a great head of white hair, perfectly trimmed. Regal in bearing, he favored shimmering blue pinstripe suits. To see Mr. Bingham was to imagine him as an ambassador sipping fine wines at state dinners.

Not so much with Earl Cox. The sports editor favored rumpled khakis. He worked with shirtsleeves rolled up. His loosely knotted ties came with mustard stains. He was no one's idea of an ambassador and everyone's idea of a sportswriter.

He grew up in a small Kentucky town and was a University of Kentucky graduate. He had been a high school sports reporter for the *Lexington Herald-Leader* before moving to Louisville and rising to the department's top job at age thirty-five. Pugnacious, abrupt, and crotchety, he loved underdogs, overdogs, and stories that rattled Kentucky coffee cups from Ashland in the east to Paducah in the west.

We sat in the sports department's little space tucked into a corner of the fourth-floor newsroom.

"We like you," he said, "but we can't offer you what you want."

Oh.

"I know you want to write," he said.

Yes.

The *Editor & Publisher* ad had offered two jobs at the Courier-Journal & Times, one company publishing two papers, the *C-J* in the morning, the *Times* in the afternoon.

"But what we have now is the copyediting job. We had two good candidates, and the *Times* got first choice," Cox said. "They hired the writer. I can tell you something will happen soon on the *C-J* side. One of our guys is taking a job outside the newspaper. I can't promise golf, but that's where you'd start. I see you've done golf."

Yes.

"For now I can offer you the copy desk job. And you can write anytime you want."

Really?

"If you find a story, write it, we'll get it in the paper."

Cox did not suggest more pay for more work. No need for that. I would have paid *him*.

I started on the copy desk in December of 1965 at $135 a week, a $10 raise from the *Pantagraph*. The next month, Cheryl started at Our Lady of Peace, a private psychiatric hospital in Louisville.

EVERYTHING WAS FINE ON MY FIRST NIGHT, EXCEPT I LOST MY CAR.

Cheryl had returned to Illinois to pack up for the move and check Louisville real estate ads. The *Courier-Journal* put me up for a month in the local YMCA, on Broadway, four blocks east of the newspaper building. The Y room had a skinny bed and an end table, with a bathroom down the hall. A blinking neon light on Broadway shone through the flimsy shade on my room's single window. The arrangement did not speak of big-time journalism. But if the job meant sleeping under a blinking neon light, I could do that—as soon as I found my car.

That first night, done with the 4:00 p.m. to 1:00 a.m. shift, I went out to Sixth Street. I had parked at the curb next to the building.

The car was not there. At one thirty in the morning, walking up and down Sixth Street, I saw only a big-city streetscape made eerie by flickering fluorescent lights. Had I forgotten where I parked? Had the car been stolen? Such a rube, inviting thieves to take a Mustang with Illinois plates. I went a block west and a block east. No cars anywhere.

Back in the sports department, I told a friend, "My car's gone."

He asked, "Where'd you park?"

"Right outside the building."

"There's no parking on Sixth after three."

"No parking?" I said. "I parked there."

"You've been towed."

It was a long first night, eight hours of copyediting followed by a lesson in Louisville's parking laws. I got a ride across town to a tow-in lot at 4:00 a.m. I paid a cop seventy-five dollars ransom to get my car out of impoundment.

ASSUMING I WOULD LEARN WHERE TO PARK—FIVE DOLLARS IN A REAL parking lot—the important question remained. Could a kid up from the *Pantagraph* do the work at one of America's top-ten newspapers?

The *Pantagraph's* circulation was about forty thousand, most of it within a half hour's drive from Bloomington into rural Illinois. We had a four-man sports department. From ripping wire copy off the Associated Press teletype to editing part-timers' copy to designing pages and writing every headline and every photo caption, I often produced a sports section by myself, which was, at the *Pantagraph*, the definition of my job.

The Courier-Journal & Times sports department had fifty men and women. The papers had two photographers who were also pilots who flew to news stories. C-J circulation was 250,000. Its reach extended four hundred miles across Kentucky and two hundred miles north to south. The paper covered all 120 counties in Kentucky and another 20 in Indiana. It had news bureaus in the state capital, Frankfort, and in the mountains at Hazard. From the National Press Building in Washington, DC, the C-J and the *Times* covered Kentucky's congressional delegation. Every afternoon except Sunday the *Times* delivered fifty thousand papers.

In a week, I knew I was ready, at least ready to edit copy. The type-setting process began with a typist punching tape that was fed into a machine producing hot-metal type. I had asked the *Pantagraph* tape-puncher for advice. He said, "Give it to me the way you want it to look in the paper." He wanted no typing mistakes, no x'd-out words, no penciled-in scrawls. That sounded reasonable and professional. I became obsessive about clean copy. (Obsessive meant retyping any page with a typing mistake. I filled wastebaskets with crumpled-up paper.)

To my surprise, I saw no clean copy in Louisville. I decided that x'd-out, penciled-in copy was the norm.

There came a night in the winter of 1965–1966. The most important stories in the sports section were on University of Kentucky basketball and its legendary coach, Adolph Rupp. UK was undefeated, ranked No. 1 in the country, and with no starter taller than six foot five, nationally known as "Rupp's Runts." Somehow, UK stories fell to me for editing.

Copy arrived typewritten on paper. Pages of paper were cut and glued together. The glue was a white paste delivered from a glass "pot," a jar of the kind my grandmother used to can tomatoes. From the "paste pot," we slathered the glue onto paper with a brush attached to the pot's lid. "Pass the paste pot, boys," is a century-old deadline phrase. As for cutting copy paper? The *Courier-Journal* people did it with large iron scissors attached to heavy chains connected to bolts screwed into the desk.

I asked Cox, "Those scissors, why are they chained to the desk?"

"Chain's so you can't try to stab the guy across the desk. Happened."

That first month on the desk, I understood the possibility of blood on the scissors. I edited a reporter's deadline copy faxed in from a UK road game. The copy was bad. What to do? Let it pass? Fix it? The reporter was a veteran star. He had reached for cutesy lines. He may have been worried about brain lock on deadline; he had written the game story's early paragraphs *before* the game. I rewrote it into a straight game story. The next day, Cox came by the copy desk and asked, "Who handled Kentucky last night?" I raised a hand. "Good," he said, and I resumed breathing.

Cheryl and I bought a house in Louisville, nice and neat in a good neighborhood. It cost $17,500, more than double my annual salary. The purchase was possible because we were ahead of our time as young marrieds, both with full-time jobs. Cheryl made the payments on a second mortgage.

With Cheryl at the hospital five mornings a week, I was the worst kind of Mr. Mom. I did nothing at home to make her life easier. The 4-H queen of the Straight Row Chicks tried to teach me how to make the bed. I failed. I did not pull the top sheet tight. I could not tuck in the corners in that magic "nurses' corners" way that allows the sheet to drape just so. And I did not notice we had put the top sheet on with the top of the sheet at the bottom, causing her to say, "Why'd you let me put the top at the bottom?" And I said, "How do you tell the difference?" And she said, "The seam!" Before I could explain that writers know nothing except how to spell, she said, "Good thing you know how to spell."

Anyway, my failures as Mr. Mom included the way I tended to our son while Cheryl was saving lives at the hospital. I drove downtown to the newspaper office and took Jeff with me. He was three years old. With the *C-J* newsroom empty at that hour, I gave him a doughnut, set him at a typewriter, and showed him how to hit the keys. Meanwhile, I worked the phones in search of a story.

I found one in February of '66. I called El Paso, Texas. *Courier-Journal* readers knew everything about Kentucky. They knew nothing about the No. 3 team in the country, undefeated in twenty games. I wrote about Texas Western, soon to become a team Kentuckians would never forget.

Texas Western College is this kind of place: Its campus, just a few Gila-monster hops from the Rio Grande, resembles a Tibetan monastery . . . a disc jockey who calls himself "The Big D" is its best basketball player . . . and the coach of its undefeated basketball team is an expert coyote caller.

Gila monsters, Tibet, and coyotes? Talk about cutesy. The paper's executive editor, Norman Isaacs, later would advise me to quit trying so hard. (I tried hard to quit trying so hard. I often failed.) The good thing was, Cox had come through on his promise that if I found a story and wrote it, he would get it in the paper. A month later, in a game that made basketball history, Texas Western defeated Kentucky for the national championship.

That summer, Cox moved me off the copy desk to cover golf. That winter, I became the beat man on Kentucky and Rupp. For the first time, I would be a writer full-time.

I HAD NEVER WANTED TO BE ANYTHING ELSE. MY HIGH SCHOOL PRINCI-pal suggested law school. Dad once took me with him on a roofing job in July, making sure I would never be a carpenter boiling on a roof. I thought of politics, which is sports, only with words. But I knew nothing about politics and everything about baseball. Also, I was too shy to talk out loud, which ruled out radio and TV.

I had made money only on two jobs. I detasseled corn, a dollar an hour, a two-week summer job. That same summer of 1955, Dad paid me a penny a brick to scrape mortar off old bricks. It took a lot of scraping to pay for a cheeseburger and milkshake at Deuterman's. I scraped for one day, Dad again teaching me the burdens of manual labor. Even as a grown-up, I worked the desk at the *Pantagraph* only as a required part of the scholarship deal. At the *Courier-Journal*, I was marking time on the desk until I could write.

I did not know it then and would not fully realize it for a long time, but my life changed on the Mr. Mom morning of October 26, 1966.

Cox said, "Clay's in town, go find him."

I knew Cassius Marcellus Clay Jr. was born and raised in Louisville. He won the heavyweight championship in 1964 and confirmed that he had joined the Nation of Islam, a segregationist sect. Later he renounced Clay as a slave name; he would be Muhammad Ali. In February of '66, after having said, "I ain't got no quarrel with them Viet Cong," he refused induction into the US Army. The *Courier-Journal* called him "Cassius Clay, also known as Muhammad Ali."

And the boss said Clay's in town, go find him.

As if I knew how to do that . . .

I was the kid who couldn't find his car . . .

As if I knew what to do if I found Ali . . .

Me, the *Pantagraph* bowling columnist, I'm supposed to find the most famous man in the world . . .

"Go to Cash's place," Cox said. "He'll know where he is."

Cash?

"Cash Senior, Clay's dad. The old man's got what he calls an 'art gallery.' Two blocks from here."

That day I learned a great lesson in journalism. You can be scared as hell. Just do it. Take what little information you have—"Go to Cash's place"—and start asking questions.

I walked west on Broadway to the storefront that Cassius Marcellus Clay Sr. used as a gallery for his artwork and painting business.

Cash Senior said, "Go down to Grand, by our house, maybe he's there."

"Where's Grand?" I said, and Cash Senior pointed to his right.

My memory of that day is at once vivid and untrustworthy. I gathered up Jeff and drove into a place I had never been. Grand Avenue was in Louisville's West End, home to most of the city's African Americans. In my Ozzie and Harriet world of small-town Illinois, I had never met a black person. Driving in the West End of this major metropolitan city, I was lost.

I rolled down the car window and asked passersby, "Seen Cassius today?"

Second lesson of the day. Ask questions, you will get lucky.

Everybody had seen Cassius; he was *everywhere*. I found him on a street corner entertaining friends. Somehow, he wound up in our car and we drove around.

Get lucky? I had never been so lucky. Ali was a sweetheart. He wanted to show me a telephone pole. He said Joe Louis had leaned against a telephone pole in his neighborhood, and he had leaned against it as a boy, and though we never found that pole, if it even existed, Ali told me it was the only pole of all the poles in the world that two heavyweight champions had leaned against.

All day, Ali carried Jeff on his lap. We stopped somewhere that had a giant scale, probably in the *Courier-Journal* pressroom. Ali got on the scale and posed for photographs with Jeff in his arms. (I have searched for such a photograph without finding it.) I remember those moments, and surely there were more, for in the next fifty years I was never in Ali's presence without feeling that each day of his life could be made into a movie.

That day, I did good by finding Ali. Still, I was in over my head. We did not talk about the Viet Cong. We did not talk about his next title fight, coming up against Cleveland Williams. I managed to do a routine story reporting that Ali was in town to raise money for a children's hospital. My story began . . .

Cassius Clay does this. . . . He stands on the Fourth Street sidewalk, scoops into the air a pig-tailed girl, hugs her, and thanks the girl's mother for letting him do it.

Ali visited the children's hospital. He told the Louisville Quarterback Club it was "worth the sacrifice" to lose millions of dollars in endorsements to stand up for his Nation of Islam beliefs. At a Fourth Street jewelry store, he bought a white-gold diamond ring. It matched a platinum watch he'd bought in Germany. He said, "I can remember when five dollars was just so much money."

That day in 1966, Muhammad Ali was twenty-four years old. I was twenty-five. We would grow old together, the fighter and the writer, and in time I would know what to do when I found him.

THE *COURIER-JOURNAL* LIBRARY RECEIVED DAILY NEWSPAPERS FROM around the country. During dead time on the four-to-one copy desk shift, I walked down a flight of stairs to the library, known by newspaper people as the "morgue." All the bodies were buried there, clippings of news stories decades old, every reference book a journalist would need. The best stuff came with the out-of-town papers, called "exchanges" because we sent you ours if you sent us yours. The *Courier-Journal* library in 1966 was my graduate school in journalism. I came to think of every column in every exchange as Required Reading.

The best columns were in the *New York World Journal Tribune* (a doomed consolidation of three major papers, but alive with columnists who shaped my thinking forever). Red Smith and Jimmy Cannon ran on the front page of the sports section, Smith's music down the left side, Cannon's drama down the right. Inside the paper,

Jimmy Breslin and Dick Schaap did the gritty work of badass report-ers telling the city's stories. "New Journalism," the use of novelistic techniques in journalism, claims many creators. I first saw it in Tom Wolfe's stuff for the *World Journal Tribune*.

What those columnists did, I wanted to do.

I wanted to be Red Smith today, Jimmy Cannon tomorrow, and Jimmy Breslin the week after. Not that I dared dream out loud. I was a kid from nowhere Illinois lucky to be editing copy at one of Amer-ica's best newspapers—and especially lucky to be in a town where they ran the Kentucky Derby every May.

Derby Week was all hands on deck, with a kid copy editor set loose to help fill the space. In 1968 I wrote every day from Churchill Downs. Mornings on the back side were full of stories from train-ers, jockeys, grooms, all the eccentrics of a unique culture. I also met Smith, Cannon, and the *Washington Post*'s legendary columnist Shirley Povich. Long after that week in '68, I learned that Povich had read my little color pieces and proposed that his sports editor, Martie Zad, give me a call. Cheryl answered that call and told me, "A man from Washington wants to talk to you."

"Washington?"

"The post office, I think," she said.

An hour later, I explained to my beloved that the *Washington Post* wanted to hire me.

"Oh, no," she said. She had in her hand a paint brochure with a picture of a house she wanted to build.

Zad offered me a job as beat man on navy basketball and backup on the Washington Redskins. Two years away from the *Pantagraph*, I was thrilled to be noticed. But in 1968, the *Post* was not yet the *Post* of Ben Bradlee, Bob Woodward, and Watergate. Navy basketball had no Adolph Rupp. The Redskins were sad sacks with no reason to think Vince Lombardi was about to become their coach. I thanked

Zad and began stammering. Thanks, those are good jobs, thanks, and, maybe someday, not that this could ever happen, but what I'd really like to do, if I was ever any good, was try, y'know, to be a columnist, if that could ever happen.

Zad then did three great things: (1) He ignored my stammerings. (2) He said, "I'll keep track of you. We'll talk again someday." (3) He gave me my first lesson in how to use a job offer at one place to get what you want where you are. "Now," Zad said, "go tell Earl Cox that we talked."

THE MECHANICS OF NEWSPAPERS FASCINATED ME. AT THE *PANTAGRAPH*, I stood in the composing room and watched printers drop the metal type of stories and photographs into rectangular iron forms called "chases" that sat on iron tables atop four-wheeled carts. Through a series of magical processes, that metal became printed pages on tens of thousands of newspapers rolling through presses two stories tall. The papers were packed into waiting trucks. They were delivered to distant locations. An agent, most likely a teenage boy, gathered up his bundle of papers and, depending on the accuracy of his throwing arm, caused that morning's miracle to land on your front porch or at least in the flowers out front.

The *Pantagraph* taught me what it could in the same way a Minor League Baseball team gets a shortstop ready for the next level. Now the *Courier-Journal* had called me up. It is an exaggeration to say everything I did in the rest of my newspaper career I did first at the *Courier-Journal*. It is certain, however, that everything I did in Louisville prepared me to do any story anywhere at any time.

Cox and his editors recognized my ambition. *Sure, go ahead, Mr. Mom, in your spare time write something.* They let me call down to

El Paso and write about Gila monsters and Texas Western's basketball team. They sent me into the unknown to find "Cassius Clay, also known as Muhammad Ali."

In April of 1967, they sent me to Augusta, Georgia.

At eleven fifteen on a Tuesday morning, I stood at the entrance to the Quonset hut that was the Masters press building. I asked the woman checking credentials, "Can you show me where Red Smith sits?"

I was there to cover the golf tournament. I would do that, right after I saw Ben Hogan and Red Smith.

"Red's in the back there," the woman said. "At the end of the second row, on the right side. It's seat J15."

He was a small man, sixty-one years old, with thinning hair, once red, gone white. He wore a brown suit coat. I watched as he threaded a sheet of paper into an upright typewriter. He used both hands, one on each side of the paper. I saw why. His hands trembled. I chose a seat on the left side of the Quonset hut, three rows from the front, excited to be in the same pressroom with the great man but far enough away to hide my boy-reporter excitement.

The next day, I arose before dawn to watch Hogan on the range. His hands looked like my father's carpenter hands, thick and strong. Every shot with every club flew two yards left of the target and fell two yards right, a fade two decades in the making, the ball dropping in his caddy's shadow, to be gathered up for the next drill. Hogan had last won a major in 1953, four years after being broken into pieces in a head-on collision with a Greyhound bus on a forlorn Texas highway. Now, fifty-four years old, his knees were no good and every step brought him pain.

I was in the press building on Saturday afternoon when we saw red numbers going up on Hogan's scorecard. Back then, television showed only the last nine holes. The red numbers meant that

Hogan—Hogan? Hogan!—had birdied the tenth, eleventh, twelfth, and thirteenth holes. Someone said, "We better get out there!"

I did not see Hogan until he appeared on the eighteenth fairway. It is a long, wide, ascending aisle in Augusta's cathedral of loblolly pines. From both sides, as Hogan limped up the hill, came the gallery's sound of hands clapping. No shouts, no whistles, just a sound like soft rain dancing on a tin roof.

Hogan had put a 5-iron second shot twenty-five feet above the hole at 18. That day, from the first row of a press tower alongside the eighteenth green, I saw the little man in the white cap standing over that slick, downhill, scary putt. The yips owned him. For a player of Hogan's dignity, it became an act of courage to draw back the putter when that action might provoke a spastic jab at the ball. Yet he had made five birdie putts that day and now could make a sixth. He later said, "I apologize to everyone for taking so long to putt. I still freeze some, but I'm trying. I can hear people in the gallery saying why doesn't that man go ahead and putt. I wish I knew the answer."

Journalists root for stories. Whatever happens, good or bad, OK, just make it something we can write. Sometimes we get lucky and the best story is the one we want to write. I wanted Hogan to make that putt. It would give him a record-tying 30 on the back nine and 66 for the day. With one more round to play, he would be two shots behind the tournament leader. He stood over that evil downhiller until, at last, he moved the putter away from the ball and back to it. Just touching the ball, really, and down the hill it rolled, slowly, almost too slowly, until it dropped out of sight. Hogan had made the thing, and the day's soft rain of applause gave way to the patient people in the gallery sending up a waterfall's roar.

It was 1967, a prehistoric time in sports media. No national TV interview of Hogan, no ESPN highlights of his four-birdie run, no Golf Channel analyses, no social media, no Twitterverse. Only seven or eight sportswriters followed Hogan to the clubhouse. Some sat beside him, some knelt in front. He had become a great player by force of discipline so severe that the Scots, in admiration, called him "the wee ice mon." He had been that man at work on this Saturday in Augusta.

Now smiling with warmth, he said, "There's a lot of fellas that have got to fall dead for me to win. But I don't mind telling you, I'll play just as hard as I've ever played in my life."

He sat on a padded bench with his back to a window bearing white lace curtains. Afternoon's fading sunlight came through the curtains. It fell soft and golden around the old man's head, a halo.

He shot 77 on Sunday and finished tenth. It did not matter. On Saturday, he was Ben Hogan.

ALI WAS BIG. THE MASTERS WAS BIG. THE DERBY, TOO. NONE OF IT WAS as big in Kentucky as basketball.

Cheryl and I had a son, two mortgages, and two jobs. She would be out of the house at five thirty in the morning to drive in the dark to Our Lady of Peace. No longer chained to the copy desk's bloody scissors, I would go wandering in Kentucky to find another hoop on another barn. From one end of the state to the other, Adolph Rupp was Good God Almighty, or to spell it the way the coach would say it when riled up, "Goodgawdamighty!"

An early suggestion of Rupp's almightiness came from a hollow-cheeked man sitting in a rocking chair on the rickety front porch of his general store along KY 7 in Letcher County. Joe Begley was his name. He was a kindly soul who hated the strip mining that ripped the beauty out of his eastern Kentucky mountains. He hated strip mining with the same passion he hated deep-underground mining, but he saved the greater fury of his hate for the distant, faceless, soulless corporations that stole the coal and rendered the mountains' men and boys useless to anybody, mostly themselves. When I asked Joe Begley how big basketball was in Kentucky, he teetered back in his rocker. "If a lump of coal ain't Jesus Christ," he said, "basketball is."

I found basketball everywhere. Customers at a grocery store on the Mountain Parkway could shoot jump shots from the bread shelves at a hoop in the parking lot. At Jackson, basketballs fell through a hoop onto a funeral home's hearse. Hoops need not be fancy. I saw a clothes basket, with the bottom still in it, tacked to an abandoned church near Hazard. Not far from Monkey's Eyebrow, a bicycle tire rim (with the spokes removed) hung sideways from a tree. In Maytown, two clothes hangers had been reconfigured into an oval big enough for a ball to pass through. I saw new nets, no nets, ripped nets, nets of chains, and twine nets. They were nailed to trees, telephone poles, garages, work sheds, great white mansions, and a doghouse in Hardinsburg. No matter if the backboard was corrugated tin in Elizabethtown, whether the shooter stood on Burnaugh's railroad tracks or in a dirt backyard in Turners Station—no matter how they did it, chances were they all did it because Adolph Rupp had come to Kentucky and started winning basketball games in 1932.

I shot layups in the Hell for Certain community center, named for the mountain creek running outside the building.

I watched Kingdom Come Settlement School lose a game in the sandstone building's tiny second-story gym with a potbellied stove heating the place and wire over the windows keeping the basketballs indoors.

In 1975 I went to a girls high school game in Earlington, one of the first girls games in rural Kentucky since Title IX became law. As basketball, it was dreadful. No one could run, jump, or handle. But Earlington's coach, Francis Bibb, had the right idea. Twenty-two years old. Taught remedial math in grades 1 through 4. Learned basketball "playing knockdown, drag-out with my two brothers." What did Ms. Bibb first teach her team? "Well, like, 'This is a basketball, and that's a goal.'" They had lost all ten games. No never mind. Ms. Bibb got all evangelistic about basketball helping timid girls become strong women.

"The girls become more confident—they develop a new awareness," she said. "They feel emotions they've never even noticed before. They begin to find out things about themselves. I have some girls who always had been very quiet. One hid in corners. Walking down the hall at school, she'd press against the wall. They've begun to come out of their shells, to be more interested in themselves. They've begun to look at things with a different perspective. They're looking for challenges now."

I went to a state prison in Eddyville and heard the recreation director say they once had a great player who scored 74 points in a game and he did not know where that fellow was anymore. Then he added, "I hate to wish it on anybody that he should wind up in Eddyville, but if he has to go to prison again, I hope it's here."

So there was basketball everywhere, all of it revolving around the almighty man himself, Adolph Rupp.

His Kentucky teams won four national championships from 1948 to 1958. He was a legend when John Wooden was a rookie high school coach in a Kentucky village along the Ohio River. In 1966, for the first of hundreds of times, I drove the eighty miles from Louisville to Lexington and wandered inside Kentucky's Memorial Coliseum. There was Rupp, outside his office door.

His face was soft and deeply lined, his ears a size too large with fleshy earlobes that jiggled when he talked. He stood tall and straight; he once coached in a steel-ribbed leather corset after spinal surgery. Long beset by diabetes, Rupp had worn an eye patch on the bench and propped up an infected foot on a stool. He had survived hundreds of basketball games worried so much that "my stomach feels like I've swallowed a bottle of lye." That day in the Coliseum, he was sixty-five years old.

Soon, I became an eager listener to tales of the Rupp legend, many told by the legend himself. He said he came to Kentucky at age thirty, straight off a high school coaching job in Illinois, but only after giving the university good reason to hire him. "Because," he said, "I'm the best damned basketball coach in the nation." Incidentally, that spinal surgery was not done by an ordinary surgeon. "By the same doctor, Glenn Spurling, who they flew over to Europe to operate on General Patton."

Rupp did not like the university's mandatory retirement age of seventy. "Retire? What would I do? Time would hang heavy on my hands. It's the competitiveness I like—taking a bunch of boys and seeing what I can do with them. These young squirts come in as coaches at other places, and they say they're going to put an end to Rupp and Kentucky. Well, we'll see about that."

As for the bunch of boys, those boys had something to say about the coach's methods. Bill Spivey, one of his two dozen All-Americans, said Rupp was unique. "He wanted everybody to hate him—and he succeeded. He called us names some of us had never heard before." Vernon Hatton said, "It takes six or eight years to get over playing for Coach Rupp. Once you get over it, you get to like him." I saw Rupp upbraid a player who hesitated and had a layup blocked. "You get the ball like this—" Rupp held an imaginary basketball that he raised slowly overhead—"and then you say, 'Our father who art in heaven, hallowed be thy name, thy kingdom come, thy will be done, I am now going to shoot the damned basketball.'"

Rupp's biography was epic Americana. In the late nineteenth century, his German immigrant parents settled on the unforgiving plains of southeastern Kansas. Three straight crop failures preceded his father's death in 1910. Dolph, as his family called him, was nine years old, one of five boys helping their mother, Anna, farm 160 acres of no-good land. He made money by working in neighbors' wheat fields and stocking shelves at Williams' Grocery in Halstead, a small town seven miles from the Rupp farm. He swam and fished in Little Emma Creek. He played basketball in the dirt at Harvey County's District 33 one-room school and at home, where the boys rigged up a barrel-stave hoop and threw a gunnysack full of grain at it. "That ball never bounced too good," Rupp said.

He installed himself as Halstead High School's basketball coach in 1919 when the real coach went off to World War I. Dolph enrolled at Kansas University and played on the KU basketball team. Though he never played much, he profited from exposure to the school's ambitious new coach, Forrest (Phog) Allen, and to James Naismith, the very inventor of basketball, who had returned from the war to resume work as KU's manager of athletics. From there Rupp moved to Freeport, Illinois, and on to Kentucky, where the school put him up in the local YMCA. He told me, "I had a room that wasn't fit for a cat. I said, 'Goodgawdamighty, what kind of place is this Kentucky?'"

I crossed rhetorical swords with Rupp. "Gawdammit," he said, wolfing down a bowl of chili, "what do you mean, writing that I 'wolfed down' my chili?" (Another culinary note: In my year as the UK beat man, Rupp's '66–'67 team went 13–13, his worst season ever. At dinner one night, he claimed to sort prospects from suspects by watching them eat. "Why, if a boy is aggressive with his eating, then he's going to be aggressive on the basketball floor. Lordy, you should have seen Cliff Hagan!" He poked at his eight-ounce filet mignon. "See this? Hagan would have eaten this in three bites— chomp, chomp, CHOMP!")

In Rupp's glory years, college basketball was overwhelmingly a white man's game. That changed with Texas Western. Rupp's five white starters lost to Don Haskins's five black starters. Even schools in the Deep South began recruiting black players. That 1966 national championship game became the historical basis for suggestions that Rupp was a racist. For what it's worth, he had recruited black players at least two years earlier. In 1964 he gained a scholarship commitment from a black Kentucky All-Stater, Butch Beard, only to have Beard switch at the last minute to the University of Louisville. When Rupp also lost out on another black Kentuckian, Wes Unseld, who joined Beard at Louisville, many critics labeled Rupp a racist. Arguing against that narrative, I cited the Beard and Unseld recruitings. I quoted Spivey on Rupp and race: "He cared about one thing, winning ball games, and he didn't care if you were green, blue, purple if you could help him win." I also asked: Is it fair, in the case of a white man born of German immigrants in Kansas in 1901, to find him guilty at age sixty-five of failing to be the Martin Luther King Jr. of college basketball? Rupp was seventy when he signed his first black player.

He had passed the university's normal retirement age of sixty-five. At seventy he had campaigned for—and failed to achieve—exemption from mandatory retirement. Meanwhile, the world around him kept getting younger. The year Rupp retired, Louisville hired Denny Crum away from John Wooden's staff at UCLA, and Indiana hired Bobby Knight, who had won big with West Point's undersized cadets. At an afternoon practice in his last season, I sat with Rupp in Memorial Coliseum. His eyes fell shut. He began talking. "The legislature should pass a law," he said, "that at three o'clock every afternoon, any basketball coach who is seventy years old gets a shot of bourbon." Eyes popping open, he smiled. "These damned bouncing, bouncing, bouncing basketballs are putting me to sleep."

Charmed as often as not, I yet wrote it was time for the cantankerous old man to retire. Rupp noticed my opinion and had an opinion of his own. He made that opinion clear to my colleague, Dick Fenlon. Then the *Louisville Times* sports columnist, Fenlon had called the coach at home.

"Fenlon? Fenlon?" Rupp said. "I know two guys in Louisville. One's Fenlon, the other one's Kindred. One's a good guy, the other one's a son of a bitch. Which one are you?"

Fenlon claimed, correctly, he was the good guy.

Retire? We know what Rupp thought of that. *"Retire? What would I do? Time would hang heavy on my hands. It's the competitiveness I like—taking a bunch of boys and seeing what I can do with them. These young squirts come in as coaches at other places, and they say they're going to put an end to Rupp and Kentucky. Well, we'll see about that."*

He was Adolph Frederick Rupp, a basketball coach from Halstead to Freeport to Lexington. He did not want to be anything less. I should have argued that he had earned the right to leave only when he wanted to leave.

The Kentucky job went to a Rupp assistant, a Kentuckian, Joe B. Hall. Led by a cadre of black stars, Hall's 1978 team won the national championship. By then, Kentucky had moved out of Memorial Coliseum into a twenty-two-thousand-seat basketball palace. It was called Rupp Arena.

AS MARTIE ZAD SUGGESTED AFTER THE '68 DERBY, I TOLD COX I HAD turned down the *Post's* offer because I wanted, someday, to be a columnist.

Soon after our talk, things happened.

The *Courier-Journal* columnist, Earl Ruby, retired. The *Times* columnist, Dean Eagle, moved over to take Ruby's place. And on January 1, 1969, I became the *Times* columnist.

Cheryl and I were twenty-seven years old. I told her that now we could build that new house. We would be in Louisville forever. Maybe. Probably. Unless the *New York Times* called. Or the *Washington Post*.

ALWAYS, THERE WAS MUHAMMAD ALI.

October 26, 1970, four years after my Mr. Mom day with him, I saw him again in Atlanta, Georgia. He returned to the ring after a three-and-a-half-year exile imposed on him by boxing commissions for refusing the draft. It was my first time ringside at an Ali fight. No one, not Ring Lardner, A. J. Liebling, or Red Smith had ever seen commotion, hullabaloo, and pandemonium matching that night's phantasmagoria. I wrote up a storm. . . .

Raucous celebrants, intoxicated by a moment of sports, cultural, political, and racial history, jammed into the Hyatt Regency Hotel. They wore ermine-trimmed hats with brims drooping to their shoulders. They outfitted themselves in purple velvet and golden silk. Mink coats came to their ankles above pointy-toed purple suede shoes. And those were the men. They came to Atlanta, pimps and platoons of plumed ladies arriving in yellow Rolls-Royces and psychedelic Stutz Bearcats with curlicue fenders and hoodlum tires, "every black man and woman in America who could scratch up the change," the author and boxing aficionado Budd Schulberg said, "high rollers from the biggest floating crap games in the land."

It was a dreamscape of America's black Mafia and black intellectual elite, drawn to a city famous for William Tecumseh Sherman's fire, for Scarlett and Rhett and a way of life gone with the wind. Bill Cosby and Sidney Poitier and Harry Belafonte and the Supremes and Mr. T—all drawn to Atlanta by Muhammad Ali, the great-grandson of slaves, both repository and carrier of black pride. A lawyer and Rhodes scholar, Stan Sanders, told Schulberg, "You know the day will come when our sons will be asking us, 'Daddy, where were you on the night they let Muhammad Ali come back to the ring?'"

Ali defeated Jerry Quarry by TKO in three rounds. To get near Ali in his dressing room, I bumped aside the supreme Supreme, Diana Ross.

Ali's plan was clear. During his exile, Ali's heavyweight champion title had been given to Joe Frazier. Ali wanted it back. Quarry was the first step. Six weeks after the Quarry fight, Ali endured thirteen hard rounds with the Argentinian Oscar Bonavena and won by a knockout in the fourteenth.

Before he would fight Frazier, I went to see Ali at home. After that Mr. Mom day, I had become "Louisville," his hometown newspaper guy. I had talked with him in courthouses, law firm conference rooms, and once in the tiny shower room at Miami Beach's 5th Street Gym. Now I met him at the oddest place of all. It was an extravagant house in Cherry Hill, New Jersey, a gilded palace with Louis XIV furnishings, mirrored walls, and twenty-two telephones.

Down a flight of stairs, a figure lost in the darkness answered when Ali called out, "Cash? You awake? Come on."

Having roused his father, Ali asked me, "Want to go for a ride?"

He drove a Rolls-Royce to a Philadelphia rowhouse funeral home, where the three of us looked into an open coffin.

We had passed down a narrow, dark hallway into a small room with five or six rows of wooden folding chairs set on a gray linoleum floor. The room's only light came from single bare bulbs on floor lamps at each end of the coffin. The man in the coffin had been shot by an off-duty policeman after pulling a knife in an argument during the Ali-Bonavena fight.

Ali talked with the funeral director.

"What was his name?"

"He was Leslie Scott."

"Have a family?"

"Two children about grown," the funeral man said.

"How about his wife? She take it pretty hard?" Ali spoke softly, almost a whisper.

"Very, very hard. She took it hard."

Ali put his hands on the coffin's edge. "What's he feel like? Is he hard?"

"Like clay," Cash said. "Putty. Not hard."

With his right index finger, Ali touched the dead man. He pushed against the body, first on the thigh, then between the thumb and fingers, finally on the cheek.

"Cold," he said. "His cheek is hard."

"Sometimes," Cash said, "they put cotton in their cheeks."

"They do?" He stared at the dead man. "He was a big man."

"About your size."

"Yeah."

Ali traced his fingertips on the coffin's edge. "Life is pitiful. One second, this man is alive. He's arguing that I'm a better fighter than Joe Frazier. The next second, he's dead."

Ali walked away.

"I ain't worth dying for," he said.

I wrote those words after the Bonavena fight, and later, after Frazier, these . . .

On fight night, along Seventh Avenue between Thirty-first Street and Thirty-third, at the entrance to Madison Square Garden, a caravan of long, sleek, black limousines delivered their ladies and gentlemen in formal evening dress, gowns and tuxedoes, hot pants and mink-trimmed jumpsuits, peacocks all, movie stars and astronauts, senators and singers, Joe Namath with a goatee, Hugh Hefner with a Playmate in see-through chiffon, not at the Atlanta show only because in New York the sensational was de rigueur. More than twenty thousand people gathered for The Fight, the promoters claiming that closed-circuit television to thirty-five countries would reach three hundred million people from London to Hong Kong to Christchurch, New Zealand. . . .

Only the least emotionally involved or the most experienced fight-watcher sees both men in the ring. Neither description fit me on March 8, 1971. I was Ali's Louisville reporter. I had known him four years. He had held my son in his arms. The loudmouth stuff, the Nation of Islam and its mothership, Malcolm X, refusing the draft, putting his career and millions of dollars at stake on a principle, the contemptible slurs against opponents—all that was entertaining, inspiring, disturbing, confusing. I knew one thing for sure. He was the greatest athlete I would ever see in a lifetime of sportswriting. When he was in the ring, I saw him. Always, the other guy had been a blurred figure, a pale shadow, nothing really.

But not this time. This time, even I saw Joe Frazier.

I was at ringside, the first row, across from Ali's corner. Above the roar of the crowd, I could hear Ali in the ring. He shouted at Frazier, "Don't you know I'm God?" Leaning against the ropes, letting Frazier beat on him, Ali once looked down at ringside, at me, and roared, "No contest. Noooo contest!" Between rounds, as Ali sat on his corner stool, I heard his trainer, Angelo Dundee, say, "Stop playing. Do you want to blow this fight? Do you want to blow everything?"

After ten rounds, Frazier's face had become a grotesquerie of hematomas bulging from his jawline, cheekbones, and brow, squeezing his eyes to slits, his swollen lips pulled back from a mouthpiece once white and now red. Ali no longer danced even the minute of earlier rounds; now he moved on the same plane as Frazier. What notes I made were hieroglyphics of anxiety, unreadable. . . .

It became apparent that Ali believed he needed a knockout. He started the last round, the fifteenth, with two left-right combinations. He wanted then to throw a right uppercut. A fighter who drops his right hand to start an uppercut has no defense against a left hook. At that moment, Frazier's hook thundered against Ali's head. He went down. . . .

Ali landed hard on his back and rose quickly. . . .

And then the referee Mercante put himself between Ali and Frazier. The fight was over. I had heard no bell because the crowd's roar was so loud I could barely move, let alone hear, and then the only sound that mattered was the voice of the ring announcer.

I heard the decision, unanimous for Frazier, who had been a relentless, punishing aggressor for fifteen rounds. And yet to look upon his misshapen face and call him the winner was to defy reason, at least the reason of a man who once had been at Ali's side looking at a dead man in a coffin. That night it was a good thing I worked for an afternoon newspaper with a 6:00 a.m. deadline. I needed most of the dark hours of the night to figure out how to write about Ali in defeat. He had not come to a postfight media conference; instead, he went to a hospital for treatment of a swollen jaw. I finally started typing . . .

He began it arrogantly, as always, and he ended it in silence, as never before.

The next morning, in his hotel room, Ali met with reporters. He was gracious in defeat and full of praise for Frazier. The *New York Times* man, Robert Lipsyte, reminded Ali that he once said no man would ever beat him twice. His face still swollen and scratched, Ali smiled. "I remember that. And you know what I say now? Get me Frazier. No man ever beat me twice." His voice rose. "I'll get by Joe this time. I'll straighten this out. Joe, you hear me?" Now shouting. "Joe, if you beat me this time, you'll really be the greatest."

EARLY IN 1972, EARL COX SAID, "YOU EVER BEEN TO THE OLYMPICS?"

I had been to the Logan County Fair.

"Get your passport up to date."

I would be the Courier-Journal & Times man at the 1972 Olympics in Munich, Germany. Cheryl and I did the young lovers' grand tour through London, Paris, Zurich, Rome, and Madrid. In Munich we stayed with a local family. While I worked, Cheryl wandered around the Olympic Park with Marcy Mizell, whose husband, Hubert, was the *St. Petersburg (FL) Times* columnist. Each night we caught a taxi home from a downtown beer hall. Such a good time.

Until it happened.

The morning of September 5, when Cheryl and I came downstairs, the family's television was on. I remember it as a black-and-white portable showing shadowy figures on the screen, men wearing combat gear marked POLIZEI. We understood none of the TV commentary, only that its tone was ominous. The one member of the family who spoke English was Karl-Heinz, ten years old. He looked from the TV to us and said, "We bad people."

At the media compound I learned that a terrorist group known as Black September had taken Israeli athletes and officials hostage. I listened to the official briefings. Then I did the only thing I knew to do. I walked toward Building 31, where the Israelis had lived. I was not sure what to expect, but I did not expect what I felt when I stood on a hillside overlooking the building.

There was no sense of terror. Whatever was happening was happening out of sight. Spectators walked past the building. For an hour I sat among tourists on that hillside, as if we had found a nice picnic place—albeit a picnic place with a view of a masked man on a balcony carrying a machine gun, standing guard outside the Israelis' rooms.

The world was out of kilter. Even as killers held Israelis hostage, tourists sat on a hillside watching a man with a machine gun, and somewhere, in a stadium not far away, the Olympics went on.

The week before had been beautiful. We had seen the Soviet wunderkind, gymnast Olga Korbut, take flights of imagination. We had seen John Akii-Bua of Uganda dance over hurdles after winning his nation's first gold medal ever.

Now the joy was gone, replaced by a chilling fear. The week before the games began, Cheryl and I had gone to Dachau, twelve miles from the Olympics site. Jews had been exterminated there a generation before. We walked in Dachau's gardens created in memory of those who died. We saw Dachau's ovens. We had heard the little German boy Karl-Heinz say, "We bad people." Karl-Heinz had no more understanding of the event than I did, but, like me, he knew Germany's history. My father had been a GI who landed at Normandy on D-Day +13. He had marched into Germany in 1945. Now I sat on a hillside in Munich a quarter mile from men killing Jews.

Still, the Games went on.

JOE FRAZIER NEVER DEFEATED ALI AGAIN. I WAS THERE FOR ALI-Frazier II, a dull fight in Madison Square Garden in which Ali mostly held Frazier more than he fought him, winning by decision. There would be an Ali-Frazier III, the "Thrilla in Manila," won by Ali when Frazier did not come out for the fifteenth round. I was not there. The *Courier-Journal* said it was too expensive to send a man to the Philippines. Nor was I in Zaire the year before when Ali regained the heavyweight championship by knocking out George Foreman.

Too deferential to buck authority, I had watched those fights on closed-circuit television. I should have paid my own way ($600 for a chartered flight and accommodations in Zaire). I should have thrown Earl Cox through a window. That, or at least a typewriter.

OTHERWISE, I SAW EVERYTHING.

I saw Hogan be Hogan. I saw Ali in a rowhouse funeral home. I saw a killer on Building 31.

May 1969, I flew out of Louisville with "Chargin' Charlie" Glotz-bach, a big-time stock car driver. He had his own plane. He was flying to Indianapolis to qualify for the 500. As we descended to Eagle

Creek airfield, a plane appeared directly beneath us, apparently aiming to land in the same pasture. "Charlie?" I said. He did something that made us go straight up. The ascent also caused a buzzer to go off and a red light to come on. Under the light, I saw STALL. I said again, "Charlie?" He said, "We got thirty seconds." We had gone from going down to going straight up and then to leveling off and coming down again, all without getting anyone killed. Then came the harrowing part. I rode shotgun as Charlie drove his pickup truck to Indianapolis Motor Speedway at seventy-five miles per hour on blind-corner country roads. After that, I never went anywhere with Charlie.

My first Super Bowl was number IV. It was 1970, Minnesota–Kansas City, Tulane Stadium, New Orleans. I sat next to the *Dayton (OH) Daily News* columnist, Si Burick, a gentle man and a sneaky punster. Before kickoff, a stripper from Bourbon Street, baring her wares, flounced onto the field. Four policemen chased her down. "And they took her away," Si said, "two abreast."

In Norman, Oklahoma, 1972, Nebraska beat the Sooners, 35–31, and I wrote they could quit playing college football, that at last they had played the perfect game.

Secretariat won the 1973 Belmont Stakes by an astonishing thirty-one lengths. He was the first Triple Crown winner since Citation in '48. I stood alongside the Detroit columnist, Joe Falls, who nudged me with an elbow and said, "Citation, my ass."

There was the night Bob Knight cuffed Joe Hall upside the head— then did not want to talk about it. December 1974. Knight's first good team had Kentucky down by about thirty late. Knight stood at midcourt with Hall as the game flowed past them. Knight dropped his right hand behind Hall's back and brought it up swiftly, cuffing the back of Hall's head. Knight dropped the hand in front of Hall as if the intent all along had been to shake hands. Hall refused to play.

In the pressroom, people asked questions designed to God-up Indiana. Finally, I raised my hand. I had known Knight a couple years. I knew his combative, combustible personality, and I was about to know it better. "Coach," I said, "what happened there with you and Joe?" Knight looked around the room. "We're here to talk about basketball. Anybody got a basketball question?" The dutiful press, sitting in little desk-chairs like sixth graders, asked basketball questions. I raised my hand again. "Coach, you and Coach Hall there at midcourt, what was going on?" Knight said, "We're here to talk about basketball. Anybody got a basketball question?"

Now I was more afraid, professionally, to not ask my question than I was to ask it in the first place. Still, I asked it a third time, and Knight kept talking about basketball—until finally he turned his coal-black eyes my way. "Now, David, what did you want to know?"

I said, "Coach, seventeen thousand people saw you hit the other team's coach. What happened between you and Coach Hall?"

Knight gave a nonanswer about how his cuffing someone on the back of the head was a sign of respect and admiration, something he did to his players all the time.

Well, OK, yeah, sure, we all believe that. Later, writing, I saw a bear lumbering across the basketball court. Big, strong, no shoulders. I turned to my neighbor in the press row and said, "This can't be good." Knight climbed up to my row and said, "How do I get myself into these things?" He seemed remorseful, even a touch human. I again asked him my question, and I did a virtual live column, just typing in his answers.

We got along well from then on, though getting along with Knight was a full-time job that asked you to understand that you would never understand him. My default position on Knight was not knee-jerk condemnation but an effort, however futile, at understanding, perhaps even helping him understand himself. As my pal Tom Callahan often said, "Knight gets all the big things right and the little things wrong." I admired his honesty—a belligerent honesty, to be sure—in the cutthroat world of big-time college basketball recruiting. And no one ever doubted his basketball brilliance, a coach creative at both ends of the court and spectacularly successful at pushing players to near their full potential—and I say that knowing he often treated players despicably. (A misogynist, he once placed a tampon in a player's locker.) His sense of humor ran from raw to crude, usually expressed in four-letter words, sometimes in twelve-letter words. To call him volatile was to understate his volatility. No one ever demanded more discipline from his teams, and no one was ever less disciplined than Knight. He could move from control to rage with no warning. In the end, by failing to confront his flaws, he created his undoing.

I called him in 2018. We agreed that I would come visit him in Lubbock, Texas. I would do a Knight-in-retirement story for the *Athletic*. The next day, his best and oldest friend, Indiana newspaperman Bob Hammel, asked me to cancel the interview. He said Knight was often lost to dementia. "He's known you for fifty years," Hammel said. "But he called me yesterday and said, 'Who's Dave Kindred?' Some things, he has no memory of. It's sad." I did not go to Lubbock. I did not want to see that Bob Knight.

In Fenway Park, the 1975 World Series, Game 6, at 12:30 a.m., I was up against a final-edition deadline. The Red Sox catcher, Carlton Fisk, came to bat in the twelfth inning of a four-hour game on a freezing night. Out of necessity, I was filing a running column, one paragraph after another (basically live-tweeting from my Smith-Corona long before God invented Twitter). That's when Fisk did his hero thing. I said a silent hooray and began typing, fast.

Hold the coffee. Carlton Fisk just hit one. It's high, going out to left, toward the Green Monster. It's a home run. Pandemonium, as they say, is breaking out. It's 12:33. Boston wins, 7–6. Good night.

Every May for twenty years I sat against a chain-link fence at Turn One, awed and terrified by the thirty-three-car thunder of Indianapolis 500 starts, and at a Daytona 500 I watched, awed and terrified, as NASCAR's great rivals, Richard Petty and David Pearson, crashed together out of Turn Four at 180 miles per hour, Pearson's car spinning, dying, finally coughing to life and lurching across the finish line.

On a cold November day in 1976, I sat with Adolph Rupp. He had come home after twenty-five days in a hospital for repairs he did not want to mention. "Just say I'm awful weak." We talked for an hour, a coach and a writer, the coach who once called the writer a son of a bitch. "I'm as happy as I'll ever be," he said. "And I'm not a bit bitter about anything." He walked me to the door, limping. Snow covered his yard. He said, "I'm looking forward to spring." He was seventy-five years old.

THEN THE *WASHINGTON POST* CALLED. I HAD SPENT A DESULTORY NINE months from late '72 into '73 as the third man in the Courier-Journal & Times Washington bureau. I had played with the idea of leaving sports, perhaps to write politics, and had applied for the papers' one-year rotation in the Washington bureau. One year there, then I would return to the mother paper. I was mostly miserable keeping tabs on Kentucky's congressional delegation. Reporting the distribution of federal tax revenue to eastern Kentucky counties did not satisfy an addict's need for the adrenaline rush of sports.

At the '73 Preakness Stakes, I met George Solomon, then a deputy sports editor at the *Post*. We had mutual friends in the business. He asked how I liked it in Washington. "If I never hear of another Army Corps of Engineer project," I said, "it will be too soon. And Cheryl hates living on the sixteenth floor of an apartment building. We can't wait to go home."

Late in 1976, I was in my office at the *Courier-Journal* when Solomon called. He had become the *Post* sports editor. He asked my opinion on a columnist he might want to hire. After hearing my scouting report, Solomon said, "You wouldn't be interested, would you?"

"Why," I said, "would you say that?"

"Last time we talked, you didn't seem happy being in Washington."

"The town, I loved. The bureau job wasn't my thing. I'd be very interested."

NEWSPAPERS WERE NEVER BETTER, NOR DID THEY EVER MATTER MORE than in those days when they were rich with cash and ambition. Before the Internet, before Facebook, Twitter, and Instagram, newspapers were important in ways that social media could never be—as trusted messengers of the day's news. Earl Cox was passionate about the newspaper that had shaped his life. He believed the *Courier-Journal* was one thing all Kentuckians had in common. That passion made Earl a great newspaperman, made the *Courier-Journal* a great newspaper, and made me proud every day that I walked into that grand lobby at Sixth and Broadway.

At the *Pantagraph*, I had covered Minonk-Dana-Rutland High School. A year later, I was in Memorial Coliseum annoying Adolph Rupp. By 1969, I was a columnist going to the Masters and following

Muhammad Ali around. When George Solomon called, I went to Cox. Only later did he tell me he had already talked to Solomon, who had asked if I was ready. "I told him," Earl said, "you've been ready."

I was not looking to leave Louisville. But it was the *Washington Post*. It had become America's most famous newspaper, the *All the President's Men* newspaper, Ben Bradlee's newspaper.

I drove home. We had built the house Cheryl had seen on a paint brochure. We even painted it the same rich chocolate color. We had fireplaces in the family room and master bedroom. We had plans to add two decks, one outside the kitchen, the other a small balcony off the master. We would live there forever. Unless . . .

As I walked in, Cheryl was leaning against a kitchen countertop. I said, "Remember when I told you we were here for good, that we wouldn't move, unless, maybe, the *New York Times* or the *Washington Post* called?"

My beloved said, "Oh, shit."

3

. . . .

W AIT. I HAVE SKIPPED OVER A PLOT TWIST IN THIS STORY. SIX months before Solomon called, I had been offered a columnist's job at the *Chicago Sun-Times*.

It was 1976. The *Sun-Times* sports editor was Lewis Grizzard, later known as a southern humorist writing books with titles such as *Don't Bend Over in the Garden, Granny, You Know Them Taters Got Eyes*. We met in the *Sun-Times* sports department on a freezing January day. Deep in his son of Georgia's soul, Grizzard hated Chicago's wind and ice. The only thing he hated more was the *Sun-Times* sports department. He called it "a retirement home for broken-down sportswriters who knew George Halas back when."

He had a scheme in mind. "You come here," he said, "and us young guys will get rid of the old guys."

Two things wrong with that. Why would I want to sign up with a guy so miserable that he might be on the next Delta flight to Atlanta? (He later wrote a *Sun-Times* memoir: *If I Ever Get Back to Georgia, I'm Gonna Nail My Feet to the Ground*.) Besides, I had grown up riding my bike from Grandma Lena's house to the Lincoln train station to fetch the Chicago papers. I had come to know those sportswriters he wanted me to throw under the bus. Bill Gleason was a Chicago South Side tough guy who knew a fraud when he saw one and counted Grizzard as one. Also, Grizzard wanted Jerome Holtzman gone, Holtzman who for forty years had known everything worth knowing about baseball and had written a classic oral history of sportswriting, *No Cheering in the Press Box*.

Grizzard earned a place in sports editor lore by ordering Holtzman back from spring training for a lecture on how to do his job. "You're using too many clichés," Grizzard said.

Holtzman asked for examples and, on hearing them, said, "Those are *my* clichés, I invented them," after which Grizzard allowed him to return to spring training.

With no such memorable line, I just said no to the *Sun-Times*.

Six months later, I sat with Ben Bradlee.

Solomon and I had been to lunch at Duke Zeibert's restaurant, the favored gathering place of politicians and journalists in the nation's capital. The next order of business was a meeting with Bradlee. I was nervous. I saw it as a pro forma meeting in which my job was to not say anything stupid and please, God, do not let me ask for his autograph.

Bradlee made it easy. He was a sports fan, a regular at Washington Redskins football games and a buddy of the team president, the quintessential Washington lawyer, Edward Bennett Williams. Bradlee talked about all the fun he had going to Carlisle, Pennsylvania, where the Redskins trained. In our meeting, he asked one question.

"What do you think of George Allen?"

Allen was the Redskins' coach, a great coach and a flawed person. "I think he's Nixon with a whistle," I said.

Thank heaven, Bradlee laughed out loud.

When I returned to George's office, he slid a piece of folded paper across his desk and said, "That's what we can pay you."

No one had ever suggested my salary by way of a folded note. Then it got more unusual. The figure on George's piece of paper was $300 a week less than Grizzard's offer. George said, "What do you think?" I said nothing. George sensed a problem and named the sports columnist at the *New York Times*. "It's what Dave Anderson makes."

I said, "OK, George. But tell me, how do I explain to Cheryl that I've taken a job in Washington, DC, for $15,000 less than I turned down six months ago in Chicago?"

George answered with a sentence that had the sound of having been said before.

"The *Washington Post* rewards well those who do well," he said.

That line I would remember.

WE SOLD CHERYL'S DREAM HOUSE IN LOUISVILLE AND BOUGHT A BRICK ranch down the Mount Vernon Parkway that ran along the Potomac River. We were five minutes from Mount Vernon itself. Cheryl decided the brick-colored brick on our brick ranch needed pizzazz. She painted the bricks red, better than red, louder than red. It was the red you see coming down the street on a big truck with its siren wailing. Neighbors knew our house as "the one that lady from Kentucky painted."

My first week at the *Post*, the publisher, Don Graham, said hello. He was an extraordinary man, born to wealth, a Harvard graduate who enlisted for duty in Vietnam and chose to be a District of Columbia cop before entering the family business. His grandfather, Eugene Meyer, had bought the failing *Washington Post* at auction in

1930. His mother, Katharine Meyer Graham, became publisher on the death of her husband, Phil Graham. Donnie, as he was universally known, worked at many levels of the *Post*, including a year as sports editor, with Martie Zad and George Solomon on his staff.

Now he stood at my desk. "Welcome to the *Post*," he said.

"It's great to be here," I said.

"You got a place to live yet?"

"We bought a house down by Mount Vernon. My wife's already painted it red."

The publisher paused. "You *bought* a house?"

In Louisville we had bought one house and built another. So why not buy in Washington? This was different from my year in the C-J & Times Washington bureau; that was a one-year assignment. I figured being hired by the *Washington Post* was a permanent thing. Only later did I realize it was no sure thing that I would be around long enough to make buying a house a wise decision. I was the second man hired to succeed Shirley Povich; the first was a veteran writer with a big-league résumé. He wrote three-thousand-word columns, missed deadlines, and soon sought other work. Yet here I was, up from Triple-A Louisville telling the publisher that we did not rent a house, we *bought* a house in George Washington's neighborhood and my wife had painted it fire-engine red. He must have wondered if I was confident or naive. I was both.

"Good luck," Donnie said.

I HAD ASTONISHING LUCK. SOLOMON USED TO SAY, "I HIRE 'EM YOUNG, single, and hungry." I was not that young, thirty-six, and I had been married fifteen years. I made up for those failings by being very hungry. My life became a succession of thrill rides, beginning that first year. I remember a walk to ringside for a fight at Robert F. Kennedy Stadium.

It was a cool evening, twilight coming. I walked alongside Shirley Povich, a small, courtly, gentle man who for decades had written one of newspapers' great sports columns under the signature logo "This Morning." He had sat on Walter Johnson's front porch reminiscing with the Washington Senators' pitcher about good times in the 1924 World Series. In 1939 he had been in Yankee Stadium for Lou Gehrig's "luckiest man on earth" speech.

Now I carried my typewriter and walked with him to ringside fifty years after he wrote, "Out of the maze of doubt of the cross-fire that has questioned his supremacy, the shadows that would be-cloud his claim, Gene Tunney today stands against the pugilistic horizon in bold relief, the heavyweight champion of the world, and worthy of the crown. . . . By right of might, Gene Tunney proved his claim last night at Soldier Field. Against Jack Dempsey he proved himself a champion in every sense."

Shirley had been among the 150,000 people at the "long count" fight on September 27, 1927. I had moved from my nights of reading sports history to walking with a man whose experience, vision, and judgment had helped create that history. Not that long since my days as the *Pantagraph* bowling columnist, I was about to inherit "This Morning."

The first week, I made a point of meeting the most important man in town.

Not Jimmy Carter.

Nixon with a whistle.

I drove from the *Post* on Washington's Fourteenth Street into exurban Virginia. There, in the Redskins' office building, I passed a relic of another time that in the twenty-first century would be banished from sight—a wooden Indian painted in Redskins' burgundy and gold.

From afar, I had thought of George Allen as another obsessive football coach. Vince Lombardi had established the monomaniacal standard by saying, "Winning isn't everything, it's the only thing." Allen upped the ante. He said, "Losing is like dying."

Up close, I liked him the way a columnist likes eccentrics, outliers, and other rogues. They are good copy. What Allen believed, he believed with unabashed enthusiasm and wanted you to believe it for your own good. Once, after winning at St. Louis, he stopped on his way to the team bus to shout, "This is a great victory for the Redskins, for the city, and for the NATION!" After victories he often led his sweaty warriors in a raucous singing of the team fight song, "Hail to the Redskins!" Redskin Park's walls carried photographs of the team's stars. He pointed to a picture and shouted, "Eddie Brown, that seventy-one-yard punt return!" Allen had designed the complex. "Everything here is here for a purpose," he said, and there was no forgetting that purpose. A sign on the coach's desk, turned toward visitors, asked, "What have you done today to help us win?"

Eccentrics, outliers, and other rogues . . .

Jack Kent Cooke, the Redskins' owner, was a self-made billionaire up from selling encyclopedias door-to-door in the wilds of Canada. He never let us forget he was the One & Only Jack Kent Cooke. He wore tweeds and silk cravats, favored operatic oratory over common speech, and in his eighties dated a young South American beauty billed in the tabloids as "the Bolivian Bombshell." The last time I saw Cooke, at age eighty-two, we conjured names of friends and sports figures long dead. At each name, the Bombshell asked, for reasons best known to her, "And how old was he?"

I was jammed in cheek by jowl with Edward Bennett Williams and a couple dozen other worried people stranded on an elevator in Baltimore's rickety Memorial Stadium. With each minute the elevator refused to move, EBW grew increasingly nervous, overheated, frightened. Finally, the man who had defended Jimmy Hoffa commanded, "LET US PRAY!" His face glistening with sweat, Williams boomed out the Lord's Prayer. No sooner did he get to "forever and ever, amen!" than the elevator jerked into motion and dropped down to a jarring stop. A short drop, three inches, it was better than spending the night suspended above imagined calamity. Williams was first off.

I was in the Oval Office when Sugar Ray Leonard visited Ronald Reagan. Leonard, a local hero out of the DC suburbs and an Olympic gold medalist, had defended his welterweight boxing championship against Thomas Hearns. A reporter called out, "Sugar Ray, any ideas on how to balance the budget?" Reagan, an old sportscaster, took over. "If we get too desperate," the president said, "we might ask him to do a few benefits." Leonard pronounced himself honored to be there. People keeping score knew it had taken five years and eight victories in world title fights to get the invite. On the way out, Leonard said, "If I win two more championships, maybe I can meet the man on the moon."

At a Super Bowl press conference in 1983, the Redskins' star, John Riggins, showed up wearing a "5 O'clock Club" T-shirt. To join that "semi-elite club" that met after practice, Riggins said, "You buy a Budweiser." He wore camouflage pants, an elephant-gun belt buckle, and cowboy boots. It was the NFL Mercenary look. He had quit football for a year, wanting a better deal, and then Joe Gibbs, newly hired as the Redskins coach, showed up at his door in Kansas. It was nine o'clock one morning. Riggins answered with a beer in hand. "I don't know if Joe goes for that," he said. "But I do."

A reporter asked Riggins if he had a drinking problem.

"Only," he said, "when I'm hanging from the rafters by my knees."

John Riggins! A triple-threat character, at once an eccentric, outlier, and rogue. After that year hunkered down on the Kansas plains, he came back to be a Hall of Fame fullback. Behind offensive linemen famous as the Hogs—brutes who scrounged in the muck— Riggins carried the football when it most needed carrying. On January 15, 1983, the Redskins beat Minnesota, 21–7, to advance to the NFC championship game. Riggins carried thirty-seven times for 186 yards. I began my column in the *Post* . . .

> Handsome as the night is long, smiling in the sunlight of a day he'll love always, John Riggins took his helmet off at midfield and with a flourish of gallantry did a deep bow, his arm across his waist, bowing first to the folks on the south side of RFK Stadium and then spinning to say thanks to those on the north, the 54,000 or so screaming mee- mies who loved it as much as Riggins did.
>
> Paint a picture of the moment. Get the blotch of mud on his cheek. Leave the grass stains on the white of his jersey. Remember that his pants were ripped, a pad peeking out on his thigh, and when you're done with the picture, hang it somewhere important, like in the White House or, better, in Pig Alley where the hallowed Hogs hang out.

Only four men in pro football history had carried the ball more often in a career than Riggins, and only six had gained more yards. None did it the way Riggins did it, a six-foot-two, 240-pounder run- ning around, through, and over people. Holding grievances against the press, Riggins refused to answer questions that day. But his super- powers did not include invisibility. I followed him around the locker room and out.

Riggins stayed in character. Olivier probably did no interviews on his motivation playing Hamlet. Riggins playing Riggins picked up his hiking boots, sent a man to get his saddlebags, and left the sta- dium. He stashed his saddlebags in the car trunk (no briefcase for a man who once rode his motorcycle from Kansas to Washington) and then took a beer from hometown buddies waiting to tell him, as one did, "Best game ever, John. High school, college, pro, anywhere. Best." Riggins sipped at the beer, threw back a swig of tequila, and said to his buddy, "Hey," before driving away.

Later, at age thirty-three, in his eleventh season, Riggins explained how he had lasted so long.

"Formaldehyde," he said.

For a team party early in the '83 Super Bowl week, Riggins showed up not as a mercenary but as a stylish performer, a dandy in top hat and tails, literally dancing on tabletops while twirling a cane. Then came the role Riggins liked most. He played a football hero in Pasadena's Rose Bowl. I wrote . . .

Dreamy, so dreamy, floating in a rosy jewel of a bowl at the foot of mountains caressed by clouds and snow, the Washington Redskins today won the world championship they last held 40 years ago. The Hog who wears top hat and tails, John Riggins, made the earth tilt the Redskins' way as the chill of night and defeat settled on Miami's Dolphins, 27–17.

With an 18-wheeler load of Nagurski brutishness and a touch of Astaire's fanciful grace, Riggins broke every important running record (38 carries, 166 yards) in Super Bowl lore. He gave the Redskins their first lead at 20–17, running 43 yards on a fourth-and-inches play with 10:01 left in the game.

President Reagan called to congratulate the Redskins. Riggins was suddenly voluble. "At least for tonight, Ron is president," he said, "but I'm the king."

HERE IS HOW IT CAN GO IN THE PRESS BOX ON DEADLINE. TWO PARA-graphs back, there is a sentence beginning, "He gave the Redskins . . ."

I did not write that sentence.

I began writing the column from Pasadena with an East Coast deadline closing down hard. Past midnight back home, editors waited for the column. It would run as the lead-all on Super Bowl coverage under a banner headline stripped across the top of page 1. But first I had to get it there.

I was good on deadline. It might not be pretty, but pretty runs second to fast on deadline. Getting it done quickly is especially tricky when you must write about a game while watching it without knowing how it would end. The Riggins touchdown had given the Redskins that 20–17 lead with maybe a half hour of real time to go. OK, time to get on it. I started typing, fast.

I accounted for Riggins's sensational game, the feel of it, the glamour, and the numbers. In my adrenaline rush, I swooshed right over his game-turning touchdown on fourth-and-inches. He roared off left tackle, pulling away from a falling Dolphin defender, and I did not catch the wonder of that run. Only the most famous play in Redskins history. Only won a Super Bowl. Only a moment that would forever define a Hall of Fame runner's career.

George Solomon, reading over my shoulder and urgent-whispering reminders of time passing, saved me.

He whispered, "Riggins's run."

And he wrote it in, bless him.

"GOOD LUCK," DONNIE GRAHAM HAD SAID, AND I HAD THE BEST OF good luck in my time at the *Post*.

We worked in Ben Bradlee's newsroom. Bob Woodward sat near David Maraniss across from Dana Priest and Walter Pincus. The bright young David Remnick, later the editor of the *New Yorker*, covered fights for the sports department. No one ever wrote baseball more passionately than Thomas Boswell, unless it was Shirley Povich, and Shirley often visited us, raising the room's elegance quotient. My partners in crime: Solomon, his deputy Leonard Shapiro, Paul Attner, Ken Denlinger, and John Feinstein (who knew where the *z*'s went in *Krzyzewski*), Jane Leavy, Barry Lorge, and Tony Kornheiser (who wrote eighty-eight inches so he could hold aloft a printout of his feature on seven-foot-four Ralph Sampson and say, "This tall!"). There were Michael Wilbon, Betty Cuniberti, the irreplaceable night editor O. D. Wilson, Suzanne Tobin, Bill Gildea, Bob Fachet, George Minot, the outdoorsman Angus Phillips (who went fishing with G. H. W. Bush, "a bright, funny guy"), Sandra Bailey, Gary Pomerantz, Peter Richmond, John Ed Bradley (with novels in the works), Dave Brady, and Peter Mehlman (misplaced on Solomon's desk, freed for TV by Howard Cosell en route to writing/producing *Seinfeld*, a career arc full of comic possibilities).

If not for that astonishing good luck, how else would a kid from Illinois cornfields wind up in the press gallery at Wimbledon's Centre Court? Close enough to the royal box that he could study the aquiline profile of Princess Diana and write, "Quite the babe."

Ken Stabler, the great old Raiders quarterback, a rogue's rogue, was playing out the string with the Houston Oilers. I read to him the Jack London declaration: "I would rather be ashes than dust! I would rather be a superb meteor, every atom of me in magnificent glow, than a sleepy and permanent planet." I asked Stabler what London meant by that. The old pirate grinned. He said, "Throw deep."

The night before a funeral in Las Vegas, I sat in the dark with Muhammad Ali in his hotel room. Ali had said he did not want to end up like Joe Louis, poor Joe, poor, broke Joe. Now, his voice a whisper, Ali took it back. "Look at Joe's life. Everybody loved Joe. Joe would have been marked as evil if he was evil, but everybody loved Joe. From black folks to redneck Mississippi crackers, they loved him. They're all crying. That shows you. Howard Hughes dies, with all his billions, not a tear. Joe Louis, everybody cried." The next day, Jesse Jackson stood in a boxing ring under the tin roof of a sports pavilion behind the Caesars Palace casino. He stood by a casket bearing Joe Louis, and he preached on the power of a man's life. "When we were vulnerable and the scent of the Depression was still in our clothes . . . when lynching mobs threatened our existence and we were defenseless without legal, political, economic, or military protection, God built a fence around us and Joe was anointed and appointed the gatekeeper. He was our Samson, he was our David who slew Goliath."

The phone rang in my *Post* office. "Howard Cosell here," the caller said, and damned if it was not Cosell. He liked a recent column. "You are a most perspicacious young man," the most obstreperous television broadcaster in America said. We spoke for the next seventeen years. Sometimes he even listened.

I was one set of seats over from a princess at Centre Court and near enough to the court to see Martina Navratilova burn with uncommon fire. She would win Wimbledon's singles title eight times, a record, including six times in a row. She had come to America at eighteen, from Czechoslovakia. Her world, once gray, became a Technicolor wonder. "Oh my God, how did I do it?" she said, having left her home and parents, maybe forever. I sat with Barry Lorge, the *Post*'s great tennis writer, to talk with Navratilova, who said she had no reason to go home again. We had heard about a beloved grandmother's death. I asked, "Was she kind of a last link?" There was another grandmother, Martina said, but not so close. She turned away. She leaned against a wall and wept for five minutes. Sorry, she said, she did not know that would happen. She walked off, down a corridor, stopping to sign an autograph for a small girl. We left a note. We, too, were sorry. The next day, we learned that Andela Subertova was eighty-four years old in 1979, the one time she visited her granddaughter Martina in Dallas. A year later there came in Navratilova's mail a card from Czechoslovakia, a black-edged card of mourning. It was the first Martina knew of her grandmother's death.

Best I know, I was in the presence of only one man who survived a duel. We stood in the cool morning air outside Barn 40 at Churchill Downs. Horatio Luro was eighty years old. He had trained two Kentucky Derby winners, Decidedly and Northern Dancer. He came in 1981 with Tap Shoes (who would finish fourteenth). A dashing figure, heir to an Argentine fortune, Luro set his cap at a rakish angle and trimmed his mustache pencil-thin. Either his hair was dyed, or it was naturally orange, but in any case he brought elegance to the stables. "The Cary Grant of trainers," a man said. Luro had danced with the movie goddess Lana Turner. ("Ah, Lana," is the way he put it.) He once cold-cocked a French nobleman who had insulted him, prompting a duel in which Luro won the choice of weapons. Swords! ("He had been shooting lions in Brazil.") The Frenchman knocked back a shot of brandy and leaped to the matter. "He was so violent that I cut him on the arm, and he started to bleed like hell . . . they stopped the duel." Luro sighed in memory of blessed victory. "This is just one of those things in life you have to face."

And there was Jack Kent Cooke.

Who hired Joe Gibbs in 1981.

The single most important event in Redskins modern history.

George Allen had taken his whistle and left town rather than argue contract law with Ed Williams, who ran the franchise while Cooke lived in Los Angeles. EBW hired Jack Pardee, who quickly failed. Finishing up a nasty divorce, Cooke moved to Washington for "the third act of my life." In the first two acts, the Canadian entrepreneur had made himself the billionaire owner of the Redskins, the Los Angeles Lakers, the Los Angeles Kings, the *Los Angeles Daily News*, a cable-TV empire, and New York's Chrysler Building. "Doing a business deal," he said, "is better than fornication, don't you think?"

With a coach to hire, we knew Cooke would not sit still.

Most of the "we" was Paul Attner. A *Post* veteran, the beat man on the Redskins, Attner was a persistent and meticulous reporter who knew everything, usually before it happened. He had already reported Cooke's foundational decision. Faced with a coach and general manager who differed on how to rebuild the team, Cooke chose to let Pardee go and keep Bobby Beathard. When it came time to hire a coach, Attner knew (1) it was Cooke's call, and (2) after giving Beathard the GM's job, Cooke would not ignore his advice.

"Still," I said, "no way Cooke hires Gibbs. He doesn't even know who Joe Gibbs is."

"Bobby has had Joe in mind for a long time, that if he ever had a chance to hire a head coach, it'd be Joe," Attner said. "Bobby will sell him."

Cooke had a good track record in sports. Among his trinkets had been a Triple-A baseball team, the Toronto Maple Leafs. There he had hired a manager, an unknown utility infielder, thirty years old. It was Sparky Anderson's first managerial job in a Hall of Fame career. In the fourteen years Cooke owned the Lakers, they reached the NBA Finals seven times, winning once, in 1972. Hiring a football coach would not be his first rodeo.

On meeting Cooke, I had fun answering his unannounced quizzes. "What do you think of Jim Murray?" he asked. (The *LA Times*'s sports columnist.) I said, "He's a sweetheart who can write funny better than anybody else can write serious." Cooke asked, "Mel Durslag?" (Another LA columnist.) "I'd like his stuff more if he used fewer dollar signs." "Atta boy," Cooke said, and when it came time, a year later, to find a Redskins coach, Cooke knew me well enough to share his thoughts, sometimes on the record.

The first week in January 1981, triangulating what Attner and I knew, I said to Joe Gibbs, "Can you come over here?" We moved behind a coaching blackboard. This was after the San Diego Chargers lost to Buffalo in a playoff game. Gibbs was the Chargers' offensive coordinator. His season was over.

"I know you're flying from here to New York with Bobby Beathard to meet Mr. Cooke," I said. "I'm going to make the same flight. I think you'll get the job."

Gibbs said, "You know more about that franchise than I do. I hope you're right."

That night I met Gibbs and Beathard at a hotel in Los Angeles and met them again the next morning when Beathard said, "Did you sleep through that last night?"

"Through what?"

"The fire alarm," Beathard said.

"What fire alarm?"

"They evacuated us," he said.

"You let me sleep through a fire?"

Beathard, eternally cool, an ageless California surfer, said, "It must not have been a problem on your floor."

In the first-class section of our flight, I interviewed Gibbs from LA to Chicago. Back in coach, I began typing an hour before we reached New York, three or four hours before we were to meet Cooke in his Waldorf Astoria suite. What I wrote on the plane might stand up or it might not, depending on how that meeting went. But deadlines do not bend to the vagaries of transcontinental flights and high-dollar meetings. I got a head start by typing a prospective lead for the next day's column. . . .

Fresh off the plowed fields out back of his house in the hills of western North Carolina, the county sheriff's oldest boy didn't know what to do with all the fancy football equipment they issued him at the big California high school.

"The only football I'd ever played was pickup games with the guys around home," Joe Gibbs said. "When we moved to Santa Fe Springs, just outside Los Angeles, the first day I went to school for the ninth grade, I saw a sign, 'Sign Up for Football.' All the gear they gave me, I was putting everything on wrong."

Eight years later, good enough at this new game to have been a first stringer at quarterback, tight end and linebacker in high school and at San Diego State, Joe Gibbs asked Don Coryell if he could join the coach's staff as a graduate assistant.

"Graduate assistant" is also known as a gofer. "John Madden was on the staff working for Don then," Gibbs said. "It was a great staff. . . . I was the guy who went out and got hamburgers for everybody. And they reamed me out good if I forgot the sauce."

In his Waldorf suite, Cooke was dressed elegantly. Though Beathard preferred shorts, flip-flops, and Hawaiian shirts, for this he came dressed to the nines, which, by his standards, meant khaki pants, a button-down shirt, a blazer, and, purchased at the last hour, a tie, a loosely knotted tie, a purple tie. Gibbs came dressed as a coach-in-waiting. I was in sportswriter chic, of course.

Some sports columnists like to hire and fire, just to hear themselves shout. I was never a shouter. Yet there I was in the middle of a coaching hire. I was there with an owner and his team's general manager. They were about to hire the most important man in the nation's capital. Beathard and Gibbs sat upright in chairs alongside the owner, and I lounged on a sofa across the way. My nonchalance ended when the billionaire began reading aloud from a newspaper column.

I recognized it.

It was my column from the week before.

On why the Redskins should hire Joe Gibbs.

He's an outstanding offensive mind, in tune with the day's game.

He's great at the blackboard, great communicator, demanding teacher.

Cooke's dramatic reading suggested he was about to offer Gibbs the job. That part made me uncomfortable. I did not want to cross the line between reporting news and creating news. "I gotta leave," I said. "I don't belong here right now."

The good thing was, I did not need to report news. Attner, citing sources, had nailed down the story the day before.

In twelve seasons, Gibbs led Cooke's Redskins to four Super Bowls, winning three, each time with a different quarterback, each time with a different star running back. At this writing, he remains the only coach who ever did that.

MEANWHILE, AS I WAS THERE IN 1966 WITH THE YOUNG MUHAMMAD ALI in Louisville, I was there in 1980 with the old Muhammad Ali in Las Vegas.

He had retired two years earlier. Now he had come back to fight for the heavyweight championship once more, this time against Larry Holmes.

I had seen him earlier that year when he shilled for a fight in Montreal. He weighed 260 pounds. His face was puffy, his eyes streaked by blood lines and coated with a veil of tear water. He had that viscous and lifeless look of men who sleep on street grates. His voice was a gritty, stuttering whisper and at one point he said, "I have surpassed storps" before adding a repair to the sentence, "er, sports."

"See how good I look?" he said. He looked a mess, rheumy-eyed, gray at the temples, shirt unbuttoned at the throat, his tie pulled askew. The index and middle fingers of his right hand trembled. The trainer Ray Arcel, a master of the game for half a century, would say, "All those fights after the Manila fight destroyed Muhammad Ali." In three years after Manila, Ali fought eight more times, going fifteen rounds six times.

When I arrived in Vegas three days before the Holmes fight, Ali, always the master illusionist, looked good. "Montreal," he said, "that was my thyroid acting up. I took two pills a day for a month and it's all cleared up now." He had lost thirty-five pounds. His eyes were bright, his voice again in full cry, the gray hair gone ("Black hair rinse," he said).

Still, those of us who had seen him for years knew the sad truth. The day before the fight, I wrote that Holmes would win, probably by a knockout before the tenth round. He was much too good for the Ali who, lying to himself, promised to "dance fifteen rounds" when for the previous five years he had been a stand-still fighter.

I sat below Ali's corner. At the end of the second round, he shouted to Holmes, "You about ready? You ready?" A round later: "You're through." He had neither landed a punch nor stopped one. Late in the fourth round, the twenty-five thousand spectators, once cheering for Ali, went silent. They had been silent for Ruffhouse Walker, a prelim fighter, a pug no one cared about, and then they fell silent for Ali. By the sixth round, the silence born of mourning had been replaced by boos.

Years later, in an interview for a Ken Burns documentary on Ali, I recalled my wishful thinking of that night. . . .

All right, he's done nothing the first round. He's done nothing the second round. Any minute now, he's going to be Muhammad Ali again. Third round, it became clear that he was not going to do anything, and then it was sad. Then it was like a train wreck, like a friend getting run over by a truck. . . . I'd seen Larry Holmes when he was 19 years old sparring at Deer Lake with Ali, and he was a great fighter, and now he's the champion in the ring asking the referee, "Stop this!" . . . And you start thinking, "I don't want to watch this, I don't want to see this anymore." I've seen all the magic. The magic is gone now. That was as emotional a night as I've ever spent as a sportswriter. Because I cared about him. I liked him, and if he lost, that was one thing. But don't get killed in there.

Ali did not come out for the tenth round.

Fourteen months later, Ali tried one more time. In an improvised ring set up on a kids' baseball diamond, Ali lost a unanimous decision to Trevor Berbick, a journeyman of small distinction. From a phone hooked up to a pole near a small wooden hut that served as Ali's dressing room, I called the office and dictated my last Ali fight column.

NASSAU, Bahamas, Dec. 11—Muhammad Ali, five weeks short of his 40th birthday, lost tonight to the invisible opponent who is undefeated now and always.

"I couldn't beat Father Time," Ali said. . . . "This is it."

Someone said to Ali, "Six months from now, Muhammad, will you smile at us and say you were only kidding about, 'This is it'?"

Ali said, "No, it's too late now. The body can't do it anymore."

THE WASHINGTON POST WOULD NOT BE MY LAST NEWSPAPER JOB. I AM not sure when I decided that. I had heard George Solomon say, "The *Washington Post* rewards well those who do well," and yet, a year and a half later, knowing he had hired me on the cheap, Solomon had not caused my salary to change. I did "This Morning" three and four times a week, pitched in an occasional long-form piece, and was still hungry to do well. But there had been no rewards that help pay a mortgage.

Solomon finally told me a raise was coming. "Got you twenty-five dollars a week."

Still confident and a touch less naive, I knew the twenty-five dollars was not a merit raise but a raise guaranteed by the Newspaper Guild's labor contract with the *Post*.

"George, that's the union raise and it's the smallest raise I have ever got," I said. "To get it, all I had to do is stay alive."

"There'll be more," he said.

I was thirty-eight years old and I had never cared about money. Whatever the *Pantagraph* paid me, fine. If Dad offered a penny a brick for scraping mortar off 'em, it was a penny more than I had a minute ago. I was a quiet Midwest kid bowing to authority. I told George, "I hate this arguing about money."

"We're not arguing," he said, trying to be light about it. "We're negotiating."

That was another line I would remember.

By then I knew Gerald Strine, a hard-edged veteran writing a football betting column for the sports section. "Don't let the *Post* use you," he said. "Newspapers use us and toss us aside when we're no longer useful. When you can, you use the *Post*." Was that a cynic's view or a realist's? I had asked Red Smith why he had not written a memoir. He was my hero, the best sports columnist ever, a Pulitzer Prize winner at the *New York Times*. "I'm saving the memoir," Red said, "for when the *Times* fires me." He did not laugh. I decided then that if Red Smith made plans for being fired, common folks should also get ready.

The *Post* was the ultimate journalism destination. Succeeding Shirley Povich was the honor of a lifetime. Yet I knew I would leave. Cheryl was unhappy. The capital of the free world did not impress a Straight Row Chick. "Everybody thinks they're SO IMPORTANT," she said. Our telephone ringing set her off. "George again! Where's he sending you this time?" I had become Pavlov's dog, leaping to answer every bell.

It was one thing to be in a huff about the sports editor's management strategy. It was another to be disappointed in myself for ceding control of my life to a job.

I felt the disappointment most intensely after that dreamy, so dreamy game. Long before the team earned a spot in that Super Bowl, the Kindreds made plans to join the Attners, Paul and Mary Ellen, for a week's vacation in Hawaii. Then everything changed. The Redskins won, and the nation's capital went gaga. There would be a parade. Solomon ordered us to cancel Hawaii to help cover the parade.

We returned but were not assigned to write a word of parade fluff. George wanted us back in case he needed us. It was infuriating. I was forty-one years old. My life was not my own. Events owned me. The *Post* owned me. Work owned me. I decided to change all that.

I had moved beyond naivete. I let sportswriting gossipers know I was restless at the *Post*. I talked to the sports editor at *USA Today*, an ambitious start-up with a national audience. The *Chicago Tribune* called, twice. The second time, Solomon said I should let Howard Simons know. He was the *Post* managing editor, No. 2 to Bradlee.

"You've been in here about the *Tribune* before," Simons said. My memory of our second meeting consisted of the managing editor's testaments to the power and glory of the *Post*.

"Here you move with the heavy hitters," he said. "There's psychic income here." He also said, "Don't come in here again like this."

Simon's words sounded like a dare. He dared me to think of leaving the *Post*. That was a mistake.

We had moved from George Washington's neighborhood along the Potomac. We bought a century-old house up a country lane in suburban Maryland. As always, Cheryl went to work on the house. She was her own general contractor, construction crew, painter, drywaller, plasterer, and multipurpose handywoman.

She was hammering on a kitchen sink the night Van McKenzie called.

I knew him. He was a friend of a friend. He had heard from that friend that I was restless. (Word does get out.) A year earlier, he had become the executive sports editor at the *Atlanta Journal-Constitution*.

He said, "We're already good. We want to be the best sports section in America. You'd make us the best. Would you be interested?"

I said, "Let's talk."

4

W E TALKED FOR A MONTH. VAN MCKENZIE DID NOT MENTION PSY-
chic income. He talked about doing good work for good
money.

Before taking over in Atlanta, McKenzie had been the sports editor of the *St. Petersburg Times* for ten years. He had been a design
savant producing extravagant sections that were voted among the top
ten in the nation. I asked around. He was unique, a high school graduate who had started in a clerk's job at *Cocoa Today* and earned his
way to *St. Pete*, one of America's best dailies. His staffers would go to
war for him. A bearded, rough-edged Falstaffian figure, McKenzie
scarfed down Mexican lunches liquefied by Dos Equis while study-
ing the day's dog track entries.

He said I could have the job and make it whatever I wanted. The
best part of that was I believed him. For the first time, I would be in
charge of me. Whatever happened, it would be on me, good, bad, or
indifferent. Van laughed at my *Post* salary. "Seven years there," he
said, "and you're making that? If we do this right, you'll start at double that. My bosses are going to make you an offer you can't refuse."

I had never been asked to the prom. This was like that.

Ed Sears, the Atlanta managing editor, tall and slender, silky smooth, was the archetype of the modern executive. We sat for lunch at a fancy Washington hotel. In an alcove high above the glittering room, a woman in a diaphanous white dress plucked at a golden harp. The music seemed heaven-sent. I asked Sears, "Did you hire the harpist?"

"Wish I'd thought of it," he said.

Sears came with a good question: Would I miss the prestige of the *Post*? It was a graceful way of asking what other folks would soon ask: Kindred is doing *what*? Leaving the *Washington Post* for *where*?

For some people, the *Post* became their identity. A George Smith, to make up a name, would think of himself not as George Smith but as "George Smith of the *Washington Post*." I was never that person. But I understood how it happened.

The *Post* was Woodward, Bernstein, and Watergate, Redford and Hoffman in *All the President's Men*. We shared in the power and confidence of an aggressive daily newspaper in the capital of the free world. The roster was filled with journalists who won Pulitzers and wrote big-idea books. In the Watergate years, the *Post* was the Everest of newspaper journalism, towering over foothills in the hinterlands. Though the *Atlanta Journal-Constitution* was a major metropolitan newspaper, its reach seldom extended beyond the Deep South. The *AJC* admitted it had failed in coverage of the 1960s civil rights movement led by Martin Luther King Jr., an Atlanta native and once pastor at the city's historic church, Ebenezer Baptist.

I had turned toward prestige's glow, but I had not sold my soul for it. Since the day I hunted-and-pecked Stan Musial's given name, I wanted one thing: to play in the big leagues. Now I had done that, not, alas, in baseball, but in the next-best world, journalism. In answer to the Sears question on prestige, I quoted Red Smith: "Red said, 'I'm a reporter trying to write better than I can.' That works for me. I love what I've done, and I want to keep doing it. Van tells me that's what you all want. I am ready."

Atlanta offered real money inside a contract promising lifetime security. The *Post's* response was an offer of a $15,000 raise. It would have moved me to the salary I had turned down in Chicago. I said yes to Atlanta. The next morning a man appeared at my office door in the *Post* sports department. I had not seen that man in a couple years. He had told me to never come to his office again.

"Bad for the paper," Howard Simons said, "worse for you."

"Something I had to do," I said.

"Like the Baptist preacher following the call of God to more money," Simons said. I tried to imagine the *Post* as a going-broke rag unable to fight off competition. I tried to imagine the paper that brought down a president as a local weekly staffed with volunteer wannabe reporters building clip files. In those attempts at imagination, I failed.

Cheryl had long been ready to move. Our son, Jeff, then twenty-one years old, had his own place. I was on the road so much I sent home postcards signed "The Phantom." Our earlier moves from Illinois to Kentucky to the *Post* had been my calls. This time Cheryl had spoken. We left town smiling. We may be the only people who ever traded the nation's capital for the county seat of Coweta County, Georgia.

Rather than fight big-city traffic again, we looked outside Atlanta. We drove a half hour southwest on I-85 to an exit marked "Newnan." The 1980 census put that city's population at 11,449. From the interstate, through a night mist, we could see a light atop the Coweta County courthouse. The road into town was four lanes, divided by light towers. We wandered through the small town's neighborhoods until Cheryl said, "Look at THAT house!" A big, beautiful Victorian. On a rise above College Street. With a wrap-around porch. A turret reached above the second floor. A giant oak tree stood high over a side yard at the intersection of College and Wesley Streets. I said, "Look at that SIGN." The place was for sale.

We moved in early in 1984. Within the year, Cheryl's mother, Hazel, came to live in our upstairs apartment. It was perfect, except for a ghostly derelict of a house across the street. Neighbors called it "Lillian's place," Lillian being the ancient witchy woman who lived in the dark there and believed we could not see her on the sidewalk if she turned sideways behind the metal pole holding up the corner stop sign.

When Lillian died, an empire-building church wanted to replace the house with a gymnasium. We did the greatest, happiest, silliest thing ever. We bought Lillian's place for $60,000.

What Cheryl saw, no one else saw. She did not see a derelict building hopelessly beyond repair. She saw a glorious Queen Anne Victorian. So what if it had been unattended for most of a century? She saw it as one of those Painted Lady Victorians on the hills of San Francisco. Only Cheryl saw that in a small Georgia town, and only Cheryl could make it happen.

Again her own contractor, she went to work. She scraped layers of paint off the house from foundation to turret. Once she had removed the peeling, faded, cracked paint, she sanded the wood until it revealed its original golden tones. Done with sanding, she primed the wood for painting. She painted the house with two coats from bottom to top. By the end, in seven different procedures, she had touched every square inch of the exterior of that house.

She did work you could not pay most people to do. She stacked twenty feet of scaffolding on the porch roof to reach medallions under the turret eaves. Wearing a surgical mask, she reclined on the scaffolding and painted those medallions above her head, the way Michelangelo did the ceiling of the Sistine Chapel.

One day, as she climbed up the scaffolding, her mother said, "What if you fall off?"

"If I fall," Cheryl said, "you'll know that I died happy."

Done with the exterior, she did the interior. Again, she first undid decades of neglect. To say she stripped paint from wainscoting in a bathroom is to make the work seem simple. She spent a month in that little bathroom off the kitchen. A quarter inch here, a half inch there, she stripped white paint from blue from red until she reached the wood itself. Then she painted it all anew. She did that in every room, on every pocket door, on every archway, on every step of every staircase. As on the outside, on the inside she had her hands on every square inch.

She lived with that house for three years. Then, one day, she was done, and she was alive, and she was happy. It had been Lillian's wreck. It became Cheryl's masterpiece. She sold it for $240,000, about a dollar an hour for her work.

We loved Newnan. We always said you could go farther south than Newnan, but you could not get more southern. The town's mayor drove a Cadillac with a deer stand attached to the front bumper. The high school football coach had played for Bear Bryant. I watched a wizened black man fondle a pearl-handled revolver while enduring a Ku Klux Klan rally at the courthouse. We brought to our new house a portrait of Abraham Lincoln that caused a Newnan matron to say, "I s'pose it's OK, y'all *are* Yahnkees." For the first time since we left Louisville, we knew our neighbors. There was the mayor, also famous for an act of official business that involved using his daughter's pink shotgun to shoot a downtown burglar alarm that had been going off for hours. An evening's walk might take us to a photographer, three lawyers, an artist, two airline captains (husband/wife), and a pair of spinster sisters who hired Cheryl to pretty up their home. I told friends, "It's like living in *To Kill a Mockingbird*. I expect to meet Boo Radley any day."

Best of all—or so I thought at the time—Jeff, his wife, Lynn, and their twin sons, Jared and Jacob, just past a year old, moved from Virginia to live across the street from us.

THE FIRST SPRING IN ATLANTA, 1984, I WENT TO THE BRAVES' SPRING training camp in Florida—and who do I meet again?

Lewis Grizzard was taking the sun in a box seat along the first baseline. The once-suffering soul had made his escape from Chicago's wind and ice. He was writing a news-side column for the *Atlanta Journal-Constitution*. We were teammates.

"I thought I'd come home and be Mike Royko," Grizzard said. Royko's column in the *Chicago Tribune* was as good as such things get. "Yeah, boy, I'd be like Royko raising hell about low doings in high places. Then one day I wrote about my dog, Herschel. I never got a letter from readers about politics, but I got a hundred letters about Herschel. I kept writing about Herschel." (Yes, named for Herschel Walker, Georgia's almighty running back of 1980, later fumbling into national politics.)

Howard Simons had said of my move to Atlanta "Bad for the paper, worse for you." He was wrong. The *Post* had brilliant writers ready to move into my space. And I would be fine, free to follow advice from the *Sports Illustrated* master Dan Jenkins, who said, "Write what you'd like to read." In Atlanta, like Grizzard, I was a boy having fun in his new newspaper. . . .

I wrote the Goodwill Games from Red Square in Moscow, the Winter Olympics from a mountaintop in Yugoslavia, and the

America's Cup from the Indian Ocean coastline of Australia. The Atlanta Braves finally won a World Series. (More on that later.) After the bombing at the 1996 Olympics, Richard Jewell's lawyer filed libel suits against everybody, including me. (Much more later.) I saw the preternatural Tiger Woods at age nineteen in the 1995 Masters, saw him win it for the first time in '97, the last time in 2019, and three times in between. In the visiting team's clubhouse, Pete Rose did not blink as he denied everything that in the next century he would admit.

On June 9, 1988, I read an incredible story about Muhammad Ali, truly incredible in that none of it was credible. The *Washington Post* story carried the headline ALI STILL HAS A WAY WITH WORDS. The writer, a news-side veteran with no previous exposure to Ali, reminded readers of the truth that Ali's speech in recent years had been slurred and slow. "Now," the story went on, "he's talking like a machine gun, floating and stinging, jabbing and stabbing, like the Ali of old and about everything that pops into his head from Jesse L. Jackson to Mikhail Gorbachev. . . . The thoughts, his words tumble out faster than a reporter can note them down." An important detail: the reporter said the conversation took place by telephone.

In that call, Ali offered opinions on Virginia's governor and senator, the evolving nature of Strom Thurmond's politics, and the current troubles of Attorney General Edwin Meese III. He called Utah senator Orrin Hatch "a very trustworthy person" and noted that Ted Kennedy "seems real concerned about abuses in the judicial system."

I knew that was not Ali talking. He never thought that way. He could no longer machine-gun a full sentence. The question became, who was it on the phone with the *Post* reporter? And why? To find out, I took time away from the daily column. The time turned out to be three months. I skipped the Olympics in Seoul to stay on this story, the strangest of all Ali stories.

Because the *Post's* front-page piece had mentioned Ali's lawyer, Richard M. Hirschfeld, I called and asked if he could arrange an Ali interview. My pitch: the Democratic Convention would start in Atlanta soon and I would be covering it. I would like to hear Ali's views.

The next night, Ali called.

More precisely, the Ali voice called.

In twenty-two years, I had been a happy captive audience to hundreds of Ali's rambling monologues, soliloquies, and one-man shows. With this "Ali," I had a back-and-forth conversation that went on forty minutes. "Ali" was good, with the right whisper of air in the voice and suggestions of the young Ali's wit and charm. The hoaxer's mistake was in going too far. He sprinkled in words such as "dispossessed" and "fallacious." He even recited a poem about his political leanings. "I don't wear any particular label," he said. "I'll support any man who's honest and able." Near the end of our talk, "Ali" said, "You know the movie *Mr. Smith Goes to Washington*? This is *Mr. Ali Goes to Washington*."

All this sent Mr. Kindred to Washington.

My reporting showed that "Ali" had made hundreds of phone calls to at least fifty-one politicians, Capitol Hill staffers, and journalists. The climax of the act was Ali appearing personally. He visited seven US senators, all on the Judiciary Committee: Thurmond, Hatch, Kennedy, John Warner, Arlen Specter, Joe Biden, and Sam Nunn. Each of the senatorial offices reported that the visits had two things in common. Ali stood mute while his lawyer, Richard Hirschfeld, did the talking.

Hirschfeld was a tiny man who compensated with a chipmunk's chattering bravado. He had been in a dozen kinds of con man trouble since earning his law degree from the University of Virginia. A family friend invested in a Hirschfeld banking venture only to see his money vanish. "Richie would rather lie for a dime," he said, "than tell the truth for a dollar." Hirschfeld's schemes, nefarious deals, and finaglings reached not only into Ali's life. Stories came from across the Atlantic and Pacific Oceans about a dead accomplice in Europe and a treasure hunt for Ferdinand Marcos's gold bullion in the Philippines.

Hirschfeld pressed the US Senate for legislation that would allow Ali to sue the federal government for damages stemming from his draft-refusal conviction in 1971. At the time of the Supreme Court's reversal of the conviction, Ali said no to any suit. He finally filed suit in 1984 asking for $50 million in damages. His lawyer then: Richard M. Hirschfeld. On September 6, 1988, that suit was dismissed as filed ten years past a statute of limitations. Hirschfeld persuaded Orrin Hatch to create work-around legislation called a "concession of error remedy." Such a law would allow Ali to resume his chase for the $50 million jackpot.

I first confronted Ali with the story at a dinner that month. I said, "I think Richie's been imitating your voice all year in phone calls to politicians and reporters."

"How's Richie gonna talk like me?" Ali said. "Sounds crazy. Sounds crazy, don't it?" He stopped. "I smell trouble. I'm through talking about it."

Within two weeks, the Hatch proposal died for lack of senatorial sponsors.

I did not care about Orrin Hatch. The story was the Hirschfeld-Ali con game run against senators beguiled by Ali's presence in their offices.

On November 7, 1988, in Las Vegas, I went to Ali at ringside of a Sugar Ray Leonard fight. "Ali, I've gotta talk to you about politics again."

A twinkle in his eye, Ali whispered, "You're gonna get your ass sued."

"What?"

"You're gonna get your ass sued."

"I just want to get the story right, Ali."

"That little Jewish lawyer's gonna sue your ass."

"OK. But I gotta ask you again. Did you make those political phone calls?"

"I didn't call 'em. Why would a Black Muslim fuck with politicians? I don't care."

"Did you know the calls were being made?"

He shook his head no.

"No idea?" I said.

Shook his head again.

"Who made the calls?"

He indicated he did not know, and I said, "What about Richie? People have told me he sounds like you."

"Naw. He's white. How could he sound like me?"

"But people have told me . . ."

"I can't see Richie doing it."

I said, "Why did you go to Capitol Hill with him?"

"The senators, Richie said they wanted to see me."

Now Ali was on the record denying he made the calls. Back in Atlanta, I wrote. For the only time in our years together, Van McKenzie acted as a line editor on one of my stories. He called me into his office. He was on his back on the floor.

"Back's killing me," he said. "Listen, great stuff here, Pulitzer stuff," he said. He held a printout above his face. "But you gotta do one thing."

"Sure, what?"

"People will want to read about Ali. You've got too much up high about that turd Hirschfeld. Get him outta there. Ali's the story. Get the little turd in later."

The story ran on the front page of the *AJC*. It began, "In an act of political deception aimed at the U.S. Senate, an imposter using Muhammad Ali's name and voice . . ."

The turd got into the story in the eighth paragraph.

Four days later, Ali called a press conference on the steps of the US Capitol. He told reporters he had made the calls to senators. He had lied to me, he said, "just to get him off my back." He also gave reporters a handwritten statement that included this sentence: "Richard Hirschfeld, my lawyer, said I should not have this press conference because I will make this Dave Kindred famous, like I did Howard Cosell."

I called Cosell to pass along the mention.

"Save it for the memoirs," he said.

Two postscripts:

—I would see Ali again twice, first eight years later, 1996, at the Atlanta Olympics. He said nothing about our last meetings. In August of 2003, all had been forgiven, or forgotten. I was at work on a book about him and Cosell. Ali invited me to his home in Berrien Springs, Michigan. He greeted me at the door, "My man!" (More on those occasions later.)

—On January 13, 2005, the *Washington Post* reported:

Richard M. Hirschfeld, a flamboyant lawyer and confidant to Muhammad Ali whose shadowy life on the fringes of high finance, politics and espionage led him to prison and, eventually, to life as a fugitive, committed suicide Jan. 11 at a federal jail in Miami.

Mr. Hirschfeld, 57, was captured Oct. 1 in Fort Lauderdale, Fla., and was about to be transferred to Norfolk to stand trial on a variety of federal charges. He apparently hanged himself with plastic wrap in a jailhouse laundry room.

would include a story about the Last Train from Zagreb.

February 1984. Rowdy sportswriters drinking their way to Sarajevo for the Winter Olympics . . .

As we 70 sportswriters dragged into the Hotel Esplanade in Zagreb, after 15½ hours flying from New York, women in peasant costumes met us at the door. They carried silver trays. On those trays were teeny-tiny glasses only half-filled with a clear liquid.

"Slivovitz?" they said, smiling.

"Why not?" we said. Sportswriters are brave, thrifty, kind, thoughtful and always willing to be the grateful guests of hosts bearing drinks.

Slivovitz, let me tell you, could be used for rocket fuel.

I had a second.

I may have had a third.

Things got fuzzy.

Anyway, we hung around the Hotel Esplanade for four hours. The Olimpik Ekspress was to leave at 3:30 that afternoon for Sarajevo, 300 miles east. . . . You've heard of bullet trains. This was a bow-and-arrow train. It took seven hours to go the 300 miles. We hostage sportswriters became magicians. We made cases of beer disappear. Soon enough there came proof on the TV set in each passenger car that we had made sanity disappear, too.

That great American, Bugs Bunny, appeared on those TVs. Bugs spoke Serbian. "What's up, Doc?" became . . .

Kako ste, Dok?

Some homesick scribbler had brought along a tape deck on which he played Beach Boys songs as we creeped through the night at seventeen miles per hour. He caused "California Girls" to echo across the tundra passing by our train windows. Deep into the trip, the homesick Beach Boys boy was discovered sleeping on the landing between train cars. It was then I heard a voice that sounded like mine, only in a far-off, disconnected, out-of-body way. The voice cried out in Serbian . . .

"*Pivo*, Behrka."

Behrka, the young woman tending our needs, would deliver more beer, *pivo*.

RED SMITH SAID PEOPLE GO TO GAMES TO HAVE FUN AND THEY READ the paper the next morning to have fun again. Van McKenzie, never a word guy, made mornings fun for *AJC* sports readers. He loved big football preview sections. In 1985 he wanted a cover photo of Auburn's great running back Bo Jackson. He did not want another cliché photo of a hero outlined against a blue-gray October sky. Working from the premise that the southern universe thought Bo was Superman, Van wanted Bo in a Superman outfit, Bo in blue tights, with the red cape, Bo in the full and glorious faster-than-a-speeding-bullet package. So *AJC* readers woke up one morning to a full-page color photo of Bo Jackson stepping out of a telephone booth as Superman. (The photo became a trading-cards classic for sale on eBay.com.)

Through the last two decades of the twentieth century, the *Atlanta Journal-Constitution* was a big-time player in a golden era of sports journalism, there with the *Washington Post, Boston Globe,*

Los Angeles Times, Dallas Times-Herald, Chicago Tribune, Detroit Free Press, Philadelphia Inquirer and *Daily News, New York Times,* and NYC's screaming tabloids. Everyone had a star columnist, or two stars. "Sports columnists then were a more exclusive club than the United States Senate," Glenn Hannigan, a McKenzie assistant, said.

We knew in January at a college football bowl game that we would convene for a Super Bowl in February before an NCAA Final Four that would end on Monday night, giving us time to get to Augusta for the Masters. Like a traveling theater company, we played all the big stages: the Indianapolis 500, NBA Finals, US Opens (golf and tennis), World Series. We would throw in an Olympics (winter/summer) every two years, drop into Las Vegas for a fight, and make room for a Billie Jean King–Bobby Riggs extravaganza. Then, the next year, do it all again, perhaps adding a side trip to the Snake River Canyon in Idaho to see if Evel Knievel could defeat gravity. (He could not.)

Las Vegas! It is impossible to speak of Las Vegas without mention of the time Ali raised a corner of his bedsheet and addressed me: "Louisville, come here." I was there to ask about a fight coming up. He was in bed, resting. Because his hotel suite was filled with a shouting mass of hangers-on, he could not hear me and I could not hear him. I got in. One of us had on clothes. He pulled the sheets over our heads. We talked. I made notes. I left. Just another day in the life.

And George Kimball! George was the *Boston Herald*'s columnist at big fights, a sweetheart with a pirate's look, a scruffy guy, scraggly red beard, a belly too big for its britches. He had one good eye and one glass eye. Over beers at a Vegas dive bar, George told us that as a college student in Kansas he ran for county sheriff. His opponent had a withered right hand. One-eyed George put up campaign posters saying WE NEED A TWO-FISTED SHERIFF.

Anyway, we were drinking when *Sports Illustrated*'s fight man, Pat Putnam, left to tend to other business and told George, "Keep an eye on my beer."

As Pat disappeared, George popped his glass eye into his hand. Dropped it into Pat's beer.

Growled through that beard, "You heard him ask for it, right?"

WHAT DID I LIKE TO READ? AT THE START, BASEBALL. I TOOK *THE FIRESIDE Book of Baseball* to bed along with the *Baseball Encyclopedia*. I learned that Ty Cobb had 4,191 hits. Stan Musial was born in Donora, Pennsylvania. Fans on their way to the Brooklyn ballpark dodged streetcars, and their heroes became Dodgers. I tore a full-color photograph out of *SPORT* magazine and tacked it to my bedroom wall so that every day I would see Mickey Mantle at bat left-handed, dazzling in Yankee pinstripes. I liked the way he rolled his cap bill.

Mrs. Pryor's seventh-grade readings from Jack London expanded my universe. I read *The Kon-Tiki Expedition: By Raft Across the South Seas*, an account by Thor Heyerdahl of his 4,300-mile journey from Peru to a South Pacific island that appeared on no map. After *Kon-Tiki*, I went to Ernest Hemingway's *The Old Man and the Sea*. (Santiago, the fisherman, admired Joe DiMaggio and Red Smith.)

Yes, my father had won that race. Yes, that Jack Chick monster had frightened a teenage boy. Yes, I had mastered only the Mantle roll of my cap bill. I fully accepted those cold truths in my senior season at Illinois Wesleyan. I was a five-foot-seven, 140-pound banjo hitter who never outran anyone. But being a good-hands second baseman is better than not being a good-hands second baseman. I got by at the Division III level and was there to meet a new double-play partner, a freshman shortstop named Doug Rader. He was six foot two and 200 pounds, a phenom out of suburban Chicago. One day, on a ground ball that hopped over the third baseman's head, Rader sprinted to his right, leaped for that ball, came down, and threw out the hitter. Not even in my dreams, I could never do that.

One of us became a Major League Baseball star who hit 155 home runs and won five Gold Gloves in eleven seasons.

Meanwhile, I read a lot.

The first textbook assigned to English majors at Illinois Wesleyan in 1959 was *English Literature and Its Backgrounds*. I met Chaucer, Marlowe, Shakespeare, Milton, and a hundred lesser phenoms. They all wrote in a language with which I was not familiar. But being valedictorian in a high school of a hundred students is better than not being valedictorian. I got by in English lit and upon graduation went to the more accessible prose of James Bond novels by Ian Fleming. Reading everything, I discovered my bible, *The Elements of Style*.

It is the classic work of William Strunk Jr., a professor of English at Cornell University, and E. B. White, the *New Yorker* essayist. Strunk called it "the little book." It is little only in number of pages. One chapter alone makes it huge. That chapter, "Principles of Composition," presents Strunk's famous Rule 17. "Vigorous writing is concise," he wrote. "A sentence should contain no unnecessary words, a paragraph no unnecessary sentences, for the same reason that a drawing should have no unnecessary lines and a machine no unnecessary parts. This requires not that the writer make all sentences short or avoid all details and treat subjects only in outline, but that every word tell."

White remembered sitting as a student in Strunk's classroom and hearing the professor speak about brevity with such relish that he found he had nothing more to say in the time allotted the class. White wrote:

Will Strunk got out of his predicament by a simple trick: he uttered every sentence three times. When he delivered his oration on brevity to the class, he leaned forward over his desk, grasped his coat lapels in his hands, and, in a husky, conspiratorial voice, said, "Rule Seventeen: Omit needless words! Omit needless words! Omit needless words!"

The Jenkins advice to write what you'd like to read had nothing to do with fundamentals but everything to do with the way you look at the world. I thought of sports as fun. It was great fun to see Spud Webb of the Atlanta Hawks, the shortest man in professional basketball, win the NBA's Slam Dunk contest in 1986. Laughing while typing . . .

Spud Webb, we bow before you. Master of the skies, we worship at your winged heels. Gravity defeats us, but you sail on. We stand bound to the earth, while you rise on the warm zephyrs of imagination. We look up at the rim, an orange ring a ladder's length away from our Lilliputian leaden feet. We look up. And there you are, up there.

Spud Webb, a little man, 5-foot-5½, your face is in the net, the orange ring a hand's length away. What we mortals dream, you make real. Spud Webb, the Spudnik of basketball orbitry, you can dunk it, slam it, throw it down, reverse it, 360 it, goodgawdamighty it.

Also, absolutely, omit needless words! Write what you would like to read! Easier said than done, so read everything and write all the time. You will learn stuff you did not know you needed to learn, and you will make writing mistakes so painful you will never make those mistakes again.

Here is my version of Rule 17: Pay attention! Pay attention! Pay attention! You will see something you have never seen before, then write about it. Not 90 percent of the time, not 95 percent, 100 percent of the time something will happen you have never seen before. You just must have paid attention long enough at enough games to know what the thing is. It does not mean the thing has never happened; it's just that you have never seen it before and now you have a chance to learn something and pass it along to readers with the enthusiasm that comes with discovery. Like this. At Augusta once, I told an Atlanta buddy, Steve Hummer, "Let's go out," meaning out of the media building. We walked to a spot behind the second green. The South African pro Louis Oosthuizen, from the top of a distant hill, hit a shot that flew forever, landed on the left side of the green, then turned toward the flagstick, rolling, rolling, the crowd's noise rising as the ball rolled forever, always toward the hole—until it fell in. A double eagle. We started interviewing people. We had not been waiting in the media building for news to be handed to us. We had been paying attention and we saw news happen. We wrote about that.

Also, when you read something you like, do the hard things hidden deep in the Jenkins advice: figure out why you like it, and then do it. Do not despair on your first failure. One day you will succeed. You will say what you meant to say, only better. You will rise in joy.

IN 1986 THE *ATLANTA JOURNAL-CONSTITUTION* HAD AN AWAKENING. IT hired a new executive editor, Bill Kovach, a fiercely competitive and ambitious veteran, most recently the *New York Times*'s Washington bureau chief. His hiring in Atlanta and immediate expansion of staff and coverage were seen as signals of a decision that Atlanta would be a serious player in national journalism. Van McKenzie said, "At last, we'll have a newspaper the sports department can be proud of."

Kovach enlisted McKenzie and his lieutenants to produce special convention sections every day of the 1988 Democratic National Convention. I wrote two columns a day for those sections, morning and evening. The last night of the convention, as we stood in the composing room watching a page take shape, Kovach wrapped an arm around my neck. "We did it," he said.

What a future we had.

It ended three months later.

Kovach was gone in a resignation/firing brought on by corporate disputes over his authority. I told a local TV reporter, "They'll never be able to hire another editor as good as Bill Kovach." I left the *AJC* soon after, partly in disappointment, mostly to jump on board for a daring adventure into the unknown, a nationally distributed sports newspaper, the *National*. Turned out it was too daring. The *National* had a run even shorter than Kovach's. It folded in a year and a half, gone by June 1991. I went to work at *Golf Digest* and the *Sporting News*. In 1995, still living in Newnan, I returned to the Atlanta papers in time to cover three dramatic moments in the city's history.

THE FIRST WAS THE BRAVES' VICTORY IN THE 1995 WORLD SERIES, Atlanta's first championship in any of the four major sports leagues. The second was Muhammad Ali's lighting of the flame opening the 1996 Olympics. The third was a story fraught with such tragic overtones that *Vanity Fair* magazine called it "AMERICAN NIGHTMARE: The Ballad of Richard Jewell."

For the dynastic Atlanta Braves at the turn of the twenty-first century, a thousand heroes strutted onstage. The Braves won fourteen division championships and played in five World Series. I gave one man a lion's share of credit—Bobby Cox. The team's general manager from 1986 to 1989, Cox remade the organization from the bottom up. In 1990 he became the Braves field manager. Future Hall of Famers filled the dugout: Cox himself, Greg Maddux, Tom Glavine, John Smoltz, and Chipper Jones.

Then the Olympic Games came to Atlanta. On opening night, July 19, 1996, the last relay runner carrying a torch climbed to the top of a mighty tower. There she would hand off the torch to someone—that person's identity a secret—who would light the flame signifying the opening of the games. The start of my *AJC* column that night . . .

There was no one there . . . until . . . a spectral figure, wearing the torchbearers' whites, came into a spotlight, as if materializing before the world's eyes.

There, Muhammad Ali.

He had been gone from public view for 15 years. Now, suddenly, wonderfully, Ali stood above the rim of the Olympic stadium, outlined against the night's darkness. The relay runner touched her torch to Ali's, and he moved slowly, stiffly, raising his burning torch high. There arose in the stadium, from the assembled thousands, a waterfall's roar of delight.

The next morning, I sat with Ali in his Atlanta hotel room. The torch, with a flame's scorched mark on it, leaned against a wall. He rested on a bed with a pillow under his head. Jerry Izenberg of the *Newark Star-Ledger* was also there. To hear Ali's mumbled, slurred answers to our questions, I sat on a corner of the bed. Ali's body trembled from his shoulders to his feet. The bed shuddered like a boat on troubled waters.

Ali explained the anxious moments of the night before when his torch seemed reluctant to light the flame. "It wouldn't catch," he said. "I looked around." But no one was there to help. "Then I puffed on it." His eyes a scamp's, he pantomimed puffing. "The whole world is watching. Three billion people, and I look like a fool." He said he felt the fire's heat against his wrist until, finally, it caught. "Whoosh," he said.

I asked, "What did the night mean for you?"

"An honor," Ali said.

"In what way?"

"Mankind coming together. Martin Luther King's home. Muslims seeing me with the torch."

Red Smith closed his notebook when he had enough grist for the day's typing. He would say, "I'm rich." Again, Ali had left me rich.

Years later, on his podcast, the author Jeff Pearlman asked, "Do we at all overstate or overrate Ali's greatness and meaning? I'm not referring to his boxing skills. I mean more along the lines of his late-life status as a holy, near-Gandhi-like figure." I said . . .

"Ali was whatever you wanted or needed him to be. A sweet-hearted saint? OK. A crueler-than-hell sinner? OK. That is no answer to the ultimate question, but is the best answer to the mystery of a man once reviled and finally, in his years of brain-damaged silence, revered. He was a follower, not a leader; he was a symbol, not an actor. He gave us reason to despise him and he gave us reason to love him. It was up to each of us to decide what we wanted him to represent. If we think of him as a great man of principle—for refusing the draft, for being willing to go to prison for his beliefs—we should also know that he did not refuse the draft so much on principle; he had no idea what that war was about—as he refused on orders from the leader of a racist cult/religion, Elijah Muhammad. That said, it is also true that his refusal inspired thousands, if not millions, of protesters against that war. Those he inspired did not care if he could find Vietnam on the globe and they did not care if he had never heard of dominoes falling in Asia or that he simply did not like the idea of getting shot. They cared only that the most famous man on earth stood with them at risk of his career and life. Ali's resistance against the most powerful government in the world was no small thing, however it came to be. He gave courage to lots of folks, black and white, in lots of ways."

EIGHT DAYS LATER, ON JULY 27, ALI'S APPEARANCE BECAME A FOOT-note in the history of Atlanta's Olympics. I was awakened at 3:00 a.m. by a call from the *AJC* newsroom. Someone said, "A bomb went off in Centennial Park. We don't know details yet. Come on in if you can."

I had been in Munich in 1972. Every Olympics since had been an armed camp. Every major sports event had prepared for disaster. I was in the office within the hour. One person had been killed, hundreds injured.

Days later, the FBI identified a low-level security guard as the focus of its investigation into the bombing. That information was leaked to an *AJC* reporter, Kathy Scruggs, whose story naming Richard Jewell was published in a special edition on July 31. That day I drove to an apartment complex on Buford Highway. Its parking lot was full of television crews set up with their cameras directed at an apartment staircase. For three days I had seen Jewell on television hailed as a hero for having discovered the bomb and helping move hundreds of people away before it exploded. Now I saw him for the first time as a suspect. For the *AJC* . . .

He sat in the shadows with his back to the world. He wore a white T-shirt, white shorts, and black sneakers. Occasionally, he turned his thick body and looked through the staircase toward the firing line of cameras, every lens fixed on him. He sat on the stairs outside his mother's apartment because, inside, federal agents were at work.

They brought in a dog, a ladder, and boxes. Men wore latex gloves. A white van with Virginia tags unloaded members of the FBI Evidence Response Unit. . . . Hero or fool, he sat on the steps and leaned to his right to make room for agents passing on the staircase. An agent might sit with him a while, talking about whatever FBI agents talk about with men who are suspects in murderous bombings.

Once upon a horrible time, federal agents came to this town to deal with another suspect who lived with his mother. Like this one, that suspect was drawn to the blue lights and sirens of police work. Like this one, he became famous in the aftermath of murder. His name was Wayne Williams. This one is Richard Jewell.

I stood beside a television photographer, Dave Busse of KABC in Los Angeles, a veteran of TV stakeouts. "Reading the body language," Busse said, "the agent in the blue shirt there has been up all night and he's saying, 'We're not finding anything.' And the other guy is on the cell phone every ten minutes to Washington saying, 'We can't put a guy in jail with what we've got here.'"

He sat with his back to us. He'd sat with network television stars this week. Now he sat in the shadows, alone, making room when a neighbor, Leonard Shinew, came down the stairs, pausing to put his hand on the man's shoulder.

Shinew walked to his car. He was seventy-eight years old and had lived in the complex ten years. "I just said, 'Are you all right, Richard?' He said, 'OK.' Richard's just a regular fella. If you needed something done, who should you ask? Richard. Get my car started.

Give me a ride somewhere. Regular fella, and I don't want him and his mother to have to move out. They're good neighbors, like everybody here."

Maybe the regular fella had nothing to do with the bomb; the FBI has often sat on a suspect and come up empty. But when the FBI sat on Wayne Williams in 1981, it gathered enough to convict him for two murders.

The Wayne Williams story had happened before my time in Atlanta. He had killed children. I had not thought of Williams until I left the parking lot stakeout. On the way out, Ken Hawkins, a freelance photographer, said, "Did you see the FBI take those little vacuum cleaners into Jewell's apartment? It's exactly what they did with Wayne Williams. And, like this one, they were in Williams's place all day." In the office, preparing to write, I talked with an editor, Hyde Post, who had reported the Wayne Williams story. As Hawkins had done, Post also noted the similarities in the men's stories. I ended my column with lines that showed a man's life hanging in the balance, as another man's life once had hung in the balance. . . .

Richard Jewell sits in the shadows today.
Wayne Williams sits in prison forever.

Muhammad Ali and his lawyer, Richard Hirschfeld, never followed through on threats to sue me over the hoax they ran on the US Senate. But Richard Jewell and his lawyer, Lin Wood, named me in a libel suit against the *Atlanta Journal-Constitution*. Many readers thought that I had portrayed Jewell as the equivalent of a serial killer of children. I considered it an honest column that said let's wait and see what happens to the beleaguered regular fella.

Several media organizations also sued by Jewell/Wood settled their cases by handing over hundreds of thousands of dollars. The AJC did not settle. In 2012 the suit naming the AJC ended when the Georgia Supreme Court let stand a lower court's decision dismissing it. Truth was the newspaper's defense. Jewell had in fact been identified by the FBI as the focus of its investigation. The court also made a ruling on my column.

Jewell, clearly troubled by any comparison to Williams (a convicted child serial killer), argues that the column was false and defamatory to the extent it implied any similarity between the two men. And while we do not agree with the Media Defendants that Jewell's position requires a "tortured reading" of the column or that his arguments are "illusory," we nonetheless conclude that the column is not actionable.

Our holding in this regard is supported by the legal principles discussed supra. To support a defamation action, a statement must be one of objective fact. Non-literal commentary that cannot reasonably be interpreted as stating actual facts about an individual is not actionable. The Kindred column falls into this category. Kindred's conjectural comparisons between Jewell and Williams "consist of the sort of loose, figurative language that no reasonable person would believe presented facts." And Kindred did not suggest that he had access to or was otherwise premising his comparison on undisclosed facts beyond those available to the reader. Indeed, Kindred expressly acknowledged within the column the scarcity of evidence upon which it would have been reasonable to make such a comparison. It follows, then, that the Kindred column cannot form the basis of a defamation action.

On October 28, two days short of three months after the bombing, Jewell appeared at a press conference in a downtown hotel. The

FBI had cleared him. "As I told you on July 30, as the government has admitted to you two days ago," he said, "I am not the Olympic Park bomber." He took no questions and left the dais immediately. Eighty-eight days of federal investigation had led to an answer. Hero or fool? He left the room, a hand on his mother's elbow. He no longer sat in the shadows. Richard Jewell, hero.

5

● ●

HAD LEFT THE *AJC* FOR THE *NATIONAL* AND RETURNED IN TIME FOR THE Braves' great years and the Olympics. But with Bill Kovach gone, the place had new bosses of small ambition. Partly to satisfy a long interest in political journalism, partly to be near Jeff and his family again (slow learner here), I asked for a transfer to the paper's Washington bureau. There, one day in 2003, my newspaper career ended.

Lafayette Park, across from the White House, was often the gathering place for political protesters, among them Tibetans denouncing China's centuries-old occupation of their tiny mountaintop region in the Himalayas. Because Tom Callahan and I had been in Beijing in 1993, I used that experience as background for the day's column. We had walked through Tiananmen Square, where in 1989 the government's soldiers had massacred Chinese citizens protesting for democracy. So in 2003, reporting the Lafayette Park protest, I wrote about the mismatch, China's nukes against the Dalai Lama's robes.

The column did not appear in the next morning's *Atlanta Journal-Constitution*.

Asking what had happened, I was told to stay in my lane, that I was in Washington to write "feature" columns, not news-based columns. No one had ever defined such boundaries for my columns. I had endured my share of run-ins with angry readers and litigious lawyers, but never with my bosses. If the job meant I would write columns with no opinion, no viewpoint, and nothing that suggested a human thought, I did not want that job.

So I left the paper, again, for good.

We had settled on a farm in Virginia, 175 acres, an hour's drive from Thomas Jefferson's Monticello. It was idyllic. Everything we could see, we owned. The farm pond spilled over a waterfall into a creek, Russell Run, that flowed into the Rapidan River on its way to the Rappahannock River before emptying into the Chesapeake Bay and the Atlantic Ocean. In Christmas letters to friends signed "Dave & Cheryl," we portrayed country life as delightful and befuddling, often at the same time. From our first Christmas . . .

Snow makes Dave younger. Beginning one December midnight, it snowed so much that by noon Dave was 13 years old. He then did what young adventurers on the farm have done for centuries. He went walking in the woods. Of course, he got lost. It's a little farm. But when snow makes everything look alike and you're in the dark woods at sunset, it's easy to get lost if you're the kind of guy who can follow directions only when they lead to a Victoria's Secret store.

Another Christmas . . .

Live in the country long enough, you get to be on speaking terms with snakes. This is our third Christmas season on the glorious Civil War lands of central Virginia. One afternoon I said to a copperhead, "Excuse me, I'll be leaving now." I set NCAA, Olympic, and AARP records for Old Man Running While Zipping Up after Seeing a Big Copperhead at His Feet.

One more . . .

This will be a great day. This is the day Dave goes into the woods and brings back a Christmas tree. It will not be a perfect Christmas tree. It will be a skinny, crooked, scraggly, poor relative of the store-bought trees. Cheryl will say, "Another Charlie Brown tree?" Dave will say, "You bet." She'll say, "Can't wait."

We had each other, and we would always have each other, but we wanted more. Jeff, Lynn, and our twin grandsons, Jared and Jacob, had followed us to Georgia, buying a house across the street. The joy we felt at that time was so complete that we imagined it never ending. We had discounted friends' suggestions of our naivete. We were told how very exceptional we were in coexisting with a grown child and his family living next door. Everyone seemed to believe parents needed to be at a distance from their children and grandchildren, perhaps even a great distance, and certainly never just across the street, a proximity certain to breed squabbles, bickerings, and lesser annoyances.

What no one ever said but what I heard every time was a warning: "Just wait, Gramps, an anvil's gonna fall on your head." We were stubborn. We could not get enough of the indefatigable sweetheart grandsons. Whatever everyone thought, I was confident that anyone who knew the Kindreds knew our arrangement worked for everyone involved. How blind I was. The anvil dangled from a thinning rope.

It fell after two years there. Jeff called us over for dinner and said, "The real reason we asked you over is to tell you that we're going back to Virginia." He was not happy at work, and Lynn was not happy in our little southern town. ("Newnan doesn't even have a bowling alley.") We later learned their marriage had come apart, and they hoped to repair it by returning to Virginia.

That night I wrote in my journal, "I wanted nothing more than to spend the rest of my life being around the boys. I couldn't go to sleep until four in the morning, and Cheryl cried all night." The day they left town, Jeff and I embraced, trembling in the emotion of the moment. He said, "I'm going to make it better, Dad, or make it worse." It got worse. Divorce ensued. Jeff remarried. The Georgia idyll was over.

Our reaction to all that was predictable if pathetic. Four years later, we moved to the Virginia farm and helped Jeff buy a place nearby. We wanted a second chance, this time with Jeff, the twins, and his new wife and new son. This time it would work. This time we would learn from the mistakes of Georgia.

Yes, this time . . .

This time it rained anvils.

We were worse neighbors than before.

The Georgia mistakes, we made them and new ones in Virginia. I am here, shell-shocked and battled-scarred, to tell you what you most likely have learned for yourself in one painful way or another. Love can make you stupid.

We decided to get smart at last and move away, a long distance away. Already done with newspapers, I wrote for *Golf Digest* and the *Sporting News* while working on a dual biography of Ali and Cosell. I did not need to be in anyone's offices. We could live anywhere.

Golf Digest's top editors, Jerry Tarde and Mike O'Malley, had given me a golf writer's dream job, once commissioning what a friend called "the mother of all boondoggles." On the magazine's nickel (and with a book publisher's advance), Tom Callahan and I went around the world. In eighty-nine days we played in twenty-two countries on four continents. We started in Iceland and ended at Augusta National. We hit balls into the Atlantic, Pacific, and Indian Oceans as well as into an African lagoon filled with crocodiles. We missed Timbuktu, but we did Kathmandu, where we visited Mother Teresa's infirmary full of dying, smiling, praying people, and Tom wrote, "As we left, Dave crammed all the Nepalese money we had on us into the slot of a collection box. 'It's either $8,000 or 16 cents,' Dave said. 'I'm not sure.'"

My relationship with the *Sporting News* reached back to 1956 and the fifth grade when every week I was eager to read about the phenom Juan Pizarro dominating the Sally League. For a long time, I wanted nothing more than to be a Major League Baseball writer, one of those seamheads who knew everything about the greatest game ever invented. John Rawlings, *TSN*'s editor, plucked me off the unemployed rolls when the *National* folded, put me on the big-time sportswriting circuit again, and I became enough of a late-life seamhead that the *Sporting News* produced an anthology of my baseball columns. Forever grateful.

And yet . . .

Print journalism's death rattle was growing louder.

At newspapers and magazines across America, corporate bosses explained they needed to relieve their companies' financial distresses by relieving journalists of their jobs. I was among those relieved, twice, first by the *Sporting News*, then by *Golf Digest*. It was my great good fortune to have learned from Red Smith that we should plan for the day we become expendable. So, though losing those jobs hurt emotionally—I had never before been told to go away—we were OK financially. Cheryl, the farm girl of a guy's dreams, believed five dollars was too much to pay for anything except filet mignon and a cocktail. Besides, she had got rich at her one-dollar-an-hour job in Newnan. We owed nobody nothing.

As we decided to move to . . . well, somewhere . . . my only concern was Cheryl's health.

She was sixty years old when she suffered a transient ischemic attack, a TIA, often a precursor to a major stroke. She required carotid artery surgery. Three years later came a so-called minor stroke, a bleeding in the brain that might resolve itself; if not, a neurosurgeon said, "We'll have to do surgery, and it's surgery we don't like to do." It would be done in the middle of the brain at the weakest blood vessel in the body. Her life had become scare after scare.

The next frickin' day, I needed a stent placed in a coronary artery. Going to visit Cheryl in the hospital, I passed out in the lobby. Five minutes and twenty-six seconds into a stress test on a treadmill, the attending cardiologist shouted, "Stop it! Stop it!" I had passed out again, this time with cardiac arrest. Within seconds, I was revived. (Rule of Life: If you're going to have cardiac arrest, do it at the feet of a cardiologist in the hospital.) Doctors implanted the stent to relieve a 95 percent blockage. The Kindreds were the ICU Couple of the Year, Cheryl in neurology, me in cardiology.

Cheryl avoided the brain surgery. But a blood pressure problem persisted. Late in 2009, on our way to a movie, she frightened me. We had stopped at the top of our lane to pick up mail. Without preamble, Cheryl said, "Someday you're going to have to take care of me the rest of your life."

I said nothing. She had taken care of me. I would take care of her. We went on to the movie.

That moment reinforced the realization that we needed to change our lives. We needed new neighbors. I knew where to find them, at home, in Illinois, where every woman eating buttermilk pancakes with maple syrup at Cracker Barrel looked like every aunt we ever had, and all their husbands came with farmer tans so manly I wanted one myself.

Forty-five years gone, all the moves, all the stress, we had had enough. It was time to close the circle. We needed to be with people who cared about us. Our moves had been my calls, always made for a job. This was for better reasons. We would find a place near Morton, Illinois. Mom was ninety-three years old and living in a nursing home there. Cheryl had a boatload of cousins nearby. My sister, Sandra, was there with her husband, Jim, and their extended family of children, grandchildren, and great-grandchildren.

Cheryl agreed, mostly. "But the weather," she said.

"We lived there the first twenty-five years of our lives," I said. "How bad can it be?"

To say the possibility of a move from Virginia to Illinois puzzled our friends is to understate the pity in which they held us. My go-to sage at the *Washington Post*, Gene Weingarten, a New Yorker and twice a Pulitzer winner, said, "To Chicago, America, I hope, not some stinkweed hamlet." Even our New Zealand–born horse veterinarian wondered why anyone would exchange the rich landscape and temperate climate of Virginia for the drab flatland and arctic/tropic weather of a bankrupt flyover state whose governors made a habit of winding up in prison. She said, "What did you do wrong?"

I told our Illinois real estate agent we wanted a place in the country with one condition. "From the house, we don't want to see a cornfield."

The real estate agent laughed. "This may take a while."

We landed on a small farm about twenty miles east of Morton, two hours southwest of Chicago, between Congerville (pop. 700) and Carlock (pop. 500). Neither place had a bowling alley, and I was fine with that, but the Carlock cemetery did have a history. A local feud in the 1800s had caused Republicans to be buried on one side, Democrats on the other. Folklore had the young circuit-riding lawyer Abraham Lincoln passing by the Carlock cemetery on a horse-drawn wagon headed to court in Metamora. So, no, not just any ol' stinkweed hamlet.

We arrived in the fall of 2010, just in time for the weather Cheryl mentioned. It began snowing in November and did not stop until March, fifty-five inches of snow, a record for that part of the state.

Cheryl, bless her heart, never said I told you so.

6

T HROUGH IT ALL, A CHILD'S RHYME SPOKE TO ME.

Ride, ride the carousel,
Reach for the golden ring,
Never to finish,
But begin again,
Life is a circular thing.

I knew a bright young woman who after college had drifted from job to job, never happy and never understanding the source of her misery until she fell into a newspaper job, an intern thing, elementary reporting, just to see if she could do it. The best thing happened. She loved it. It was not so much the work she liked as the people at the paper. Newspaper people were like her, not quite right in most acceptable ways but exactly right in primate ways. "In a newsroom with all the other misfits," she said, "I had found my chimpanzee family."

From Illinois to Kentucky to Washington to Georgia, I had been a quiet guy who reached adulthood without learning to fit well with real-world people, mostly those known as neighbors. We spoke different languages. I spoke English, they spoke Gardening. More than once, Cheryl rescued me from a somnolent state of neighbor phobia by calling out, "Oh, David, another bottle of wine, please." I found my own chimpanzee family in press boxes.

My brothers, sisters, and cousins in sports journalism came in different shapes and colors but with three things in common. They could do the work, they loved the work, and they came to the bar late at night to recount their adventures.

Jenny Keller of the *New York Daily News*, an elfin charmer, charmed us by recounting a moment in the New York Jets locker room. One of the troglodytes in shoulder pads, a defensive end, thought it clever to wiggle his waggle at her.

He said, "Know what this is?"

"Looks like a penis," Jenny said, "only smaller."

The Irish Republican Army in my pal Tom Callahan often bubbled to the surface, as on the day Sonny Liston grunted nonanswers to questions from the *Baltimore Sun*'s newest sports scribe, a lanky kid fresh out of St. Mary's College. They were in a hotel suite bedroom. Tom read from a publicity sheet that Liston was thirty-six years old. "Can this be right?" he said. "Are you only thirty-six?" The ex-champ and ex-Mob leg-breaker pressed his nose against Callahan's and growled, "Anyone who says I'm not thirty-six is calling my mother a liar." Callahan grabbed two handfuls of Liston's shirt. Buttons flew off. They galumphed around the room, scattering lamps. The racket caused a hanger-on in the living room to ask, "What are you fellows doing in there, dancin'?" "Yeah, yeah," Liston said. "Dancin'."

More dancin', chimps being chimps. Done with work that night, John Feinstein stopped by a basketball tournament's hospitality room. Our *Washington Post* colleague Ken Denlinger had gone to bed. Another, Michael Wilbon, went bowling. That left Feinstein to banter with a Baltimore writer who answered a bit of repartee by hurling himself at Feinstein. They went down in a clump, and the most insightful post-clump analysis came from Dave Pritchett, a basketball coach and keen observer of ink-stained chimps in the wild. "It was the lowest moment in the history of the *Washington Post*," Pritchett said. "One reporter is doing a sleep-a-thon. One is bowling. And one is rolling on the floor with a Baltimore dockworker in an Al Capone hat and a peacoat."

A thrill ride, the sportswriting carousel, and I had never imagined getting off. Grantland Rice stayed on until he had a stroke at his typewriter and died that week. Taken to a hospital after filing his last column, Red Smith died there. Shirley Povich's last column, written the day before he died, appeared in the *Washington Post* the day after he died. It seemed almost the honorable thing to do.

I had a good start at it. I spent a year of my life in Augusta, Georgia, fifty-two Masters, meaning fifty-two weeks of columns on Arnold Palmer and Jack Nicklaus, Tom Watson and Tiger Woods. In 1951 I saw Satchel Paige pitch at Sportsman's Park. A half century later, again in St. Louis, at the foot of the Stan Musial statue outside Busch Stadium, I said, "Stan, I knew you before they bronzed you up." We were young once, and I saw the young and beautiful Muhammad Ali float like a butterfly. We grew old, and I saw him crippled and teetering on feet stuck to the earth.

For some sportswriters, Frank Deford the brilliant example, the writing came easy. Red Smith said he opened a vein and bled the words onto the page. (In Red's case, the words then sang.) Three or four generations of sportswriters envied Deford. From the 1970s into the twenty-first century, he was the brightest of stars, elegant and telegenic, a Princeton University man who first created literature for *Sports Illustrated* and later became a television commentator. An anthology of Deford's magazine work, *The World's Tallest Midget*, reminded me of my old English teacher, the matchmaking Miss Swinford. In suggesting I should aim to be a foreign correspondent, she had bought in to the "toy department" bias against sportswriting. Such critics, Deford said, dismissed any good sportswriter as "the world's tallest midget." He wrote those words only to argue against them. "I have written at length about the following subjects: death, race, religion, politics, nationality, sex, sexism, homosexuality, business, art, growing up, growing old, sickness, insanity, history." Writing about sports in America had allowed him to write about life in America. Frank was a giant.

Robert Lipsyte stood alongside Deford. Lipsyte's book, *SportsWorld: An American Dreamland*, was published in 1975. It forever changed the way a kid columnist thought about sports. It was a screed against sports' abuses and testimony to the power of athletes who challenged authority. Lipsyte showed us Billie Jean King, Kareem Abdul-Jabbar, Joe Namath, and Muhammad Ali as players in a cultural movement that defined twentieth-century sports. No one ever matched Lipsyte's decades of insight into the sociology of sports, first as a *New York Times* sportswriter (he was in Ali's Miami yard when Ali first said, "I ain't got nothin' against them Viet Cong") and later as television commentator and author.

I studied the ways Deford and Lipsyte saw the world, and Red Smith taught me to hear the music.

I heard Stan Musial—*Stanley Frank Musial*—cackle in laughter and say he had used supplements in his time. "A steak and a cocktail. They called me a low-ball hitter and a highball drinker." Every May, around Memorial Day, thirty-three cars brought percussive thunder to the First Turn at Indy. Fifteen-year-old Steve Cauthen curled up in the hay of a Churchill Downs barn, silent, sleeping, a babe in a manger.

Jack Nicklaus fired a rifle shot from a valley to a high green, a 2-iron for immortality at Winged Foot. Mike Tyson, twenty years old, in that onionskin voice, said, "Look at me, just a kid, with the belt." Henry Aaron on Willie Mays: "I did everything Willie did, only my cap didn't fall off."

Boots on the ground for the *Washington Post* in 1984, Jane Leavy walked in Sarajevo and knocked on doors and asked an old woman in that country long at war and soon to be at war again what the Olympics meant to her. In the dust on her door frame, the woman drew a heart. In Kansas City, the heroic bronze version of Oscar Charleston stood tall in the Negro Leagues Baseball Museum, and a kid sportswriter never felt so small. A hollow-cheeked stock car driver in Daytona wore a cowboy hat fluffed up with pheasant feathers, and Tom McCollister, the *AJC*'s NASCAR man, said, "Richard, talk," and Richard Petty talked until he was begged to stop.

In his 1957 memoir *Bury Me in an Old Press Box*, the *Nashville Banner*'s Fred Russell defined press boxes: "A sportswriter spends a considerable portion of his life in an elevated workshop called a press box. At most ballparks, stadiums, race tracks, etc., this extended cubicle with the picture window provides a splendid panoramic view of the proceedings below."

Russell, always dapper in a suit, tie, and fedora, recognized that organizers of sports events counted the press as essential to ticket sales and accordingly provided certain creature comforts, such as those splendid panoramic views, not to mention as many hot dogs as a newspaperman (women and television came later) might need to get through the day's proceedings.

A decade into the twenty-first century, Augusta National Golf Club created the greatest press box of all time. It was opera-theater grand. Its banked tiers of seats, gracefully curved, faced a floor-to-ceiling wall of windows overlooking the club's massive driving range. The men and women covering the Masters reclined in high-backed leather swivel chairs. Each work space had its personal computer screens providing video and audio from every corner of the golf course. Grand, all that. No grander than the media dining room. Lobster, anyone? The room was an architect's abstract rendering of the club's original Quonset hut press building, complete with a domed, ribbed ceiling. (It needed Red in bronze at seat J15.)

In Hubie Brown's time as coach of the Kentucky Colonels of the American Basketball Association, there was no press box in Freedom Hall. A kid sat at the end of the scorer's table, a chair away from Hubie, and learned new curses and basketball. For a bird's-eye view, the best place was in Baltimore's old Memorial Stadium. A one-man photographer's platform hung from the front of the press box. It had an iron cage that kept shooters from falling out. A trespassing baseball writer could lower himself into the cage, where, suspended in midair, he had the best of panoramic views. There were higher press boxes, among them the auxiliary press sections at Super Bowls and World Series, seats unsuited for high-dollar sale and thus converted into space for scribes from the hinterlands. Once, returning from a funeral in the piney woods of Mississippi, I typed in the copilot's seat of the *Courier-Journal*'s little plane, a mile-high press box.

We first worked on portable typewriters. Smith-Corona, Royal, and Olivetti Lettera 32 (the Rolls-Royce of portables). Artists all, we were also beasts of burden asked to lug suitcase-size telecopiers around America to fax our stuff to the copy desk. Computers arrived in the 1970s, among them the TeleRam Portabubble, Radio Shack's TRS-80, and Texas Instruments' maddening whatchamacallit. Steve

Jobs gave us Apple's laptops, PCs, and iPhones. (During the 1984 World Cup, I got a laptop to work by wiring it into a Madrid hotel room's air-conditioning unit. If necessity is the mother of invention, deadlines are the father.) Each evolutionary step increased the speed of communication until it was possible in the second decade of the twenty-first century to dictate a column into a device on your wrist and touch a button that bounced the words off a satellite into your grandmother's Bluetooth'd ear, provided she had not blocked you over what you wrote about Trump.

Just when the carousel seemed to be slowing to a stop, I saw that child's rhyme printed on the blocks of a wooden puzzle that Cheryl found in an antique shop.

Never to finish,
But begin again,
Life is a circular thing.

So here we go. Act Two is next.

ACT TWO

7

. . . .

M AYBE IT WAS TIME IN MY, QUOTE, RETIREMENT, TO *BEGIN AGAIN* BY writing a novel. The thought caused that whisper of a voice in my head to rise to a snarky harrumph. "You, a novelist? Get over yourself." I moved on to a study of Mary Karr's wonderful teaching tool, *The Art of Memoir*. She said all her memoirs told the same story, "I am sad. The End. By Mary Karr." I decided my memoir could only be, "I typed. I stopped. The End."

I had done six thousand columns. It seemed enough to call it a day. Laid end to end and stretched from home plate to second base, all that newsprint would be a mess and fly away if the wind blew out to left. Grantland Rice is said to have written twenty-two thousand columns and sixty-five million words. With two or three decades of magazine stuff and a handful of books, my number of words would be in the low to moderate eight figures. (Written-and-deleted words would move the number into Bill Gates bank account territory. Makes my brain hurt, and other organs, too.)

In our forty-five years gone, we had returned to Illinois every summer and Christmas, but never to the country between stinkweed hamlets in never-ending snow. Our house stood on twenty-seven acres, surrounded by timber. Cheryl went to work with a flair for design that she called "Early Barn." She ransacked antique shops for furniture from the second Grover Cleveland administration. Anything marked "primitive" found a place in our living room. She contrived for sunlight to fall through stained glass onto full-grained wood and rich earth tones. We built a small barn in the pasture outside our bedroom windows.

One morning we looked out there and saw a snapping turtle stopped alongside the driveway. We watched it digging with its back legs. We went out for a closer look and saw her drop sixteen eggs, one at a time, into a hole she had dug. She tamped each egg in with her left rear leg. Done with that, she used both rear legs to drag mud into the hole, covering the eggs. Once the hole was filled, she used her body to smooth out the mud. All this took about ten minutes, after which Ethel (the least we could do after watching her give birth was give her a name) walked back toward the pond.

Life in the country, the start. It was time to be who we were, kids coming home one more time, this time to stay.

I had no plans to write anything more.

You may know the truth. Man plans, God laughs. We had not been in Illinois long enough to find all the light switches in the house before I jumped at Dave Byrne's offer of Milk Duds for little stories on the Lady Potters.

We would cheer for Carly Crocker and her candy-striped friends. We would be three rows up in the bleachers among parents and grandmas and grandpas. The games would be pure and simple, four eight-minute quarters, no halftime shows, no media time-outs, no commercials, and no video boards demanding we GET LOUD!! After games, we would stand around on the court trading small talk with friends before driving the half hour home, first stopping at

McDonald's for ice cream. Then, at home, at the typing machine, I would *Begin again.*

ON A SNOWY, FREEZING DECEMBER NIGHT IN 2010, WITH THE PRETTIEST girl in the Atlanta High School class of '59 riding shotgun, we took our first road trip to a Lady Potters game. It would be a State Farm Holiday Classic game at Normal Community High School, a half hour's drive from Carlock east on I-74.

Last time I went to Normal Community for a basketball game, it was a boys game, of course, and I was a super-earnest kid reporter wanting to impress the sports editor because that is how super-earnest small-town kids operated. I made sure I knew all the players' names on both teams, with the correct spellings, and I talked to both teams' coaches before and after the game. I compiled the box score, then hustled back to the office to write (with no x-outs that would disturb the tape-puncher).

My first goal in covering a high school game was to not cover any more high school games or at least to do it well enough that if I ever got a more glamorous assignment, I would be ready. (All day, all night at the Pontiac!) To make sure I paid attention to the game, I did not take along my girlfriend. Even then, Cheryl had a role in my life, but that role did not place her next to me at a game saying, "Number 25, he's cute, isn't he?"

So it was different going to Lady Potters games all these years later. I did not care who played for the other team. Only two or three times ever did I know the name of a coach besides Becker. I never did a box score. I went through my play-by-play to figure only the Potters' scoring. I wrote with the idea that readers on the Lady Potters website were not hungry for big-time sportswriting on anything but the exploits of their blessed daughters and granddaughters. If someone from Metamora, say, scored 40, her name might appear in my little essays, but probably not.

At Potters' games, my girlfriend tagged along. I insisted she come. I mean, we had been married fifty years. If I got lost most nights, I wanted her to get lost with me, the wandering more fun that way. Also, if I needed another pen, she could dig into the deepest recesses of her purse—under the Kleenex, sunglasses, wallet, gum, and kitchen sink—and there she would discover a pen. She was not likely to talk during games because she had learned when to talk and when not to talk, with the do-not-talk time being most of the time. She had learned that I paid attention to games and was an even worse socializer during games than when neighbors came over to talk about their gardening.

The last time I had been to Normal Community was for the *Pantagraph*. A half century later, my girlfriend/wife and I were lost looking for the school. I stopped at a Steak 'n Shake and asked a server, "How do we get to Normal Community?"

She said, "Huh?"

"Around here, the high school, are we close?"

She said, "I dunno. I'm from Texas."

"You're lost, too?"

"I followed my boyfriend up here, four, five months ago. I just ride buses."

"Are you liking it here?"

"Not too fond of the snow." She pointed out the front door. "Try the 7-Eleven over there."

With the advantage of being from Pakistan rather than Texas, the 7-Eleven clerk said, "No, nowhere near here. Left at the third light, College Avenue. Keep going. Left at Airport Road. Next right, Raab. You'll see the school." He did not say these next words, though I heard them in his smile: "If you get to Chicago, dude, too far."

Thirty-five years after I had seen Francis Bibb's girls in Earlington, Kentucky, we had been to the Potterdome and seen the modern
girls game. We had seen enough of the Lady Potters to know we
wanted to see more.

The Potters had a D1 prospect, the sister of an NBA player. The
leading scorer was a muscled-up gym-rat dynamo of a point guard.
One forward skipped basketball in summers to go to National Guard
basic training. The webmaster's daughter was a D1 prospect-in-
training. First girl off the bench, the best sixth man in the state, a
darling in all Kindred eyes, was a dogged, scrappy competitor who
believed cheerleading was for debutantes.

The D1 prospect, Sarah Livingston, was a six-foot-one sophomore,
strong, agile, and aggressive in the paint. Her brother, Shawn Livingston, then played for the Washington Wizards.

The point guard/leading scorer was Mariah Nimmo, a five-six
senior and four-year starter. Her father, Al, was an athletic trainer at
an East Peoria sports complex; her mother, Robin, taught aerobics
and kickboxing. Two older sisters and a brother, all athletes, taught
the little kid to stand tall. Mariah said, "Whitney is five years older,
Joshua seven years, Amber ten." She laughed about the sibling bat-
tles. "Oh yeah. We played two-on-two in the driveway. They made
me suffer." (Note: Had Cheryl and I had a daughter, the name was
preselected. Mariah, as in the musical theater lyrics "the wind they
call Mariah." Robin Nimmo said Mariah's name came from the
song. Loved that about the gym rat.)

Kait Byrne, Dave Byrne's daughter, was the heir apparent at point
guard. Already six foot one with basketball skills learned at her
father's side, she would be a sensational complement to Livingston's
inside work.

Carly Jean Crocker came off the bench early, a five-eight junior,
dogged and scrappy, though neither as dogged nor as scrappy as

her best buddy, Caitlyn Vandermeer, a six-foot senior forward who took no prisoners. Any ball rolling loose, the National Guard soldier came crashing through innocent bystanders, foreshadowing a time she would become a US Army drill sergeant. She said, "Oh, I'm all bruised up. It's a physical game." Endearingly feisty, she said, "You can't be a baby and play basketball."

That night at Normal Community, the Potters came in at 11–1 on a seven-game winning streak. They lost to a Chicago team 54–47. The loss did not change the team's goal. "Of course," Carly said, "we want to go to Redbird."

"Redbird" meant Redbird Arena, the Illinois State University basketball arena, in Normal, the site of the girls state tournament Final Four.

"The first time I went to Redbird," Bob Becker said, "I wanted to take my team there."

ROBERT CANTLEY BECKER III GREW UP IN SYCAMORE, ILLINOIS, A SMALL town three hours north of Morton. His father, a lawyer, was his Little League baseball coach. Win or lose, they celebrated with ice cream at Cooley's Drive-In. The boy was a star in high school basketball and baseball. Always looking for action, he played Hearts with his mom and dad, Scrabble with his grandmother (an English teacher), and poker with his grandfather. He attended the University of Illinois. On the football stadium steps, he kissed a girl. That girl, he married.

In 1993 he took a job as an elementary school physical education teacher and assistant coach in Morton, a town he had never heard of. He coached in the first girls basketball game he saw. His freshman-sophomore team went 18–2. When the varsity coach left in '97, the school went outside for a replacement. Becker stayed on as an assistant and later said, "I still ached for my chance."

Two years later, Becker got the job, a plum only to an ambitious young man. The last time the Morton girls had won anything, Becker was eating Cooley's ice cream. The Lady Potters were lost in shadows cast by the region's best girls programs, especially the powerhouse up north, Galesburg High School, and its Illinois Hall of Fame coach, Evan Massey.

The neophyte coach went to Redbird Arena to see how far he had to go to get where he wanted to be. "Back then, if you go in Galesburg's gym," Becker said, "the banners are all through those early 1990s. They were at Redbird year after year, and I knew to get to Redbird we'd have to beat a team like a Galesburg."

"Bob got sucked in," Evelyn, the girl from the stadium steps, said. "That first year, 2000, sitting there watching Massey and his team on that floor—he was hooked." She also said, "He doesn't *like* coaching. He *loves* it." She counted the ways. "He loves it all. The homework, the video watching, the strategizing, Xs and Os, the scouting. He loves basketball.

"And you may have noticed," she said, meaning everyone noticed, "Bob is very competitive. That's as a coach. It's also even in games he creates at home." The Beckers had three children. "We call it 'PE in the backyard.' He'll draw lines on the grass to see who can throw something the farthest."

"Winning is fun," Becker said. "I remember playing games with my grandparents. My brother and I would play canasta with Grandma Becker. We were convinced she was letting us win. Well, I'm not going to let anybody win. They're going to have to earn it. My kids know, whether it was Ping-Pong or a card game or a board game, I've never had the bleeding heart where I was going to let them win. In Scrabble, Grandma Becker would prefer to teach us a new word even if it wasn't worth as many points. Me, I'd rather have the points than some great fantastic word for my vocabulary. But that was my grandma, the English teacher.

"My grandpa Becker had this one-liner, 'A fool and his money are soon parted.' One night we were playing poker, some of my high school buddies, and my grandpa was in the game. He cleaned house, and at the end of the night he tried to give everybody their money back. He didn't want these high school guys to be without their money. But he was competitive. It's just a healthy competitiveness, then we can rib each other."

IN BECKER'S FIRST SIX SEASONS, THE LADY POTTERS DID NOT GET TO Redbird Arena. At the team banquet following the 2005–2006 season in which his team went 22–6 and would have all five starters back the next year, Becker passed out T-shirts bearing the legend REDBIRD ARENA—MARCH 2007. The Potters' All-State guard, Tracy Pontius, said, "Coach knew how to push everyone's buttons."

Becker had spotted Pontius in grade school. She spent summers playing above her age against boys. As a high school freshman, she was upset that Becker did not have her in the starting lineup. "The first couple games, I didn't start varsity," she said, and she remembered hearing that the coach thought she was not tough enough. "Not 'tough enough'?" she said. "I showed him wrong. First time he put me in, I scored twenty." After that, she started every game.

I saw video of Pontius as a five-foot-seven senior. With the ball on a fast break, she made a full-speed spin move at the top of the key that left defenders wondering where she went. She was a sensational ball handler and three-point shooter who seemed certain to become the Potters' all-time leading scorer until the day Becker said, "Tracy, you can be that scorer, or you can make us a better team."

In that next season, 2006–2007, the Potters defeated Galesburg in a sectional championship game on that banner-decorated court before a raucously partisan two thousand spectators. The game went into overtime when Galesburg made an improbable last-second three-pointer from midcourt to tie it at 35–all. "Banked it in! A Hail Mary!" Pontius said. The shot set off an explosion of sound that Peoria *Journal Star* reporter Jane Miller (a Galesburg grad) called the "loudest I've ever heard at a basketball game." With Pontius scoring 7 of Morton's 9 points in overtime, the Potters won, 44–40.

Illinois girls basketball then operated on a two-class system. Eight teams in each class advanced to Redbird, among them, for the first time, the Lady Potters. There they beat the state's No. 2–ranked team, Buffalo Grove, before losing to No. 1 Bolingbrook and losing the third-place game as well. The Potters finished 31–3 that year.

"Tracy put us on the map," Becker said. For the coach, the question was not if the Lady Potters would return to the Final Four, but when.

A MONTH AFTER OUR NORMAL COMMUNITY EXPEDITION, I WAS IN A hospital robe after a routine medical procedure, if such an invasive procedure can be called routine, and everyone of a certain age knows that invasive procedure is never routine. Waiting for the wooziness to clear up, I asked a nurse, "Is it OK if I ride a couple hours in my sister's car?"

"Is it important?" the nurse said.

"Oh, yes," I lied.

"If you're not having any pain, sure, go ahead," the angel said.

"Good, no pain," I lied.

Sandy drove us north on I-74. She dawdled along at fifty-five miles per hour in deference to forecasts of icy rain changing to snow. Noticing how responsibly she drove, her passenger said, "Not raining, not snowing, game in an hour. Step on it." She motored on, now at fifty-four miles per hour.

Galesburg, the model/target/nemesis, was running a new offense. Massey had gone to the "run-n-fun" concept originated by Paul Westhead at Loyola Marymount and adapted by David Arseneault at Grinnell College. It was basketball, distorted. See the rim, shoot. Everybody, chase the rebound. Off full-court pressure, force a turnover or let 'em score so you get the ball back. Galesburg was on a thirteen-game winning streak, averaging 74.1 points.

Invited to participate in that chaos, the Potters declined. Becker's old-school stuff confused the Streaks. Morton 49–38.

The doctors in Peoria had told me to come back in five years. Then the good and right in basketball had prevailed over the eccentric. As we walked across the snow and ice to the parking lot in Galesburg, I said to my responsible sister, "I'm good to drive now."

Not even a year into this Act Two basketball, how important had the games become? If a hospital visit would not get in the way, why would a job? I had become an adjunct instructor at Bradley University. (Me, a teacher? "Just tell 'em your stories," the dean said.) In late February 2011, I stood before a sports journalism class that began at four thirty and was to end at seven o'clock on Tuesday evenings. But on this Tuesday in late February, it became five thirty and I said, "Class dismissed." Only one of the fifteen men and women in the class asked why. I said, "I have a date."

The Potters had won sixteen of their previous seventeen games, were 27–4 for the season, ranked No. 8 in the state, and that night, halfway across the state in Champaign, they would play No. 2 Springfield in a first-round sectional game. I reckoned the students could do without hearing about Game 6 of the 1975 World Series or the time I delivered Michael Jordan's shoes.

Anyway, nothing pleases a college student more than the gift of an hour and a half away from the mumblings of a rookie adjunct. My car's computer registered 1 hour and 18 minutes, eighty-nine miles at sixty-seven miles per hour on arrival at the sectional game site, Champaign's Central High School.

I did have a date, made in November and confirmed while Cheryl and I wandered all over New Antarctica in search of little gyms. Springfield was strong inside with a pair of big, seasoned, skilled players, and sensational outside with Zahna Medley, a spindly guard with Allen Iverson moves who won games by herself.

Springfield won, 57–51, Medley making four game-turning three-pointers and scoring 21 points, leaving Becker to say, "She was the kid we didn't want to beat us. And she beat us." He stood outside his team's locker room. "They dreamed big, and now they hurt big. There's a broken-up group of girls in there." Caitlyn Vandermeer had been last off the floor. She stopped and shared a fist bump and a wan smile with Mariah Nimmo. Then she went into the locker room, but for only a minute. "I had to get out of there," Vandermeer said. "I'm not good in that atmosphere." In her future drill-sergeant eyes, tears.

A MONTH LATER, MARIAH NIMMO WORE LOW-CUT CHUCKIES IN TEXAS burnt orange with white laces drawn straight across. I had never seen her in anything except a basketball uniform. There she was in a floral print sundress, turquoise in it, the gym rat prettier than a three-point rainbow. The occasion was awards night. Becker and his assistants,

Bill Davis and Erin Chan, thanked parents, grandparents, families and friends, the concession people, the ticket-takers and scorekeepers, the sandwich-makers, yard-sign makers, and the Senior Night pastry chefs who squeezed brown frosting lines on orange cupcakes to make them look like basketballs. The whole time, Mariah Nimmo's shoes shouted what most folks must have been thinking, which was: "Let's play another game, right HERE, right NOW!"

Another day, another time, the Potters could have beaten Springfield, which lost in the Final Four to the eventual state champions. In defeat the Potters yet had joined the state's elite. Becker again: "Our future is very bright. I hope you returnees all commit your off-season to building strength, improving athletically, and enhancing your basketball skills. I encourage you to SHOOT, SHOOT, SHOOT."

8

· ·

Early in the Potters' next season, 2011–2012, I was Santa Claus.

Yeah, surprised me, too.

At Apostolic Christian Restmor, my mother's nursing home, Jamie, an assistant activities director, had pointed at me and said, "Ho, ho, ho!"

I said, "Huh?"

She said, "You'll be Santa."

Basketball, I knew. The rest of this new life, I was learning. But I knew one thing for sure. Whatever Restmor wanted, I was game. So there I was in the red suit with the white beard and the big pillow of a belly, the whole jolly-reindeer-wrangler schmear.

At one o'clock, Jamie gathered Mom and me for the nursing home's Christmas party. At age ninety-four, Mom would be Mrs. Claus, in this case Santa's mother. We would hand out family gifts to residents. Mom was already in costume when I tapped her on the shoulder.

She turned and saw me in my Santa getup.

She said, "Oh, ye gods!"

I kissed her.

After the party, I was back in my sportswriter costume, jeans and sweater, and we were lost on our way to another game, though, to be fair about it, the beautiful woman was not at all lost. She was again a bewildered passenger in a car driven by a geographically challenged man. I was OK with up and down, and pretty good at left and right. But directions baffled me. I was told to drive north from Morton on I-474 and take Illinois 6 to Illinois 91. That would take me straight to Dunlap, a small town north of Peoria.

First we were lost inside the maze of a giant Peoria retail complex called Grand Prairie Mall. The more I drove, the more often I circled a restaurant, Famous Dave's Bar-B-Que. Only by accident did I pop out of the maze onto 91. It was six miles to Dunlap. We drove. We drove some more. We drove into rural America, past silos and barns and lots of cows. Soon, nothing. We had entered the eternal darkness of dead cornfields in Illinois winter.

"Where," Cheryl said, "are we?"

Then she went, "Hmm."

Followed by, "Da-VID."

We were in a narrow alley that led steeply downhill into a purgatorial abyss between dumpsters, giant furnaces, and firepits.

But wait. A person in the shadows.

"A zombie?" I said.

"Follow him," Cheryl explained.

He led us from the abyss to the Dunlap gym. We had missed most of the first quarter.

No problem there. Morton 55–38.

At Galesburg a month later, again a clash of philosophies, the Potters traditionalists, the Silver Streaks iconoclasts still using the System that some critics called "hockey on hardwood" and "five mice being let out of a shoebox." Morton, meanwhile, played basketball. Becker's idea: Don't let the other guy score. His offense: "Layups and free throws."

The Potters needed five minutes to go up 15–0. It got to be 32–13, then 52–32. When Galesburg called a time-out, Becker said an unusual thing to his happy Potters. He said, "Thank you very much." A minute later, Galesburg took another time-out. That time Becker said, "The way you're playing is a beautiful thing."

Basketball is beautiful when people move the ball quickly and surely to places where it can be put in the basket easily. It is beautiful, too, when people play defense as if it is the most fun a teenage girl can have. All that, the Potters did. Three times, Morton blocked Galesburg three-point shots.

That kind of defense had not happened in a Galesburg debate since 1858 when Abe Lincoln stuffed Stephen Douglas.

The Potters 60, Galesburg 38.

I WENT TO THESE GAMES FOR THE FUN OF IT. I LIKED BEING IN A LITTLE gym with my notebook and a line drawn down the middle of the notebook's pages. Cheryl enjoyed the treks and I enjoyed her in the seat next to me however lost we were, and sometimes the more lost we were, the more fun it was. ("If we go around Famous Dave's one more time . . . ," she said.)

Big-time coaches and athletes forever had used sports columnists to burnish their public images by telling lies they hoped to read in the newspaper. (Ben Bradlee once told a press critic, "Yes, we print lies. We print what people tell us.") I did my best to not be that sports columnist. I was not a fan of a team, a coach, a player. That relationship could only end badly either way. I was a fan of reporting and writing.

That said, I hurry to add that my pieces on the Lady Potters were little essays built on personal observations and insights (with the occasional jab at a zebra's utter blindness). The essays tended to be paternal, even grandfatherly in their admiration of the Lady Potters. In the third or fourth season, they moved off basketball and onto people we met at the games.

No professional athlete ever introduced me to his parents or asked about my family's well-being. And that was fine with me. Slowly, I understood that I cared about the Lady Potters games in ways I had not cared about all those that came before. These games were not a step up ambition's ladder; they were about connections with real people. When the wages are Milk Duds, it's everything else that matters.

On nights like these . . .

PINK Night, raising money for cancer research . . .

I had no pink shirt. "Look," I said to Cheryl as we drove down Veterans Parkway in Bloomington, "let's try that Von Maur place." Walmartians did not hang in Von Maur. It had pink shirts. I had paid less for cars. Pass.

I did have pink socks. They began life as white, only to be thrown into the wash with a red shirt. If I rolled up my jeans high enough, the pink socks might be enough. Happily, a beautiful woman saved me from my manly incompetence. My sister, Sandra, gave me a pink T-shirt. I was so with the program that when adolescent boys and girls showed up with pink highlights in their hair, I asked Cheryl, "How would I look with a pink mustache?" Her silence was eloquent.

It was a night of sweet moments. The Potters' Schultz sisters, Liz and Emily, broke away from the line of their teammates following the singing of the "Star-Spangled Banner" to embrace the singer, their mother, Mary, a cancer patient.

SENIOR Night . . .

Lisa Crocker, Carly's mother, asked, "Do you think Coach Becker will be emotional?" She wiped away tears and kept a tissue at the ready an hour before she would walk out there with her daughter. To the gathered family and friends, Bob Becker said, "We all share special memories of these seniors that make us proud. Erin Tisdale, Cortney Allenbaugh, Lexi Ellis, Carly Crocker, and Liz Schultz have worked hard and earned this tribute tonight."

Yes, the coach would be emotional. A coach does the work to be part of changing lives. It is nice when the ball moves swiftly, when your defenders are dogged, when it is all clicking, and a basketball game becomes a dance of joy. Still, it is nicer to be good people. Bob Becker made sure we knew that.

The girls in their candy-stripe warm-ups walked with their parents from the baseline to the free throw line. With laughter and tears, these moments marked joyous and poignant divides in the young women's lives.

THE NIGHT I met Joyce Domnick . . .

On Pink Night, the Potters' Erin Tisdale climbed into the bleachers to give a rose to a woman with snow-white hair, a cancer survivor. I had seen that woman somewhere. I took a seat by her. Because my best efforts at social interaction become interviews, I learned Joyce had played basketball at Morton High School in 1949, six girls on a team, three on one end of the court, three the other. You could not cross the midline, you could take only two dribbles.

"Take a guess," she said, "at how old I am."

I chose an age that fit her laughing eyes. "Sixty-three."

"C'mon," Joyce said.

I chose an age that fit her basketball history. "Eighty-three."

"Eighty-four," she said, and I flirted with that little firecracker at every Lady Potters game for six more years.

I had seen her at Restmor, a volunteer delivering mail every Wednesday. From that night on, I made a point of intercepting her on the mail route to ask, "How are you?" I knew her answer, but I wanted to hear the music in her voice when she said it again. "Thankful and blessed," she said, and she said it every time, and I never stopped asking.

At her funeral on October 29, 2021, her family played a slideshow of her life. I could not decide which Joyce was the most beautiful, Joyce at seven, Joyce at twenty-one on her wedding day, or Joyce at ninety.

THE NIGHT I first met John Bumgarner, which turned out to be the second time . . .

I had wondered about the couple who sat in the first row at the midcourt line across from the Potters' bench. They were John Bumgarner and his wife, Karin. Their daughter, Cindy, a 1980 graduate, had her number retired by the Potters before becoming an All-American at Indiana University.

A couple years in, I received a letter from the Deer Creek–Mackinaw High School football coach. He enclosed a crinkly old clip out of the *Pantagraph*. The boy reporter had done a story on the school's team in 1960. It included my Speed Graphic photo of "quarterback Denny Bumgarner."

I asked John, "Denny Bumgarner, related to you?"

"It is me," John said. "My middle name is Dennis. Everybody called me Denny." Fifty years after our boyhood meeting, poor John Dennis Bumgarner often became my copilot on wanderings to Potters games.

THE NIGHT of Twenty-One's Last Game . . .

They had come as little girls, scared. It was such a big place, and the ball was so big, the basket so high. They grew up there. It happened fast: grade school, high school, boys, cars, proms, boys, homecomings, SATs, boys, colleges to visit, dreams to make real. And then, on a snowy night in 2012, for one last game, they came to the Potterdome.

Lisa Crocker stood in a hallway outside the gym.

A man asked her, "Your last game?"

Lisa leaned against a wall and cried.

The man asked, "What's your daughter's name?"

Lisa said, "Twenty-one."

Twenty-one's mother saw every move her daughter made, just as 2's mother did, and 3's, and 4's, and 44's. Such a happy moment at game's end when mothers and fathers stood with their daughters in that gym where they had spent so many days and nights. In a circle of embraces, the girls did that thing kids can do. They turned laughter into tears and tears into laughter.

AT 27–2 FOR THE SEASON AND ON A FOURTEEN-GAME WINNING STREAK, the Lady Potters went into postseason play ranked No. 3 among Class 3A teams. In the super-sectional, they met Hillcrest Heights, ranked No. 2, one of those Chicago-area powers then dominating Illinois girls basketball. Win that night, the Potters would reach Redbird Arena.

The Potters lost in a game unlike any they had ever played. The Hillcrest coach, John Maniatis, said, "It was Muhammad Ali and Joe Frazier."

Hillcrest was Frazier, all power. Its muscle, aggressively deployed, dominated the game. The Hawks threw up crazy shots from crazy angles and then did the leaping, bumping, shoving, grasping, and clawing necessary to get rebounds and second chances to score. The Potters were Ali, all finesse. Frazier by a unanimous decision, 48–39.

THE POTTERS' BEST PLAYERS, LIVINGSTON AND BYRNE, WOULD BE BACK for the 2012–2013 season. Again, Becker wrote his players a season-end's message. "I encourage you to SHOOT, SHOOT, SHOOT. I am excited to prepare for next season. I look forward to continuing our journey in our pursuit of REDBIRD ARENA!"

9

WITHOUT TRYING, WHICH IS THE BEST WAY, WE WERE BUILDING A community of friends for the first time. The architect in charge was often Carly's mother, Lisa, a social butterfly of an irresistible kind. She believed that a person's energy level was increased by using every ounce of a person's energy. She proved her theory every day, never more convincingly than the day she said, "For your fiftieth, a costume party!"

These heartland people kept throwing things at me. First, Santa. Now, a costume party.

I said, "A costume party?"

I had never been mistaken for a person who would attend a costume party, let alone create one for my fiftieth wedding anniversary.

"It'd be so totally great," she said. "Invite the team, all the girls, and make Becker come."

Me:

Lisa: "I'll be a sixties hippie with a gold wig. Who would you be?"

Me:

Lisa: "You guys love *Gone with the Wind*. Cheryl could be Scarlett, you could be Rhett Butler."

Cheryl as Scarlett, perfect.

My sister, a gifted seamstress, created for Cheryl a replica of Scarlett O'Hara's famous paisley robe. Cheryl was Hollywood glamorous, Vivien Leigh reborn, the beautiful girl chosen by the light outside the Palace. Me, I looked like Rhett Butler's grandpa.

A dozen Potters came as themselves but somehow younger. They came in rolled-up blue jeans and ribboned pigtails. They came as a dance club, "the Sophomores."

In my mail-order Rhett Butler riverboat-gambler vest and velvet hat, I greeted guests at the door. A strapping specimen of humanity showed up, bearing no invitation. Wearing a Lady Potters warm-up jacket. Blonde hair in tangles, looked like a cheap wig. Uneven splotches of rouge on both cheeks.

"Hello," a baritone voice said, "I am transferring into Morton next season."

Your name?

"Roberta Becker," Bob Becker said.

The Sophomores did a line dance with their burly new teammate, and it was near midnight, after two or three glasses of champagne, when Rhett pressed Scarlett to his vest and whispered, "Frankly, my dear, I do give a damn."

THAT WAS IN MARCH 2012, SHORTLY AFTER THE POTTERS' SEASON ended.

Two months later, in May, I could have died, except for having the foresight to be married to a person trained to save lives.

As a person trained to spell and type, I often avoid manual labor. But a man sometimes must be the man of the house. I was mowing the yard when I ran over a hole in the ground. And out came a murderous flight of tiny bees, kamikazes all, willing to die to deliver pain. They chased me into the house. Most stung me even as my flying hands whacked them to death. (Twenty-four tiny bee bodies were recovered from inside my socks.)

I got hot. I got sweaty. I got dizzy. I got undressed. I spread-eagled on the cool tile of our kitchen floor. Cheryl prepared cool towels and draped them across me.

"I think we better go to an ER, now," she said.

While she got ready, I got dressed and went to the computer to type in my symptoms. Beestings, lots of beestings. Dizzy. Lips tingling. Google suggested anaphylactic shock. Words came up such as "severe and life-threatening allergic reaction."

Cheryl's 911 call brought an ambulance that delivered us to Normal. In the driveway at the hospital's ER, a doctor injected epinephrine into my thigh. He followed up by saying, "Uh-oh," which was not comforting, followed by, "You're having a spasm of a coronary artery." (I was wired up for an EKG. Such a spasm is a possible side effect of epinephrine.)

I was taken directly from the ambulance to an operating room where a stent—my second stent, the first, six years earlier when cardiac arrest interrupted a stress test—was implanted to clear plaque from that disturbed coronary artery.

The event led to Rule of Life 2: If you're going to have a coronary artery spasm, do it in an ambulance parked at the ER door with a cardiologist waiting in the operating room.

I joke there, but trust me, it was scary as hell. Twice in a matter of hours, I got lucky.

IN MY OLD REPORTING LIFE, I HAD SEEN LENIN'S BODY IN RED SQUARE, and I had stepped over sacred cows to get into my Kathmandu hotel. I had been with Ronald Reagan in the White House and the movie star Charlize Theron in the South Carolina moonlight. ("Scandalous, aren't I?" she said, though, alas, she was politely beautiful in a red, fringed flapper dress while talking up a golf movie set in the Roaring Twenties.)

In my new reporting life, I interviewed a ketchup bottle.

It was the first night of the 2012–2013 season. Seventeen highly energetic young men in Halloween-party costumes occupied the first two rows of bleachers across from the Potters' bench. A zombie wore a tux. A fork stood alongside a spoon. Personal trainer showed up in a four-hundred-pounder's fat suit. A lumberjack lifted a sign reading BOBBY B 4 PRESIDENT.

I asked the ketchup bottle, "What's this all about?"

Ketchup said, "We are Bobby's Boys. We are the Red Tide. We will rise at every girls game."

At Canton, the Potters ran off to a 16–2 lead. Bobby's Boys noticed their hosts' silence. They chanted. "WHY SO QUIET? . . . WHY SO QUIET?" . . . The Boys did play-by-play during Canton's ineffectual offense. "DRIBBLE . . . DRIBBLE . . . PASS . . . PASS . . . PASS." . . . When victory was assured and in recognition of Canton demographics, they reminded their heartland neighbors, "WARM UP THE TRACTORS! WARM UP THE TRACTORS!" (Morton 51–39.)

In Washington, on a blizzard's-coming night, Bobby's Boys showed up ready for the beach. They wore grass skirts, sunglasses, float rings, flip-flops, flippers, dorsal fins, purple leis, straw hats, bikini bottoms, and one dude seemed to have kidnapped Jimmy Buffet's parrot. Flexing my investigative-journalist muscles, I tracked down Jack Compton, a coconspirator in the creation of Bobby's Boys. He was the one wearing a grass skirt and a coconut-shell bra.

I said to Jack, "Explain yourself."

"We love Coach Becker. We've had 'Halloween Night,' 'NASCAR Night,' 'Army Night,' 'Come as Santa Night,' and 'Business Night.' Tonight's theme is 'Beach Night.'"

"Jack, the coconut shells?"

"Actually, they're not mine."

"What a surprise."

He said, "They're my sister's, Laura's. She's twenty-one and away at college. She heard what we were doing, and she volunteered to give me her coconuts." (Morton 51–21.)

THE POTTERS GRADUATED FOUR OF THEIR TOP SIX PLAYERS FROM THE 31–3 team that had fallen one victory short of Redbird. Livingston and Byrne would be back. Who else could play? Maybe Abbie Cox, maybe Emily Schultz. Those four Potters had a vision. Two months before their first game, they bought fake snow, cheery lights, and a miniature Christmas tree. When Bob Becker walked into the locker room, Cox explained the Christmas-in-September motif.

"Coach," she said, "this is going to be a magical season."

If that were to be true, the Potters needed help.

Help was on the way. Her name was Chandler Ryan. She would be a freshman. She had grown up down the street from Carly Crocker. They had played driveway ball together. She was five foot six, strong, aggressive, and something of a cocky little brat. Carly's scouting report: "Chandler can shoot it."

The Potters opened with two games the day after Thanksgiving. Ryan did not make one or two 3-pointers that day, or even four or five; she made nine. She had what you cannot teach. Adolph Rupp once said of his great shooter Louie Dampier, "God taught Louie how to shoot, and I took credit for it." Bob Becker knew that to be true. Even on her off nights, he told Ryan to keep shooting. "Shooters shoot," he said.

MOST NIGHTS IN THE POTTERDOME WE WOULD HAVE BEEN ANNOYED. But not the night of December 15, 2012.

There were two boys. They were maybe four years old, one all giggles and blond curls, both angel-faced and rambunctious. They bounced around in the aisle behind our bleacher seats. Most nights we would have suggested they slow down and please don't bump against our backs. Most nights we would have mentioned it to the boys' parents. Not on this night.

This was the night after Newtown. This was the night the president of the United States, Barack Obama, spoke of "beautiful little kids between the ages of five and ten years old. . . . They had their entire lives ahead of them—birthdays, graduations, weddings, kids of their own." Here the president, the father of two young daughters, touched the corners of his eyes, wiping away a tear.

"Our hearts are broken," he said. He spoke of the parents of the twenty children killed by a gunman in their school, and he spoke of those whose children lived through a day no one should ever know. And he said, "There are no words that will ease their pain."

Maybe three or four hundred people came to the Potterdome that night. Most likely they would have said they came for a girls basketball game, Morton against Washington. Cheryl and I would have said that, and our answer would have had the virtue of being true.

The whole truth is better. We almost never say it out loud, and we should say it out loud every day. We came to celebrate life. I wish we had prayed. I wish the three or four hundred people had stood in prayer for the mothers and fathers and children of Newtown. What happened in that little school in the Connecticut woods happened to us all.

So, please, you boys, you two rambunctious boy-angels, keep bumping against us. Do it from tip-off to the final buzzer. Bump against us, do it giggling, do not ever stop, and, please, someday, invite us to a birthday party, a graduation, a wedding. About eight o'clock, at the game's end, I looked for the boys again. I saw only the one with blond curls. He was asleep in his daddy's arms.

TEN WEEKS LATER, THE POTTERS WERE 28-4 AND ON A SEVENTEEN-game winning streak when they reached the super-sectional stage again, once more needing a victory to move on to Redbird Arena.

The game would be played in Pontiac, an hour's drive northeast of Morton. I wanted to be there for the going-to-Redbird moment. Proving that God has a sense of humor, I was in Las Vegas, there to report a magazine profile on the infamous old Las Vegas basketball coach Jerry Tarkanian, then eighty-two and about to die.

What to do when you are in one place and want to be in another place?

Remember BlackBerrys?

I curled up on the floor of our Vegas hotel room next to a window because that was the only place the damned BlackBerry caught the Internet. The phone's screen was the size of four postage stamps. It was like watching a flea circus. The Potters were the fleas in red uniforms.

First quarter, there would be a picture and there would be audio but never at the same time. Also, a shot might go up—a Chandler Ryan three-pointer rising on a high arc—and the screen was so small the basketball would disappear, the way Apollo rockets disappeared from Canaveral. Only when broadcaster Dee Ripka shouted—"Does she realize what a big game this is? Just playin' ball!"—did anyone know Ryan had done it again. Five 3-pointers in her 21-point night.

The issue was decided early. Second quarter, Potters up 19–15. Abbie Cox made a steal and got the ball to Kait Byrne for a fast-break layup. Then Byrne made a free throw, and Sarah Livingston added a little jumper, 2 of her 27 points. It got to be 31–17 at the half, and it was 58–35 when the BlackBerry quit. Frozen. All ten fleas stood still in silence. When the streaming resumed, Morton's lead was 63–38 with 1:34 to play and Ripka shouted, ". . . a trip to Redbird in their sights."

Morton 66, the other fleas 40.

THE POTTERS HAD EARNED A TRIP TO REDBIRD, THEIR FIRST SINCE 2007. Alas, their Final Four semifinal would be with Quincy Notre Dame. QND had won three straight state championships. It came in on a fifty-one-game winning streak. It had lost twice in its last ninety-four games. "They haven't lost to an Illinois team in a decade," Bob Becker said.

Tall, strong, and quick, QND played with the poise, composure, and confidence of stone-cold killers. Three minutes in, it was 12–0.

My note: "Uh-oh." Three minutes later, 20–5: "QND calm poise confidence pros." At quarter's end, 24–5: "QND doing to the Potters what the Potters have done to others." At 28–5, the QND student section chanted, "HOW'D YOU GET HERE? . . . HOW'D YOU GET HERE?" It was 35–8 with 3:01 left in the half.

Bobby's Boys, out in force, filled a section of Redbird's lower-bowl seats. In the game's last minute, when a late run moved the Potters within 12 points, the Boys set up one last chant: "WE ARE STILL PROUD! . . . WE ARE STILL PROUD!"

The final, 67–51.

In the third-place game the next morning, the Potters lost to a traditional power out of the Chicago suburbs, Lombard Montini, 42–38.

However fanciful it may have been in September, the Potters had made real the idea of "a magical season." They won thirty games. They won eighteen in a row before meeting Quincy Notre Dame. They won their conference, a regional, a sectional and made it to Redbird. "These kids," Becker said, "are champs in my eyes."

Abbie Cox, who had led the September shopping expedition to Walmart, said, "It has just been surreal. . . . To be here, to see that Redbird on the floor."

The junior forward had run across that Redbird center-court logo hundreds of times in two games. At the end, she walked onto a platform to receive a ribboned medal for the Potters' fourth-place finish. With her teammates and coaches, she lifted high a trophy and said, "We reached our dream."

10

THROUGH THOSE EARLY POTTERS YEARS, I HAD BEEN IN TOUCH BY phone and Facebook with our grandson, Jared. What we knew of his life was frightening. At eighteen, he'd left home to be a "travelin' kid," a modern hobo, hitching rides, hopping trains, getting where he wanted to be by any means available. He was an alcoholic who suffered seizures that had him in and out of hospitals. He was all but killed when hit by a car on an Arizona highway. Every call, I asked, "Where are you, boy?" He might be in New York or Miami, New Orleans, Seattle, or San Diego. In the fall of 2013, he said, "Headed for Philly now. We'll be at Dad's in two weeks."

On a gorgeous day in October 2013, Cheryl and I drove into Jeff's place outside Orange, Virginia, two hours south of Washington.

In the yard, waiting for us, smiling, Jared.

We had not seen him in three years.

He looked like a bum.

A beautiful bum.

He was small and slight with a scraggly, reddish beard. He wore greasy Carhartt overalls two sizes too big. A blackened bandanna hung loose at his neck. His leather boots were scuffed and dirty and had no laces. There was a rosy glow to his cheeks and a smile lit up his baby face. He was twenty-four years old.

"I'm happy, Grandpa," he said, and we wanted that to be true.

Whatever we talked about for two hours was Grandma and Grandpa talking to Jared about the lives we once had together. We did not say please stop drinking, please get off the road, please grow old with us. Cheryl and I had been there, done that, and we had failed. The boy had chosen a life, or more likely a life had chosen him, for that is the evil of addiction. All that was beyond our reach now, beyond his. All we could do that day was hug him, kiss him, and tell him we loved him.

At day's end, I told Jared and his traveling buddies, a woman named Aggro and her boyfriend, Jimbo, that I had been taking notes on Jared's wanderings. Someday I would write something.

"Tell me everything," I said. "Tell it to me from beginning to the end, don't leave anything out, and make it funny."

Jared: "Oh, we can make it funny."

Jeff: "Leave out the tragic parts."

Jared: "Yeah, no tragic."

We wanted the day to never end. After Philadelphia, Jared said, he would get to Chicago that winter and drop down to see us.

"Love you, boy," I said.

"Love you, Grandpa," he said. "Love you, Grandma."

As we drove away, Jared waved to us.

"Did you see the tears in Jared's eyes?" Cheryl said. "He cried when we left, and he tried to not let us know."

We did not know when we would see him again.

By that fall of 2013, we had been in Illinois three years. What we hoped for in the move, we had made real. The best part, sad to say, was that we no longer felt the uneasy peace of living on the same piece of land with Jeff and his second-family children. Though his house had been two hundred yards from ours on property that stretched nearly a mile from east to west, we'd rarely communicated. That was as much our fault as theirs; Cheryl no longer did well in conversation and often sought ways to remain silent, even excusing herself from planning for family get-togethers around birthdays, Thanksgiving, and Christmas. In melancholy ways, she had become the anti-Cheryl.

In Illinois, she could again laugh. Sandy's family became ours. We enjoyed happy moments with Mom at Restmor, of all places, for after seeming to be near death in a hospital, Mom had bounced back to life in the nursing home. I was working enough to feel useful; besides the Lady Potters stories, I did occasional freelance pieces for *Golf Digest*. Cheryl reconnected with cousins she had seldom seen since high school, Kathy from Lincoln, Dana from Decatur. We'd spent more time together in those three years than in the previous ten. We did movies every weekend and Scrabble most nights. We were back to long drives in the country, holding hands like kids, only now we were old marrieds hunting out roadside antique shops or on our way to Lady Potters games.

The surprise in Potters' basketball was how good it was. I should have been paying more attention to women's athletics. Title IX, enacted in 1972, ordered schools to give women equal opportunities. Thirty-eight years later, the Potters played aggressively for thirty-two minutes at both ends, handling the ball well, shooting the 3 as if they had grown up doing it. (They had.) Our first three years in town, they won eighty-eight games and lost fourteen. Illinois operated on a four-class system: 4A was mostly the Chicago-area teams, 3A was a step down in enrollment, and the smaller schools were 2A and 1A. Of the 175 teams in Class 3A, Morton was one of two that reached super-sectional games in both 2012 and 2013.

Here is how good the Potters were. I was in the Potterdome for a game in November. I watched every possession. I made notes of every score. Still, a little sophomore guard scored 19 points in a half without being seen. Chandler Ryan had achieved invisibility. Bob Becker explained she had escaped notice because her scoring came "in the natural flow of our offense," the definition of good offense.

For three quarters, Ryan was 2-for-9 on 3s, which Becker, once a shooter himself, said was no reason for a shooter to quit shooting. "We've told Chandler, 'We'll tell you when to stop.'" In the fourth quarter, she made four 3s in three minutes. She wound up 6-for-13 on 3s. Her 19 first-half points had grown to 35.

Ryan's story began with athletic parents, Bo and Liz. Bo was a scratch golfer and young sportswriter for the *Macomb Journal* when Liz was the centerfielder for the Macomb Magic, a high-level fast-pitch softball team. They connected when she bought him a beer at a Macomb pub. Their first three children, all girls, were named easily, with strong first names and delicate middle names: Keegan Elizabeth, Cagney Elayne, and Delaney Nichole. With the fourth girl, the Ryans left the hospital without a name—until Liz thought of the Matthew Perry character in *Friends*, Chandler Bing. Hmm. Chandler. Yes. Chandler Aileen she is.

For a decade and more, Liz Ryan's laundry room was full of her daughters' uniforms. Chandler was a Mid-Illini All-Conference selection in basketball, softball, and golf. She missed out on lacrosse, field hockey, shuffleboard, left-handed darts, and blind-folded hop-scotch only because no one in Morton had heard of those games. Once, asked what she liked about basketball, Ryan said, "Scoring." In the Potters' first eight games, she averaged 20 points, twice going for 26. She had a chance to break the school's career scoring record with something over 2,000.

After Ryan and Kait Byrne led Morton to four victories in its own Thanksgiving tournament, Becker said, "If our players continue to invest in each other, trusting in each other, this can be a really special team."

It was good, too, that a familiar name appeared in the Potters' starting lineup. She was a freshman, five-foot-ten Brandi Bisping, the kid sister of Brooke Bisping, a star on the Tracy Pontius team of 2007 and the program's all-time leading scorer. Brandi was a prodigy whose arrival from Bethel Lutheran's elementary school team had been anticipated, perhaps especially by Becker.

He knew her in the fourth grade. Already at work on what would become a larger-than-life personality, the little blonde made sure the coach noticed her. She had been to his summer camps, which she took as permission to sit by him while he scouted an opponent. She saw him diagramming plays and said, "Are you just *taking* their plays? Isn't that, like, *illegal*, Coach?"

No, no.

"Won't they get mad at you?"

No, no.

"Coach, you should really think up your own plays. Don't you think you're good enough to make your own? Like, why are you taking someone else's plays?"

She was ten. Fourth grade. Advising the high school coach.

Becker said, "Y'know what, Brandi. Here's some paper. You make up your own plays."

"I will," she said, and she did, with dotted lines for passes, straight lines for dribbles . . .

After the Christmas break, Ryan, Byrne, and Bisping led the Potters to third place in the State Farm Holiday Classic. Becker said,

She did not say a word. Two dozen "travelin' kids," as Jared's buddies called themselves, came from everywhere. I met his girlfriend, Maggie. I took names and contact information. I needed to know what the hell happened to the darling kid I had talked to sleep with bedtime stories as best a sportswriter could dream them up, usually featuring a child who grew up to be a star.

Ten days later, after a game, the Lady Potters invited Cheryl and me into their locker room. They gave us flowers. I told the coaches and players, "I read the other day, in situations like this, where words can't say all you mean, that a hug means more. We consider this a twenty-person hug. Thank you so very much."

Becker drew us into the team huddle. We raised our hands with the players. They shouted, "One, two, three—team!"

THE NEXT MONTH, A TUBA BUMPED ME ASIDE. THEN CAME A TRUMPET pushing me up the steps, followed by a trombone against my neck. Pretty soon, Cheryl, once a clarinetist, said, "Are we in the band again, or what?"

This was a Big Game. Washington had beaten the Potters earlier in the season, 69–56, in three overtimes. On a Saturday night in February the Washington school band swept aside all lollygaggers. Maybe eighty pieces of brass, drums, and other noisemakers rushed up the steps to transform Torry Gymnasium's silence into an orchestrated cacophony.

The longer this went on, the greater the hubbub of anticipation in the packed house—a packed house, for a girls high school basketball game, maybe a thousand people—and here came Bobby's Boys (and girls) dressed for the beach on a freezing night, Hawaiian prints, sunglasses, swimming trunks for yea, verily, a Big Game,

Morton 21–3 and ranked fifth in the state, Washington 17–2, ranked seventh.

"We came out SO ready," the Potters' Emily Schultz said. A senior co-captain, she had been the night's star. Eleven of her 17 points came in two minutes and fifty-four seconds of the second quarter. She made five straight shots, one a three-pointer, in a 19–6 run that gave Morton the halftime lead, 34–17. The final: 45–29.

"It's one–one now," the Washington coach, Maggie Mose, said. "And we'll get another crack at them."

Third time around, in a regional championship game, Washington won, 62–51, and Bob Becker called it an empty season.

"We had twenty-six wins," he said. "And we won our tournament and the Galesburg tournament."

But . . .

"We had no championships. No conference championship, no regional, no sectional, no super-sectional. So, yes, it's disappointing. We ask so much of these kids, and they're great kids who give us everything they've got. They show up at 6:00 a.m. They invest so much in it. The seniors, eight of them, put in four years of work. For them, for everybody, it hurts."

A late-season, fifteen-game winning streak suggested the Potters could win a state championship with Kait Byrne holding high the big trophy. Instead, the Potters lost two of their last three games. They wound up 26–5, a good season for most teams, a disappointment to Potters reaching for Redbird.

It had been a hard winter in Washington, another of the small towns set between cornfields in central Illinois, eight miles from Morton. In November a tornado with winds reaching 190 miles per hour destroyed everything along its two-mile path. It killed one man and injured a hundred more.

"Maybe, after the tornado," Becker said, "Washington had destiny on its side. They had a storybook season, and when you get to the postseason a good team is going to go home. That time, we were the good team going home."

A MONTH LATER, THREE MONTHS AFTER JARED'S DEATH, MY MOTHER died at Restmor.

By Mom's casket in the Quiram-Peasley Funeral Home in Atlanta, I said, "I was last in this room fifty years ago, for Dad's funeral. I was twenty-two years old, a college graduate, a husband, and a father, and I knew nothing about life, except the most important thing. I was loved by my father and mother, no matter what mistakes I made. My sister, Sandra, and I are here today to celebrate Mom's life, a life that gave us the greatest gift of all, unconditional love."

Sandy had found a little notebook. Fifty-one years earlier, Mom kept score of an Illinois Wesleyan baseball game in Jackson, Tennessee. "Dave" batted eighth. He walked, got hit by a pitch, and popped up to second. What a thing. Mom knew how to keep score. She and Dad had driven four hundred miles to Tennessee in March to see their kid pop up and boot a ground ball. ("E4" is there, too.)

Mom called herself a survivor. Many days at Restmor she said, "You gotta be brave to get old," and every day she showed us how to do it, as on the day her roommate, Lena Vignieri, died at age ninety-eight. We were worried that Lena's death would devastate Mom. But when Sandy told her, "Lena passed away yesterday," Mom said, "We are all looking forward to passing away."

That week in April, I had been at the Masters. Sandy called to say Mom was nonresponsive. I was an hour into the nine-hundred-mile drive to Illinois when our local emergency medical team called. Cheryl had passed out at breakfast and had been rushed to a hospital with a possible stroke or heart attack.

Driving across Georgia and north through Tennessee and Kentucky, I prayed. I had never been a pray-er, maybe because God had to be accepted on faith alone. Maybe because there were no provable facts. Maybe because no one taught me the language. All those maybes remind me of the famous Chicago News Bureau admonition to reporters. "If your mother says she loves you," the warning goes, "get a second source."

Please, God, take care of the women I love, my mother and my wife.

I had become a Lutheran because Cheryl insisted on it before marriage. Maybe God, on this day, was suggesting I pay closer attention. I had "prayed" for all the usual things, for forgiveness for some fool escapade, for rescue from a moment's peril. This was a prayer of a different kind. For the first time, it felt like a personal appeal. I had lived long enough to know we are promised nothing but the moment we are in. The year before, at the US Open in Pinehurst, North Carolina, I rode a press shuttle bus. As we began to move forward into an intersection, an eighteen-wheel truck, roaring from our left, ran a red light. It passed three feet in front of us. My seat was behind the driver's. Here one moment, gone the next.

My first stop in Illinois was at the hospital where Cheryl had been taken. It had been a false alarm. She would be discharged in the morning.

Thank you, God.

From there I went to Mom at Restmor. She was not awake. I talked to her and kissed her good night. The next morning, as she wished, she passed away.

For Jared, so young, we had wept.

Mom was ninety-six years old, and she knew it was time.

I remembered a Woody Allen line. He said he did not fear death, he just didn't want to be there when it happened. Once, I laughed at that. Not now. Cheryl and I were there when those we loved and those who loved us left us.

11

· ·

ARLY IN ACT TWO OF WRITING FOR MILK DUDS, I HEARD THAT THE
Bispings, who lived on a little farm at the edge of Morton, had
transformed a barn into a basketball court. Brooke was then playing
at Bradley University. Her brother Brett was a star at Sienna College
headed for pro basketball in Europe. Another brother, Braden, was
on the Potters' boys team. Brandi was still in grade school, though
already identified as an exceptional athlete, soon to be no less a
player than her sister and brothers. How perfect, a barn next to a
heartland cornfield, made over for basketball and home to stars. I
needed to see it.

Life had taken Todd and Linda Bisping from their farmland
roots in northeastern Kansas to Deer Creek, a tiny Illinois town
on glacier-smoothed, black-dirt farmlands two hours south of Chicago. Then they heard about a Morton place for sale. On first sight,
Linda declared the century-old farmhouse "a piece of junk." Before
deciding against it, she consulted higher authority. "I said, 'Lord, if
you want me to have this house, you're going to have to change my

mind.'" He did. "The third time through the house, I felt like this was where we were supposed to raise our kids."

Todd proposed a deal. Because it would be cheaper to fix up that house than to build a new one, Linda could use the saved money to make the house fit for the family. Todd's deal came with one condition. "I said, 'Can I have that one building?'"

To the untrained eye, Todd's chosen building, once a cattle barn, did not rise to the standard of junk. It was a three-sided shed of old lumber grown splintery and falling apart. Cattle had shared its dirt floor with chickens. Above the animals, a hayloft.

In all that, Todd saw basketball. Of course. Linda had been a basketball/volleyball star at Washington, Kansas, population 1,500, ten miles north of Todd's hometown, Linn, population 400. Todd had been an All-State basketball player, a six-foot-two center for the Linn Bulldogs, the 1985 Class 2A state champions. He shot 59 percent from the field, 71 percent at the line. The *Salina (KS) Journal* said he had "played effectively inside and outside throughout his brilliant career. . . . He is Mr. Consistency."

When Mr. Consistency's date was a no-show at a New Year's Eve party in Linn's Bulldog Inn, he chatted up Linda Stigge. They knew each other by name; small-town sports stars and all. They hit it off, and they danced, and they attended Kansas State University together, and Todd believed that night in the Bulldog Inn proves he was the "luckiest guy ever in northeast Kansas." Once settled in Illinois, he coached youth basketball at Morton's Bethel Lutheran Church elementary school. His teams included prospects named Brooke, Brett, Braden, and Brandi.

While Linda made the house the home she wanted, Todd went to work on the forlorn shed.

A neighbor, Mark Eigsti, who had alerted the Bispings to the place, came over to help. "We started tearing stuff out and leveling it off," Todd said. "Mark goes, 'You know what, if we tore that hayloft out, you could put two hoops on each end and one on the side.'"

Great idea, and then . . .

"We're like, if we poured this whole thing with concrete and poured it ourselves, we'd save some money."

And . . .

"It's going to get cold in the winter. We should probably wall up that other side. I got some old lumber out in the shed over here, we can probably use that and wall it up."

And . . .

"Sure enough, next thing we frame it up. And we bought a real nice collegiate backboard for the one wall and framed it up."

And . . .

"The backboard itself weighed two hundred pounds. We had to frame it up, get a special metal design. Mark did it himself and measured it all up and it's exactly ten feet. That was an engineering feat."

When I wrote for dollar bills, I had seen homemade basketball courts in rural Kentucky. They consisted of misshapen, no-net rims nailed to outbuildings floating in mud. I had hesitated in Morton. I did not want to be disappointed by the famous Bisping barn. It was three or four years before I asked Todd, "The barn, can I come see it?"

It was perfect, a twenty-first-century farm outbuilding, metal-sided, thirty-by-sixty-five and twenty feet high at the peak. We entered through a side door off a concrete step into which the Bispings had imprinted their names, handprints, and this: B-DOME, 2006.

Brooke was the first Bisping sibling in there. "Dad and I poured concrete for the floor," she said. She was then a sophomore on the 2006–2007 team that went to Redbird Arena. "I painted the lines, and Mom helped paint," she said. The lines defined the basketball court, the key, and the three-point arc.

Weather was a problem in a building that was neither heated nor insulated. "Some nights, it was freezing," Brooke said. "I mean, basketball's in the winter, and I didn't want to shoot with gloves on, so I asked Dad, 'Please get us a heater.'" A small heater arrived, only to warm the shooters' hands.

The roof was a bigger problem. Brooke, a five-foot-seven guard, was then the Lady Potters' all-time leading three-point shooter. In the B-Dome, her rainbows scraped the roof.

"I'm an engineer," Todd said, "but I'm not a structural engineer." He enlisted help to raise the roof. "I had a buddy come out and look at it with me. He goes, 'I think if you do this and this and this, you can take those rafters down, cut them off, and raise them up three feet.' Then . . ."

A pause here.

"I almost died in there."

He was on a tall extension ladder near the roof, wiring lights. Brett was his helper that day, eight years old, there to steady the tall extension ladder.

"I was tired, and I was lazy," Todd said. "I leaned over to tie the last one, and the ladder kicked out, and Brett wasn't ready for that. I fell, and I just reached up and caught a rafter with one hand. I'm just hanging there by one hand. Then I pulled up and I grabbed on with the other hand. I'm taking these little breaths, hyperventilating."

Brett, frightened, shouted, "I'm going to get Mom."

"No, you're not. Just grab the ladder and pick it up."

Big ladder. Little boy. How long did Todd hang on to that rafter? Long enough for a little boy to get a big ladder under his daddy.

From that day forward, the B-Dome became a gym away from the gym for the Bispings, their friends, and their Potters teammates.

Brandi, the youngest, said, "It was the coolest thing, just awesome. I never had an excuse to not go shoot. I'd have friends over, we'd go out and shoot. I think that was Dad's plan. 'If you have a gym right here, for what reason can you not go shoot?'

"But, really, when I think about the barn, I don't think about the actual workouts. I think about the time I spent with teammates, with Courtney, Josi, Lindsey, all those Potters girls. I think about me and Braden playing one-on-one, and him just up and deciding he was going to block my shots even though we had a rule against that. He had to play as if he was a tall girl. Otherwise, I wouldn't get anything from it. If Dad saw that, he would say no girl is going to do that to Brandi. And Braden would quit it."

Linda rebounded for the kids who wanted Mom Time. Todd worked with them on shooting mechanics. He also instituted a barn rule for the occasional party out there: "If I see one cigarette, beer, or joint, I'm going to call the cops myself." So that never happened.

Brooke did sneak into the barn one night.

"I never snuck out of the house at night," she said. "But one night, I snuck out to hang out with friends. Never, not in my whole life, except that once. Three friends wanted to hang out. They went and got Polar Pops. This is the most innocent thing in the whole world. I was, like, all right, my neighbors are out of town, 'You guys park over there and walk across the field, I'll meet you in the barn.' It's ten thirty on a Saturday night. We're doing nothing wrong. I had told Brett, 'Hey, I'm going to hang out in the barn, don't tell Mom and Dad, give me a heads-up if they think something's going on, shoot me a text.'"

A half hour later came Brett's text.

"He said, 'Dad went up into your room, doesn't know where you are. Hurry, get out of there, you got to go.'

"And I'm, like, what can I do? I grab two basketballs. I run five laps in the barn to make my face look red. I run in to the house, to the basement steps. And Dad meets me at the top of the steps. I go, 'Hey, just had to shoot a little bit in the barn.' He goes, 'OK.'"

Brandi, Brooke's little sister, was then a third grader. A year later, age ten, she drew up plays for Bob Becker. I first saw her as a freshman on Becker's varsity. In that 2013–2014 season, she came out of that cool, awesome barn by a cornfield and made cool, awesome things happen. As good as she was, the best was yet to come.

12

························

L AST THING AT PRACTICE EARLY IN THE 2014–2015 SEASON, BOB
Becker gathered his players at midcourt and said, "Kayla, got a
joke for us?"

Kayla McCormick said, "Yes, I do, Coach."

"Let's hear it."

Kayla looked around the huddle at her teammates and said, "What
do you call a pile of kittens?"

We don't know, Kayla.

"A *meow*ntain!"

A burst of laughter followed Kayla's cheesy joke, and that cheesy
joke was not even Kayla's cheesiest, and the next one really cracked
up everybody. She asked, "Do you know why the birdie went to the
hospital?"

Do tell, Kayla, why did the birdie go to the hospital?

"For *tweet*ment!"

That cheesy day, I had been writing about the Lady Potters for
four years. Even as I typed Kayla's words for the website, I asked readers' forgiveness for the trifles. But hey. Kayla made me laugh, or at

least groan happily. It was fun writing about girls basketball. The fun of it was an awakening, a revelation. This was *Hoosiers* for girls, only it was real basketball with real girls who did hero things. My movie of the '14–'15 season, if I made one, would open with the Lady Potters in close-ups, each starter expressing small hope for redemption after the "empty" and "disappointing" season of the year before.

Kayla, a five-five junior: "We lost so many seniors. Like, this season is going to be a trial."

Brandi Bisping, five-eleven sophomore: "I remember walking into the first week of camp, in open gym, all of us, the five starters, we looked around, 'Oh, gosh, let's try to get a .500 season out of this.'"

Emma Heisler, five-six senior: "You mean what I wrote down on the paper Coach gave us—or what I really thought? I wrote down 'win conference,' 'win regional,' and we all wrote down 'win State.' And we all kind of laughed at that, like, 'Yeah, right.' . . . We wouldn't have a problem on offense. But defense? We could score 80 but give up 100."

Chandler Ryan: "Twenty and ten."

Jadison Wharram, five-eight junior, was another of the Potters with basketball genes. At the wedding of her future parents, Jed Wharram was tall and handsome in a black tux. Julie Bottorff was tall and lovely in a white gown. They had been college basketball players. They met cute. He saw her on a basketball court shooting alone and asked if he could join her. The rest was love. They posed for wedding photos holding a basketball. Jadison was six or seven years old when she first threw an elbow at her father on their backyard basketball court. Ten years later, she took a cool-eyed look at the season about to start: "If we do well, we do well. If we don't, it is what it is."

Then they won their first thirteen games.

At every practice, Kayla asked and answered questions. . . .

Did you hear about the pig who knows karate?
"He does a pork *chop!*"
Why do bananas wear suntan lotion?
"So they won't *peeeeeel!*"

I TRACKED DOWN JARED'S FRIENDS, ALL OF THEM WITH STORIES ABOUT
the sweetheart I had known. He had gone from our son's place in the
Virginia woods to Philadelphia, and he died in a neighborhood infamous for drug use. The reporting was hard and painful, but I loved
him and I could not just let him go. I had to know. I had to understand his life. I would write something, a book maybe. He deserved
better than to be lost and forgotten.

WE WERE IN PEKIN'S DAWDY HAWKINS GYM ON A DECEMBER NIGHT.
Brandi Bisping woke up that morning with a 101-degree fever and
pain with every breath. She told Becker she might have to skip the
game. "Don't be a hero," he said, stay home, stay in bed.

Bisping missed the team bus and stayed home, but only until she
could stay home no more. She got a ride to Pekin. "It felt like I had
blood in my throat," she said. "And that was just from walking up
the stairs to the gym." Whatever the discomfort, she scored 18 points
and had seven rebounds in a 57–43 victory.

At home that night, Bisping posted a tweet: "All I want right now
is a shake from Steak 'n Shake."

Her phone rang, Becker calling. "What kind of shake do you
want?"

"What?"

"What kind of shake?"

"No, Coach. Seriously. I'm fine. No big deal."

"What kind?"

"OK. Double chocolate fudge."

Becker delivered to the hero's door a large double chocolate fudge shake.

If the thirteen victories announced that these Potters were better than expected, there was a more subtle signal. It came in the season's second game. Freshman guard Josi Becker, the coach's daughter, hyperextended a knee chasing a loose ball. She had to be helped off the floor. There with an arm around Becker, helping her walk, talking to her all the way, was the team's leading scorer, Chandler Ryan.

Ryan was a junior, a three-year starter, a shooter, an All-State player who would play Division I basketball. At the moment of Becker's injury, she was a teammate. Ryan had decided that no freshman would go through a freshman season like hers, "one of the worst years of my life." She had come in "probably a little cocky" and felt shut out by the team's veterans. Her sophomore year "was better in that there wasn't as much drama. But I felt stuck between being too young and being a leader. I knew exactly what everybody should do, but for good or bad I just didn't say anything."

That changed with the graduations of eight seniors. "I finally felt I could bring out what kind of player I actually was and what kind of leader I actually was," Ryan said. "Trying to lead the young kids, I wanted them to have a fun freshman year and not worry about what other people on the team were thinking. My year was awful because I was always worried about what they were saying about me."

Ryan at age fourteen was not the Ryan of seventeen. She said her summer Amateur Athletic Union (AAU) coach, Joby Crum, "taught me that I need to be a leader on the court and that means not just

182

being the person making plays, it means being the best person on the court. It's how you treat people, how you carry yourself, and doing it in a way that people watching know you are the person that people are looking up to."

In a dozen me-me-me ways, both Bisping and Ryan might have demanded that Becker create offensive schemes allowing them to score 20 a night. Instead, both were happy in a balanced offense that gave Morton multiple weapons. Becker put it on his Twitter feed: "I love our Mindset. I love that our team loves each other & I frickin love our fight & TEAMwork! Attitude & Effort & Teammates."

Ryan, McCormick, and Wharram had played on teams together since the fifth grade. But the '14–'15 team was their first in high school not dominated by older players. In a real sense, it was their first Potters team. "We were so close, we were a family," Ryan said. "Yes, our identity was that we won, we scored a lot, we shot a lot of threes. But the real thing is, we loved each other and cared for each other. And we had fun."

You have one guess as to Jadison Wharram's favorite movie. Not *Hoosiers*, not *Coach Carter*, not even *Hoop Dreams*. It was *Bridesmaids*, which has nothing to do with basketball and everything to do with Girls Having Crazy Fun. Emma Heisler said, "We always had a good time. There really wasn't any drama. I know in the past, some girls really didn't want to be at practice. But we all wanted to be there every single day. Coach wanted me to be the positive one. I know not everyone always has a perfect day. So I'd talk to everybody and make them laugh. And there'd be Kayla with her jokes."

Also, Kayla had her airballs.

In the first minute of each of the Potters' first three games, McCormick threw in three-pointers from deep in the left corner. A quick 3–0 lead. Good. Then she started missing that shot. Each time, she missed it worse. Finally, Becker brought her to the side for a talk.

"But, Coach, we're winning when I throw up an airball," she said.

"Kayla, I don't think that's why we're winning," he said.

"Coach, it's, like, our good luck charm. I throw up an airball, we win. It's *true*! It's meant to be!"

"Have a seat, Kayla."

Ryan had a better explanation for the thirteen-game winning streak. "We had people who knew how to play basketball," she said. "But we didn't have actual *basketball* players." A couple seasons earlier, Morton's starters included three six-footers. Now there were none, with only one over five eight. With all those short people, Becker said, "When we come off the bus, people say, 'Morton's bringing *that?*'"

The short people were outscoring bigger people by two dozen points a night. Bisping said, "OK, we're thirteen and zero. And I don't know what happened, but let's keep rolling with it." Wharram said, "As we got better, I thought, 'Hey, we're pretty good now. We can do this.'"

Three weeks later.
January 24, 2015.
The Potters were 20–2.

In my movie, we look down from cloud level on a yellow school bus moving north on a long straight run of I-74 through farmlands gone winter-brown with traces of snow in the shadows of the rising sun. We hear chattering voices from inside the bus as it turns off the interstate into Galesburg and right on Fremont Street to a mostly empty parking lot outside John Thiel Gymnasium. We see the

Potters, in their red-and-white candy-stripe warm-ups, walk into the great old building with a high wall full of banners. We see Becker behind them, and in a flashback, we see Becker young . . .

Becker was new to coaching when he first walked into Thiel and saw one banner honoring a boys' team of 1912. What Galesburg had, Becker wanted—victories, tradition, a self-sustaining program. The Galesburg coach, Evan Massey, had taken teams to the Final Four on his way to more than eight hundred victories. Massey was the model. In Morton's early days of success under Becker, Massey sometimes scouted games at the Potterdome. Becker once saw the veteran coach in the bleachers and sent up a slice of pizza. "Probably thought I was young and cocky," Becker said. Massey was the best. Massey was the target. Becker said, "That's the guy I want to beat more than anybody else."

The Potters' thirteen-game winning streak ended just after Christmas in a 25-point loss to Normal U High. A week later, they lost at home to Canton, 49–40.

Now, they were in Galesburg for two games against traditional state powers, Massey's Silver Streaks and Quincy Notre Dame.

Morton 61, Galesburg 45. The teams would almost certainly meet again in state tournament play.

Second game that day, Morton 65, Quincy Notre Dame 49.

However good Brandi Bisping had been, and however good she would become, that day against the best she was at her best. She scored 56 points, 27 in one game, 29 in the other. She made thirty-six of forty shots (seventeen of twenty from the field, including three of four on 3s, and nineteen of twenty at the line).

That day I sat at the top of the metal bleachers in Galesburg's secondary gym. Next to me, Linda Bisping. Brandi's mother did not say a word, not even when I kept her up to date with the point count: "Fifty for the day now . . . fifty-four . . . fifty-six." I even said that

Brandi and Ryan had done the greatest play I had ever seen in a girls game. Like this . . .

Ryan had the basketball. Only, suddenly, it was gone because, off the dribble, not wasting a nanosecond by touching the ball with her left hand, the little guard threw a pass fifty feet, and when I say she threw a pass, I mean she threw the hell out of it. She whipped it side-arm, across her body, like a shortstop, which she was, during softball season. Which is to say Ryan did not actually throw it—"throw" is so inadequate—she caused the basketball to reach a speed at which it disappeared from view until . . .

It materialized downcourt where it was caught by Bisping, per-haps the only girl anywhere who could have caught that rocket, Bisp-ing being a girl with bear-trap hands who then . . .

Turned the pass into a layup and a free throw, the whole play sym-bolic of what the Potters did in winning two games by 16 points each over programs that were legendary in Illinois. Bob Becker was aglow. "We're on the upswing," he said, "of great things happening."

"It was amazing, the way we dominated Notre Dame," Bill Davis said. Becker's assistant from the start, sixteen years before, Davis had long since earned speaking privileges in the team's locker room. At day's end, he had something to say to the Potters.

"I told them, 'When we were ten and zero, I didn't think we'd lose. I thought we might go thirty-six and zero. Then U High destroyed us and we lost to Canton and I didn't think we could win another game against a good team. Now, after today, there's only one thing left to do—and that's finish. I don't mean the regular season and win the conference. I mean, twelve more wins and the state championship.'"

"Now we need to finish it," Chandler Ryan said, "and make it thirty-four and two."

I said, "Thirty-four and two? You'd have to win 'em all the rest of the way."

She smiled.

"I'm writing it down," I said.

"Good," she said.

That day, leaving for the bus ride home, the Potters broke their team huddle by shouting, "FINISH!"

It became their mantra for another six weeks. Every drill, every practice, every game—they called out, "FINISH!" Even a second loss to Canton two weeks later did not change the Potters' belief that good things were coming. Bisping said, "That night in Canton, in the locker room, we all sat there in dead silence—until Chandler got up and said, 'Y'know, guys, thirty-three and three sounds really good to me. What about you guys?' And we all started clapping and laughing."

One month later.

February 20.

The Potters were 29–3.

They played Galesburg in the championship game of the LaSalle-Peru sectional. By now, Becker's Morton teams had beaten Massey's teams nine times in twelve meetings, including the last five in a row. All those games had been big, but not as big as this one. The winner this time appeared to have clear sailing to Redbird.

When Galesburg took a 9-point halftime lead, 25–16, Jadison Wharram was "kinda scared." She said, "I was, like, this could be it. And we can't let this be it."

She remembered freshman and sophomore games against Galesburg. She went to Kayla McCormick and Emma Heisler, who had been in those games. "I told them, 'We've been down to them more than this, by eighteen or twenty points, and beat them. We can do this.'" Down by 12 points in the third quarter, the Potters came back in the fourth quarter to tie it at 39–39 on Wharram's layup. Time to play: 4:06.

Two possessions later, still 39–all, Wharram had the ball in the free throw circle, a step behind the line. From there she did a shot fake. Her defender, a big girl, weary, did not come to her. Wharram did what she knew the moment asked of her. She shot the seventeen-footer. Good. Morton 41, Galesburg 39. Time to play: 2:23.

"After I made it," Wharram said, "I thought, 'Oh. Let's play some defense.'"

Galesburg did not score for almost five minutes of the fourth quarter. At a time-out with 1:31 to play, Becker could feel victory there for the taking. His face was flushed, his voice strained. "RIP IT!" he said, meaning it was no time for soft hands on rebounds. As he sent his team onto the court, he shouted one thing more: "FINISH!"

It was still 41–39, Morton, with 1:17 to play when Heisler missed the front end of a bonus. But Galesburg missed a layup and was forced to foul Morton's best free throw shooter, Ryan. Time to play: 0:56.1.

As Ryan walked to the line, Becker noticed Heisler at the far end, angry with herself for missing that free throw. The coach also noticed a look on McCormick's face. He called her over and put his hands on McCormick's shoulders. "I said, 'You don't want to shoot one, do you?'" She said nothing. "'Realize this, Kayla, I love you. No matter if you get fouled and miss it or make it, I love you.'" Then he thought of Heisler steaming. "'And would you go tell Emma the same thing?'" Which she did, and Heisler told me later, "I looked at Coach, like, 'What?' He was laughing over there."

Neither McCormick nor Heisler shot another free throw. With Morton up 45–44, fifteen seconds left, McCormick made a steal and quickly, even hurriedly, shuffled the ball off to someone else, anyone else. Ryan free throws wrapped up a 47–44 victory.

In Morton's locker room, the game's fire had moved out of Becker's face and left him pale. He had talked to the team, told them he loved them all. Now he crumpled onto his haunches, bumping against a wall, the last person in the room. Finally, he came back to the basketball court. There he looked up at the scoreboard and saw the numbers, 47 and 44. He looked at those numbers for a long time.

Eight days later.
March 1.
Uh-oh.

I fell on my face. Winter in Illinois can make that happen. Cheryl and I had been invited to join the Lady Potters for a celebration dinner at Alexander's, a steak house in Peoria. I slipped on ice and landed hard. Something in my left shoulder hurt like hell.

The team trainer felt around and said the shoulder was OK, nothing major.

The next day.
March 2.
The Potters were 30–3.

The shoulder was feeling major. I was not staying home. I had not missed a game because of a colonoscopy. A shoulder? Pass the ibuprofen, Nurse Kindred.

We rode the 128 miles from Morton to Romeoville, Illinois, east on I-74 and north on I-55, in a charter bus with all the comforts of home. Brooke Bisping, in her first year as an assistant to Becker, asked for a show of hands on the day's movie, *Coach Carter* or *Hoosiers*? For two hours, those Potters not doing homework, reading scouting reports, or engaging in iPhone social media-izing watched Coach Norman Dale lead Hickory High to the Indiana state championship game.

Three rows ahead of me, as Norman Dale spoke to his boys about the game's last shot, Chandler Ryan and Emma Heisler made last-minute preparations for their own big game—the Potters against Rockford Lutheran, the winner going on to Redbird Arena.

Here was how you knew Ryan and Heisler were getting ready to roll. They gathered their hair and did a series of mysterious manipulations involving twistings, turnings, and tyings that said . . .

Ponytails ready!

Then we heard Norman Dale say he would use Jimmy Chitwood as a decoy on the game's last play—until Jimmy broke an uneasy silence by saying, "I'll make it." I had never seen Jimmy miss that shot, but I had never seen him make it at the moment the Potters' fancy bus made a left turn onto Normantown Road. NORMANtown Road.

As omens of good fortune go, our arrival on NORMANtown Road was good enough to write down in my notebook.

Sure enough. Morton 55, Rockford Lutheran 42.

At Redbird, they would play Lombard Montini, a perennial power.

Back in Morton at midnight, my friend John Bumgarner drove me to an emergency room. Three hours later, after doctors declared the shoulder dislocated and manipulated its pieces to where they belonged, here came Dave Byrne, the webmaster, to drive me home. We slid sideways through an intersection on a shimmering-in-the-moonlight sheet of ice. Happily, at 3:00 a.m., we were the only car on the road.

Four days later.
March 6, 2015.
The Potters were 31–3.

My arm in a sling, I typed one-handed.

At one point, in my partisan hurry to favor the girls from the corn-fields and pumpkin patches, I characterized Lombard, Illinois, as a glossy, high-dollar suburb of Chicago where every father is a mogul, every mother is a corporate lawyer, and every long-limbed daughter is recruited to Montini Catholic High School, where she becomes a basketball-playing machine.

None of that was true, except the basketball-playing-machine part.

In four of the previous five years, Montini won the state's Class 3A championship. The very name, Montini, caused opponents to wish for a less painful challenge, such as plucking their eyebrows with Vise-Grips. Interesting, then, to hear from Brandi Bisping.

I asked what "Montini" meant to her.

"Nothin'," she said, with a nice curl to her lip.

Her sister, Brooke, prepared the coaching staff's scouting report. She said, "We're going to win. We're going to beat Montini."

Brooke said, "I saw a bunch of big, tall girls [four six-footers, including a six three and six five] running up and down the floor that could shoot the ball and that had a really big ego and a big name behind them. And I saw a bunch of our short, little girls who had bigger hearts than anybody I've ever seen in my life. And I don't care what anybody says. Heart beats height."

Sometimes you see something done so well you just laugh. You are so happy to be in the presence of excellence, you laugh at how good it feels to be there, to be alive, to see that thing done better than you could imagine it done.

So I had to laugh. The Potters would rearrange the Illinois basketball universe by defeating Montini, 58–44. They would play the next afternoon for their first state championship. But it was not even that very nice result that made me laugh. It was Jadison Wharram boxing out the big girl.

Wharram was maybe five foot eight. Montini's big girl was six foot five. As a Montini shot clanged off the rim, here is what Wharram did. She put her hind end against the big girl and pushed backward. Then she pushed some more, keeping the big girl behind her and farther from the rim with each nudge. At one point, as the two players engaged in their rebounder's dance, Wharram's hind end might have reached as high as the big girl's kneecaps.

Wharram did not get the rebound. But the ball bounced on the court, just out of everyone's reach, and then the big girl, frustrated, was called for a foul for coming over Wharram's back.

I laughed because what a thing Wharram had done by doing nothing but what every coach has asked of every inside player ever. Get position. Hold it. Keep the opponent on your back. Wharram explained later: "She was HUGE, and maybe I wasn't going to get the rebound, but she wasn't, either."

Do enough little things right, they add up to a big thing. Like this . . .

Morton's shortest, littlest girl—five-five Kayla McCormick . . . ah, Kayla . . . Kayla who charmingly insisted her airballs were omens of success . . . Kayla with her *meown*tains . . . Kayla, trusted enough that Becker allowed her a green light forever . . . it was Kayla McCormick who made "the biggest shot of the season," to quote Bill Davis.

The Potters were quickly behind Montini 5–0, and who knew what kind of killing run the perennial champions might make? But McCormick allowed the Morton faithful to exhale. She threw in a three-pointer. Then came Bisping with a put-back. It was 5–all. Five minutes into the second quarter, Morton took the lead for good at 16–15, on three Ryan free throws.

My movie's defining scene would come during a 10–0 run establishing Morton as the better team. The ball was loose. A Montini girl had it in her hands—until Bisping wanted it. She not only ripped the ball away, in the process she got an arm tangled around a Montini neck and tossed the poor girl to the floor. Bisping stared down at her for a second, and no one noticed on Bisping's face any sign of oh-I'm-so-sorry.

"Honestly, I think we had more heart than them," Heisler said. "I mean, we went out there and got it. We played our butts off."

Then I posed a question that in all my years of sports journalism I had never posed. I noticed Heisler did not play wearing her hair in the usual ponytail. Why?

"For the banquet last night, I did my hair," she said. Then she said a bunch of words about the way her hair acts after that, none of which I understood. "So I put it up in a messy bun."

Another first-ever question. "Tomorrow, the ponytail or the messy bun?"

"Messy bun!"

The Potters created a masterpiece, from their command on the court to Becker's command on the bench. By game's end, exhilaration and exhaustion, sentiment and satisfaction had combined to reduce the coach to tears.

Go back three months. His daughter, the freshman Josi Becker, shredded an ACL and sat out the season. At the time, he said, "I think it hurt me more than it did her." The coach put Josi on the roster for the super-sectional and brought her to Redbird, on the bench in uniform. If he had a chance, he would get her onto the court during a game, not to play—her knee was not ready—but to be there at one of the great father-daughter moments a coach and player could ask for.

Her chance came with 35.7 seconds to play. Becker checked in at the scorer's table and walked onto the edge of the court.

"Don't move," the coach said.

Here came Montini on an unexpected dash, brushing past Josi. When Morton rebounded and thought to hurry downcourt, Josi's first move was a player's instinctive move, a step toward the center of the court.

"DON'T MOVE," the coach/father said.

The daughter/player smiled and stood still, and when Becker was asked at a press conference about being able to get Josi in the game, he started a sentence, "It was a little bittersweet . . ." and had to stop, wiping at a tear in both eyes.

Back in his team's locker room, he told the Potters they "had knocked off the giant of 3A, but don't be satisfied," because next came Rochester, which the week before earned its trip to Redbird by beating U High, a 25-point winner over Morton in late December.

He also said, "I'm telling you, we're going to win the state championship."

The next day.
March 7.
The Potters were 32–3.

"Thirty-three and three," Chandler Ryan had said when 33–3 meant winning the seven straight games necessary for a state championship.

They did it. Morton 47, Rochester 37.

All those five-foot-and-some Potters were smart, gritty, tough, resilient, relentless, running full of moxie, all eaten up with determination and were, to most opponents, real pains in the ass—which was how Montini's coach, Jason Nichols, greeted Ryan in their teams' postgame handshake line. After Ryan's 20 points helped beat his team, Nichols held on to her hand an extra beat and said with a smile, "Chandler, you're a pain in my ass."

Which is just the way they all liked it, as they showed again in the victory over Rochester, a victory achieved from 10 points down in the third quarter. A Wharram layup cut Rochester's lead to 28–20 with 5:27 to play in the third. Becker then called for a full-court press. "We had to try to do something," he said later. "We might lose by thirty or lose by one, but whatever might happen, we had to change the momentum."

First, Ryan stole a dribble and turned it into a layup. Eleven seconds later, she stole a pass and got it to Bisping for a layup. A minute later, Ryan scored from ten feet, followed by two Bisping free throws. Next, a Heisler driving layup and two Ryan free throws.

That was a 14–0 run in six and a half minutes. From 10 down to 4 up, and the Potters then did what they had done to Galesburg in a sectional game and to Montini in that semi. They charity-striped 'em to death. Against Montini, Morton's last 20 points were free throws.

Against Rochester, Morton used one field and fifteen free throws to stay in front until wrapping it up with a 9–2 run in the last two and a half minutes.

And you get one guess as to which Potter made eight free throws in the Game Over phase.

Here is what Chandler Ryan said about those moments when, fouled, she hurried to the free throw line as if it were the only place in the world she wanted to be—which it was. "I love it," the Pain in Jason Nichols's Ass said. "I love having the ball in my hand then. I am NOT going to miss. I'm not being cocky. But I don't miss." (In the seven win-or-go-home state tournament games, Ryan made fifty-three of fifty-four free throws. In the fourth quarters of those games, she was thirty-six for thirty-six.)

In the championship game, Ryan led Morton's scoring with 20 (in addition to five steals, three assists, four rebounds). Heisler had 14 points, Bisping 10 (and eight rebounds). Wharram again starred in her specialty, the unseen game, limiting Rochester's big inside girl to three field goals. And the littlest of Morton's littles, guard Kayla McCormick, gave Becker twenty-seven minutes of flying-around defense that leaves offensive players wondering where next she will appear to bedevil them.

Nichols again: "You can't get behind Morton. When they have the lead, they're so good with the ball, they make such smart decisions, they're so efficient—and when Chandler has the ball, you're not going to take it from her, so you have to foul her, and Chandler came in against us having made 120 of 140 free throws. We knew that. We just couldn't do anything about it. Morton played the way we want to play."

Becker watched his players rush together at midcourt in celebration. Then he turned away, looked behind his team's bench into the second row of Redbird's bleachers, and hustled over to embrace his wife, Evelyn. Both had tears in their eyes. He whispered to her, "I don't believe it."

A day later.
March 8.
The Potters had a parade.

Just before one o'clock on Sunday afternoon, in the Blain's Farm & Fleet parking lot, across from Walmart and kitty-corner from Culver's, with its famous "butter burgers" so buttery they slide off the bun, two Village of Morton police cars and two fire department ladder trucks formed up to lead a parade through the Pumpkin Capital of the World.

The fire trucks' sirens wailed, their red lights flashed, and the parade moved a mile down Morton Avenue and onto Main Street through downtown Morton. Two school buses carried the team's fourteen players. The girls leaned out windows, waving to people along the route, including a happy twosome on the stoop at the Office Tap, where the burgers might not be buttery but the beer would make up for that.

You gotta love a parade in the heartland. American flags fluttered from front porches. Three women of a certain age waved silvery pom-poms they might have saved from their cheerleader days. Families came to corners with their dogs on leashes to see what the fuss was all about, and when they saw the fresh faces of the basketball players, they, too, were happy.

Behind the fire trucks and the buses came an SUV with its roof window open so Bob Becker could sit up top waving to people and embracing his new best friend, the state championship trophy, a glorious chunk of oak and brass, still draped with a basketball net, the whole thing golden and glistening in the sunlight.

13

· ·

B RANDI BISPING HAD A SLAB OF POSTGAME PIZZA IN HER HAND. SHE
waited for the team bus after the Lady Potters won at Metamora,
51–36. She was destroying that pizza, chomp, chomp, CHOMP.
Somewhere between the second and third chomps, I did the amateur interviewer thing of making a statement and hoping the player
takes it from there.

I said, "No field goals and five fouls."

Bisping said, "Tell me about it."

The three-year starter, a junior and D1 prospect without whom
her team would not have won its 2015 state championship and would
not then be undefeated in six games with the announced ambition
of winning it all again—after hearing the numbers, Bisping said,
"Like, wow, I'm bad at basketball."

She went on. "I was terrible. It was embarrassing. I disgraced the
family name."

"Nah," I said, "it wasn't that bad."

"Oh, yes," she said. "It was."

I laughed with Brandi on that day, December 3, 2015. Leaving Metamora, I told Cheryl, "Write THIS down." She dug into her purse for a pen and a scrap of paper. She took a note, "Brandi, fouled out, didn't score, ate pizza."

THREE DAYS LATER, THE LAUGHTER ENDED.

Sunday, December 6, we wanted to see a movie at the Starplex Cinema in Normal. The *Secret in Their Eyes* stars Julia Roberts playing against type as a hard-edged police detective whose daughter has been murdered. Afterward, we would grab something to eat at the Steak 'n Shake on Raab Road.

For the one o'clock matinee, a handful of people were in Theater 4. We sat in the fourth of the five rows, with Cheryl on my right on the aisle. Through the previews, she ate popcorn until I sensed she had quit moving.

Her right hand, palm up, fingers cupped, had dropped into her tray of popcorn.

I said, "What's wrong?"

Her head was tilted back, and she spoke without looking at me. Her voice was small and raspy, an airy whisper. "Nothing," she said. "I'm OK."

"You're not acting OK," I said. "What's wrong?"

Again, not turning to me, she whispered, "I'm OK."

I touched the arm of a man in the row behind us.

"Could you watch my wife?" I said. "I think she's having a stroke."

I left to call for help.

We had lived in fear of that moment. Cheryl had survived previous crises. A transient ischemic attack had foretold carotid artery surgery. Later, a bleeding in a small vessel in the middle of her brain had resolved itself without dangerous surgery; it seemed to leave no lasting damage. But doctors in Virginia and Illinois were not able to control her blood pressure. Her "brittle blood vessels," to use one doctor's words, were vulnerable to blood pressure spikes. They warned us to be careful.

When emergency personnel arrived, the theater's house lights came up and the place went silent, the movie screen blank. EMTs lifted Cheryl from her seat. She moaned, frightened and in pain, her wailing an eerie sound in the little theater. She was placed on a gurney and rolled out of the theater through the lobby to an ambulance for the three-minute drive to Advocate BroMenn hospital's ER entrance.

At the ER, I was told doctors would meet me when they could.

I waited.

Trying not to think of what was next.

A nurse took me into a hallway to see Cheryl, who, under a white blanket, was unconscious.

"We're taking her for a CAT scan," someone said.

Not long after, in a small, private room off the crowded ER waiting room, a doctor said, "Your wife has had a hemorrhagic cerebrovascular accident. Bleeding in the brain. A stroke." He showed me a CAT scan image of Cheryl's brain. Blood had flooded it. Blood had gathered in the shape of a small ball that filled a third of the image. "The first forty-eight hours are critical," the doctor said, "not only to what damage the bleeding has done, but to life itself." Later, a neurosurgeon looked at the CAT scan images and said, "It's like a bomb exploded in her brain. It will take time to know the effects. A long time."

I stayed overnight on a couch in Cheryl's ICU room, 2218. At 6:00 a.m. a doctor said a second CAT scan had shown "a little more bleeding." A coagulant drug had been ordered. At noon, the hospital's chief neurosurgeon took me into the hallway—"I don't want her to hear me"—and said the new bleeding was "three times as large" as first measured.

Fright raised my anger to a shout. "This morning I was told it was a 'little' bigger. But now you're telling me it's 'three times' bigger? It's like getting hit in the head with a sledgehammer."

The neurosurgeon said, "It was a golf ball, now it's a baseball."

The next morning, a third CAT scan showed the bleeding had stopped.

A young resident came by. We stood at Cheryl's bed. "She is in a sleep state now," the resident said, "and that may be all you get."

All you get.

All you get?

Perhaps the resident realized he should not say those words to an old man whose wife remained unconscious two days after a stroke. He added, "But it's too early to speculate."

"So," the angry old man bit off his words, "let's not fucking speculate."

The doctor on call, a general practitioner, did better. His name was Steve Kindred. No relation, but we had friends in common. He had grown up in Morton and had been a high school basketball team-mate of the Lady Potters' assistant coach, Bill Davis. He also knew the Bispings, Todd and Linda. He said, "I had a patient, eighty-three years old, who had the same hemorrhagic stroke as Cheryl. A year later, she had some cognitive slowness, but a full recovery."

Cheryl slept most of five days, opening her eyes only moments at a time. It was a week before she was awake two days in a row and able to follow commands. ("Squeeze my hand" . . . "Thumbs up.") The young resident who had angered me now apparently had moved on from his idea that Cheryl might never wake up. He said, "She's where I would expect her to be with this kind of stroke. There will be weeks of recovery, months, maybe a year."

I said, "I don't care how long. I just want to know she's on the way."

"She is," he said.

THE NIGHT OF THE STROKE, I HAD TEXTED BOB BECKER. I WROTE, "I AM only hoping she makes it thru the next 48 hours." The clock was moving slowly. It was just after eight o'clock.

The text tone on my iPhone is a harp sound. That night, I heard harps. One playing. Two, three. The music of angels on my phone, seven, eight harps. The Lady Potters, all the players, were sending us messages of hope and prayer. Somehow, they had all become our daughters. In a sports world addicted to excess—my world for so long—I came home and discovered the lasting value of understated moments.

At 8:36 p.m., Chandler Ryan wrote, "Our entire basketball family is here for you."

At 8:37, Brandi Bisping: "God always has a plan, God bless."

At 8:38, Kayla McCormick: "My family is praying for you."

At 8:40, Jadison Wharram: "I just wanted to let you know that the whole team is thinking about and praying for you and your family. We all love you very much."

I began writing about the Lady Potters in 2010. I had no agenda. It got me out of the house. It made me pay attention to something other than growing old. We met good people and shared good times. I loved it. Loved the little gyms, loved the games, loved feeling like I was twenty-five, just starting. Now I was an old guy, and when it mattered in my life, I heard harp music.

Todd and Linda Bisping, carrying grocery bags, walked into room 2218 that night. We talked and we prayed and we ate crackers, and it was all good, and before they left I said, "I don't know when I'll be at another game."

Linda said, "When you're ready, that's when."

"If I'm ever ready," I said.

"You will be. You can't quit living."

NINE DAYS LATER, ON DECEMBER 15, I WAS IN DUNLAP HIGH SCHOOL'S gym, on the first row of bleachers during the jayvee game. Chandler Ryan came over and gave me a hug. "I want you to know we're all praying for your wife," she said.

Morton beat Dunlap, 74–37. It was the undefeated Potters' ninth victory. It was also the end of Ryan's high school career. At 5:29 of the second quarter, she came down awkwardly from a layup. She hyper-extended her right knee. She heard a pop. Curled in pain on the floor, she wept. Becker left the bench and ran to her. Ryan reached up to grasp the coach's hand. She knew what had happened. A torn ACL required surgery and a year's rehabilitation.

During the second half, moving on crutches, an ice pack on her knee, Ryan returned to the Potters' bench. She once stood at the back of a time-out huddle, only briefly before moving away, crying.

I talked to her after the game. "You'll be ready when it's time for you to be ready."

She said, "I will."

It was my turn to hug her.

AT DAWN WEDNESDAY, DECEMBER 30, SNOW FELL. IT WAS SOFT AND beautiful. I had a choice to make. Drive thirty miles through the snow to a Potters holiday tournament game in Normal. Or go to Apostolic Christian Restmor and sit with Cheryl for a third week of therapy.

She had been moved into the Morton nursing home where Mom had lived and died. For years I had been repelled by the sterility and near-palpable sorrow of nursing homes. Restmor was different. It had the look of a classy hotel, with shining woodwork and pleasant art on the corridor walls. Its light fixtures were Frank Lloyd Wright designs. A fireplace warmed a seating area in the lobby.

Every day for a dozen days, I had been there with Cheryl. The morning of December 30, I changed the routine. I went to the game.

It started at 9:30 a.m., a half hour before Cheryl's daily session of occupational therapy. It was therapy that had not yet altered her sleeping state; she was seldom awake more than a minute or two. Maybe something good would happen if I were not there.

I was in the third row of bleachers behind the Potters' bench. At halftime, U High led, 21–19, and my phone rang.

I listened and scribbled a note.

Byrne calls. I'm crying. Tears rolling down my cheeks. "OK!"

Dave Byrne had gone to Cheryl's therapy session. He saw her with her eyes alive. He saw her smile when he said, "Your knucklehead husband went to a basketball game in this snow." He saw her mouthing words, silently, a full sentence, separate words, syllables formed slowly, surely. Finally, he knelt before her wheelchair and told her he had to leave for his son's game in Pekin.

"I'll be back," Byrne told Cheryl.

She said, clearly, surely, heard by both Byrne and the therapist, "OK."

It was her first word in twenty-four days.

"She's on the path, dude! On the path!" Byrne said in his text, and I passed the news on to Linda Bisping, who said, "Praise God."

The Potters came back in the second half to beat U High, 42–41. They would play again that afternoon, four hours later, giving me time to get from Normal to Restmor. The therapist told me about the "OK." She also told me she had remarked to Cheryl that it had snowed. The therapist said she nodded to a window and said, "It's bright out." And Cheryl, clearly, surely, said, "Yes."

I sat with Cheryl two hours. She said nothing and she said everything. She cocked that left eyebrow the way she did forever when in doubt about the value of my behavior. I began to sing "Sherry," the Frankie Valli hit of our youth, but I cannot sing, and Sherri knew that, and there came to her face a forgiving smile. I swear, she laughed at me. I was thrilled.

Then back to Normal. Morton defeated Springfield, 59–48, after which Becker said he liked his team's performance in the tournament. "It showed we can be pretty danged good. I'm really proud of how we bounced back from that North Lawndale game [a 48–46 loss in four overtimes the day before] to beat two really good teams. It proved we can do this. We still have a lot of work to do, and we know now that we can get it done."

Brandi Bisping recounted what the Potters learned in winning three of four games to raise their record to 13–1. "We're better than we thought we might be," she said. "I heard a lot of bad talk about us after Chan got hurt—not from the team, but from friends around school. But now we've proven that, hey, we actually can play basketball."

I thanked Ms. Bisping for her time. She did a graceful curtsy. I again returned to Restmor. I kissed my wife good night.

I LOVED MY GUYS BOB, JOHN, AND FRANK, AS PROVEN ON THE NIGHT of January 5, a month after Cheryl's stroke. I was driving the four of us to Canton on Route 29, as long and lonesome a road as there is between Morton and any Mid-Illini Conference town.

Loved 'em, I said, though I am not a hunter, not a fisherman, and I have never wondered if a downwind deer can smell my armpits. Yet for the near hour of the drive, I enjoyed listening to tales told by men who believe camo is formal wear. Somewhere between the Pekin bridge and the swampland by Banner Marsh, I heard about a monster bluegill and a turtle as big as a manhole cover and a bullfrog that ate a muskrat.

Then Bob started in. "One day," he said, "I sat against a tree."

A deer walked up on him. He was not hunting deer. He sat there. Watching. The doe came closer.

"I started giggling," Bob said.

Apparently, that is what you do when you are not hunting for deer and one walks up on you.

"She was sniffing the ground. Never knew I was there. Never saw me. Couldn't have been four feet away. Then she looked me in the eye and I looked her in the eye."

And?

"And I went 'blubba/blubba/blubba,'" he said, flapping his lips in a hunter's kind of Bronx cheer, causing the poor, frightened doe to leap straight up, spin in circles, and set the forest on fire with her sprint away from this blubbering alien sitting against a tree.

The Potters won that night, 50–47. They were 14–1.

TEN DAYS LATER IN THE POTTERDOME, MORTON 46, METAMORA 32. I sat in the third row of the bleachers surrounded by ten little girls, the Morton Heat's sixth-grade team, girls wearing jerseys with their names, among them Troxell and Krupa, Skinner and Mattson. The Heat is a girls program that starts with third graders—all with volunteer coaches, usually dads and moms. Friday night the sixth graders were invited into the locker room for pregame talks; they lined up with the Potters for the national anthem, and at halftime they played five-on-five. Some of the girls in the row behind the bench might soon play for the Lady Potters.

"The Heat is the ground floor of our high school program's success," Becker said. "I love that those little eyes are watching our players."

Chandler Ryan had been one of those girls.

"Third grade, I met Tracy Pontius," she said. "She told me I wore a good number."

Her number was 5, also Pontius's number.

"It was the most amazing moment of my life," Ryan said.

As she spoke, Chandler Ryan was the Potters' fifth-leading scorer all-time. Tracy Pontius was fourth.

By the way, that little girl by me that night, the one named Krupa? Remember her. She soon would be a big girl.

I WENT TO RESTMOR EVERY DAY THAT WINTER AND EVERY DAY AFTER that winter. I kept a journal. Someday I would write about Cheryl's days there. Writers write. I wanted to chronicle a miracle. Memory is flawed, and, consciously or not, memory can be distorted by what we want the past to be. I wanted to read the journal to Cheryl on a day she would understand every word. I wanted her to realize how far she had come.

Jan. 29, 2016. After a week of non-responsiveness, today was a godsend. Cheryl was alert when I arrived at 9:30, in her chair, but comfortable. I talked to her and started flicking her left jawline with a finger. She groaned and said, "Ouch." I saw her react to the flicking by drawing away, so, being me, I did it more. Anything to get a reaction, is what I was doing. Then Cheryl said, "Stop." I looked at Sandy sitting at the foot of the bed and said, "Did you hear what I think I heard?" Sandy said, "Yeah, she said stop." So I kept doing it. Then Cheryl said, "Quit it." It was the first sustained thought I'd heard from her since Dec. 6. I took to flicking the tops of her ears. Finally, Cheryl said, "David, will you stop it!" Said in a low, gravelly voice but loudly enough and clearly enough that Sandy heard it, too. It was the first complete sentence since Dec. 6, 54 days ago. When I said, "I'm irritating, aren't I?" Cheryl laughed. At least her face showed laugh lines. Altogether, she was as close to alive as she's been. What a great morning.

The days moved slowly, good days and bad. Stroke patients often are unable to swallow; Cheryl passed every test. Using her left hand (her right side was weakened), she could feed herself. We walked around Restmor daily. Nurses used a sling lift to move Cheryl from her bed into a full-body wheelchair known by its brand name, a Broda. With me pushing the chair through Restmor's corridors, we soon became familiar figures to residents.

A WEEK LATER, THE POTTERS' FINAL REGULAR-SEASON GAME WAS AN earache.

Morton 45, Washington 37.

The Washington High School pep band may have been the best pep band in the land. I knew only one thing. That pep band was loud. WHEN WILL MY EARDRUMS STOP QUIVERING? There were tubas and trombones and trumpets and drums and clarinets and flutes and French horns and castanets. An F-15 fighter jet seemed to have joined the saxophones.

"Never heard a high school pep band play Metallica before," a musically inclined person said. "They're playing 'Master of Puppets.'"

There were many requests made to the pep band. They kept playing, anyway.

The Potters played well. Late in the first half, for instance, the little guard Kayla McCormick had made three 3-pointers. She said, "I was just feeling it." When she made a steal near the Washington free throw line and took off for midcourt with time running out, why not be Steph Curry and throw it in from the jump circle?

Only trouble was, there were eight seconds left, time enough to sprint the length of the court. When McCormick's long shot fell several feet short, the senior did what you would expect a veteran to do. She laughed. Then she blushed. And she thought, "Oops."

McCormick did not take another shot. No need when you are a perpetual-motion machine on defense. She did not reappear until the fourth quarter when, in the paint, she saw the ball in a Washington girl's hands. The girl held it tightly—until McCormick ripped it away.

That thievery ignited a game-turning run that saw Morton go up 41–29 with 3:02 to play. The victory moved the Lady Potters to 26–3 and sent them into the state tournaments on a high.

"We beat Canton and we beat Washington," Becker said. "They're two really good teams that have—what?—fifty wins between them." (It was forty-four.) "Now, in the postseason, everybody's zero and zero. Anything can happen."

ANYTHING? YES, A THIRD DANCE WITH WASHINGTON, THIS TIME IN THE sectional championship game . . .

Morton 42, Washington 35, and I had no idea how they did it except that their littlest big girl grabbed the game by the throat and then a nervous rookie turned cool when she needed to be the coolest kid out there.

Better to explain it in four words.

Jadison Wharram, Tenley Dowell.

Wharram, a senior forward who claimed to be five foot eight, played inside with the big girls and was never bigger than in the third quarter this time. In five minutes and five seconds, she scored 11 points in a 13–2 run that brought the Potters from three down to eight up. She did it with a driving layup on the baseline, then a pair of seventeen-foot jump shots followed by two more baseline drives and a free throw. Afterward, asked about those moments, it was as if all that had happened without her notice.

"I wasn't thinking about anything like we were on a run," she said. "The baseline drives were there and I just took 'em. What I felt at that time was that the team was really coming together."

From there on, Washington never got closer than three points largely because, near the end of the frenzied game, who stepped to the free throw line for Morton except maybe the last girl you want to step to the free throw line with the game and the season depending on how she did.

Dowell was a freshman, a five-nine guard. She was good at many things, but not free throws. A 50 percent free throw shooter, she had made one of two in the first quarter and had not been back to the line until there were sixty-five seconds to play and Morton led 35–32.

"I was nervous," she said later. "I was thinking, 'I gotta make these.'"

On a scale of 1 to 10, how nervous?

"I think a 7," she said nervously.

Wednesday mornings, before school, the Potters shoot. The greatest of the Boston Celtics, Larry Bird, used to do morning sessions in high school at French Lick, Indiana. His high school team once lost a game because a kid who never showed up for the morning work missed an important free throw. Thirty years later, Bird could still tell you that kid's name.

Tenley Dowell shows up at the Potterdome on Wednesday mornings, aiming to be better than a 50–50 shooter at the line, and on the line with sixty-five seconds to play and Washington threatening, Tenley Dowell . . .

Made them both.

And twenty-three seconds later . . .

Made another.

And seven seconds after that . . .

Made two more, *swish, swish.*

She made five of six when she needed to make five of six to move Morton's lead from 35–32 to 40–33 with thirty-five seconds to play.

Morton had beaten Washington for the third time and raised its record to 30–3. It did it with the tenacious, relentless defense and grind-it-out offense that has shaped the team's identity since Chandler Ryan tore up her knee in December, twenty-four games earlier.

The victory moved Becker to praise his girls' grit, toughness, resolve, purpose, and all-around determination to do a neat trick that assistant coach Bill Davis had proposed before the game.

Dipping into his high school basketball days, Davis told the girls about a cheer he remembered. He even did it for them . . .

Rah-rah-ree,
Kick 'em in the knee!
Rah-rah-rass,
Kick 'em in the . . . other knee!

Next for the Potters, a super-sectional game in a place called Manlius. Victory there would send them to Redbird again, a second state championship now three games away.

MANLIUS TURNED OUT TO BE A TINY VILLAGE ON THE PRAIRIE OF NORTH-central Illinois, an hour and twenty minutes north of Peoria on Illinois 40. As reward for making it to the super-sectional, the Lady Potters rode in style, not in a clankety-clank school bus but again in a comfy chartered coach of the type that had carried them to NORMANtown Road the year before. It was a scenic ride if you like your scenery in Fifty Shades of Brown. Along that stretch of 40 in late February there is nothing but brown grass and brown dirt and silos and grain elevators and trees that look like witches' arthritic fingers.

We saw Singing Bird Road, Hillock Hollow Road, and the Merkle Ridge U-Cut Christmas Tree Farm. Signs pointed to Wyoming and Sparland and Osceola. In Bradford, we passed a home flying a Marine Corps flag. We passed three cemeteries. We straddled a dead skunk. We saw a '38 Packard in a barn lot. The Potters' trainer, Katie Gavin, once shouted out, "Turkeys! Two in that field!"

A couple hours later, Morton had defeated Burlington Central, 34–29. As Bob Becker climbed a ladder to cut down a net, he first kissed his sophomore point guard, his daughter, Josi, and once up there he twirled the net overhead and let it fly down to the celebrants. It landed in a player's hands, Jadison Wharram's, and the veteran did a veteran thing. She tossed the net to the precocious rookie, Tenley Dowell, who had made two free throws with 1.5 seconds to play.

"I love my kids," Becker said. "They are tough, they are resilient, they will do anything to gut it out. Guts, grit, determination, however you want to say it. They know how to win."

The victory sent the No. 1–ranked Lady Potters to Redbird again. They would play a semifinal against No. 2 Morgan Park, long a Chicago power.

ON MARCH 4, 2016, THE LADY POTTERS EMBARRASSED MORGAN PARK. It was 54–39. What we saw with Bob Becker's team were amazing events built on amazing events. I covered a World Series once, Phillies and Astros, and one game went on forever, fourteen innings or some such, and everything happened that could happen in a baseball game, and someone asked a Phillies relief pitcher, Tug McGraw, what it was like seeing all that. He said, "It was like riding a motorcycle through an art gallery."

So it is with these Lady Potters.

A piece of the art . . .

Little Kassidy Shurman, a five-foot-two sophomore, was in the game for a minute midway through the first quarter. She was in because Becker did not like a Tenley Dowell mistake on defense. And what did the little squirt Shurman do when the ball came to her in the deep right corner? She might have done the safe thing and thrown it to somebody older and bigger. Instead, she did the right thing. Left unguarded, she put up a three-point shot. It went in. It put Morton up 11–3 and sent a message to the Chicago folks: *We ain't scared*. Becker later said, "They're not intimidated by anybody, whether it's their record, or their height, or their athleticism."

Another piece . . .

Jadison Wharram was on fire. She made four straight baskets in under three minutes to move Morton from a 12–all tie to a 20–16 lead late in the second quarter. But that was not the prettiest part. That part she created with 2:11 to play in the half. From a step behind the free throw line, Wharram rose for a jump shot. She had already made her first five midrange jumpers and a layup, six for six. As her seventeen-footer floated toward the basket, Wharram floated away, holding the follow-through for a nanosecond because she was certain, floating on a shooter's high, that she soon would be seven for seven. "I was gloating for a second," she said later. "I thought, 'That feels good.'" It was. Morton led, 22–16, and Morgan Park never came closer.

That night, at the very moment that I was writing about Wharram's shot, she texted me. "That 'gloating,' please don't quote me," she said, "because that's not who I am." She had that right, it was not her. I made it "celebrating." I had never acceded to a change-my-quote request. It is also true that such a request had never been made by a player who, the day of my wife's stroke, had texted me: "I just wanted to let you know that the whole team is thinking about and praying for you and your family. We all love you very much."

One more . . .

Tenley Dowell had the ball, late in the game, dribbling away from Morgan Park's star, Deja Cage, a Division I quality player trying to foul her. Finally, exhausted, Cage grabbed a chunk of jersey. Dowell made two free throws. It was 50–34.

And what next? The Potters would play another Chicago team, North Lawndale Prep. In December's State Farm Holiday Classic, as the Potters well remembered, North Lawndale had made three improbable three-point shots to keep alive a four-overtime game that it won, 48–46.

"They're one of the three teams to beat us this season," Brandi Bisping said. "And that's not going to happen again."

ON MARCH 5, 2016, AT REDBIRD ARENA, I REMEMBERED DECEMBER 15, 2015, in the Dunlap High School gymnasium.

Back then, Chandler Ryan wept. Two notes from that day . . .

5:39, Ryan down. Crying. Knee? Holding Becker's hand. Saying something. Taken off to locker room . . .
Third quarter, Ryan on bench, crutches.

That day, Ryan's high school basketball career ended. In the season's first eight games, the little guard with a shooter's gift had scored 21.4 points a game. An All-Stater the season before when she led the Lady Potters to their first state championship, Ryan was a captain and the team's offensive heart. With her, the Potters were undefeated in eight games and worked with an unspoken commitment to a bold idea: they could repeat as state champions, they could go undefeated.

Without Ryan, the Lady Potters could have no bold ambitions.

Yet, on March 5, 2016, the Potters made the improbable happen and made it look implausibly easy, 58–41 over Chicago North Lawndale.

On that day, at halftime, Chandler Ryan came to the Potters' bench.

She had become an ex officio coach. Since surgery to repair the torn ACL, she had been at every team practice, at every meeting, at every game. For weeks she had been a mentor to the team's young guards, Dowell and Josi Becker. For weeks she had talked tactics along the bench. She made herself content with the hardest thing she had ever done. She sat, watched, and cheered.

And eighty-one days after Dunlap, she came to the bench as the second half was about to begin, Morton up 25–13.

I did not see her at first. I saw an odd thing. Morton players looked downcourt. They began to clap. Ryan was walking from the locker room, not in her black warm-ups but in the Potters' red-and-gray game uniform.

Next, the Morton student section saw her—saw her as if she were ready to play—and they knew what they saw. They saw Chandler Ryan in the uniform she had not worn since Dunlap. They saw her number 4. They sent up a roar of celebration.

Ryan wept. She touched the corner of an eye, and her face was flushed, and she smiled, and she touched the corner of the other eye, and she took a seat on the bench, everyone now knowing that, at some point, she would walk onto the Redbird Arena court, not to play—she was months from that—but to make an appearance.

Some days and nights, the Potters needed Ryan playing. Not this day. Morton allowed North Lawndale one point in the first quarter. It was 12–1 before the Potters allowed the losers a field goal. It was no contest, one team so superior in so many important ways—fundamentals, poise, basketball IQ—as to make the other seem foolish.

There were twenty-nine seconds to play when the Morton student section sent up a chant.

"WE WANT CHANDLER . . . WE WANT CHANDLER . . ."

Bob Becker looked at Ryan.

She nodded.

Becker went to a referee to explain that he would put Ryan into the game but only so she could stand at the sideline, not to move, just to be where she belonged for one more moment.

With 27.9 seconds left, Ryan stepped onto the court, and the hundreds of Morton fans in Redbird Arena let her know what they thought of her.

She blinked against tears. A second later, during a dead-ball moment, she left the game. Becker met her with an embrace and her teammates surrounded her.

"The future is bright for Morton basketball," Becker said then. Seven of his eleven Potters, including three starters, would return the next season.

"Three-peat?" said an assistant coach, Megan Hasler. "If we three-peat, I'll get a tattoo."

Say again, please?

"A tattoo."

What kind of tattoo?

"On my back, I'll get Brandi Bisping's face."

FOR TWO MONTHS, I HAD BEEN SEEING A PSYCHOLOGIST. MY PAL JANE Leavy suggested her, a woman in Champaign, Jane's buddy since their high school days. Dr. Sue's first suggestion was that I should not be with Cheryl eight hours a day, that it would be months before any appreciable change. Best to develop a schedule, an hour or two a day. Keep conversation short and simple, "Hi," "Bye," "Love you." Take care of myself, stay around family and friends. Don't be alone. Don't feel guilty, like it's my fault. "You've taken good care of her," she said. "Live your life, exercise, eat well."

Meanwhile, occupational and speech therapists had signed off on Cheryl. With no measure of progress, Medicare would no longer pay for their work. Federal rules would not allow me to pay for therapy in a Medicare-funded facility. What, to pay for therapy, I had to move her to New York? That, among many bureaucratic puzzles, made me crazy.

My best friend, Gary Pomerantz, invited me to visit him in San Francisco. We had been sportswriting colleagues at the *Washington Post* and *Atlanta Journal-Constitution* before he reinvented himself as an author and journalism instructor at Stanford University. I hated to leave Cheryl, but I thought the psychologist was right. I needed a break. A week after the Potters' second state championship victory, I left for California.

14

• •

RETURNED FROM CALIFORNIA ON THE SAME TRAIN THAT TOOK ME OUT
there, the California Zephyr, but this time bringing along Pomerantz. First day back, we went to Restmor. From the journal:

As I walked into her room, she was in a chair facing me. Her eyes
were wide open. Gary said he saw "love, relief, happiness, and tears."
I thought she recognized me and was so happy she felt like crying,
not like she thought she'd never see me again, but like she'd forgotten to miss me, then realized she did miss me and saw me all in the
same moment, a confusion of emotions. I sat with her and told her
I loved her. She reached up and put her left palm against my right
cheek, tenderly. Her hand was very warm.

A nurse asked Cheryl, "Do you know this guy?" Cheryl's left eyebrow went up, like, "Of course, I do." The nurse asked, "Can you tell
me his name?" Cheryl said, "Well, he's kinda cute."

When I told her I had been to SF and back on the train and it took
2½ days each way, she said, "You're crazy." She continues to say a few
words appropriately. Gary thinks my saying she's come "inches on a

thousand-mile journey" understates her progress. The first 15 minutes today, at 10 a.m., he thought she was totally involved in the moment.

I wanted to believe that Gary's perception was right-on. I wanted to believe a moment could become a day when Cheryl was again Cheryl and that such a day could never end. But too many times I heard doctors dismiss a sweet, kind gesture as a "moment of lucidity." Those were unexplainable moments when the blood-ravaged brain yet produced a flash of thought, a moment, a blink in time, here and gone. I understood it, and I hated it.

On my seventy-fifth birthday, April 12, 2016, Cheryl ate real food for the first time since the stroke—real, if pureed food can be thought of as real. A speech therapist, Whitney, certainly thought it was. (Stroke patients often are unable to swallow. Cheryl had been on a feeding tube four months.) Whitney fed Cheryl half teaspoons of cheesy potatoes, pork roast, green beans, and triple-berry pie, along with two glasses of nectar-thickened water. Cheryl took it all, swallowed without a problem, and Whitney declared herself "thrilled" by "a stellar day."

That evening, at six thirty, we celebrated my birthday in the nursing home's Tremont Room, a gathering place for families. Cheryl was awake and alert. When I sat by her Broda chair, she leaned in for a kiss. I made that happen five or six times. Cheryl could not sing "Happy Birthday," but she lip-synched it.

Two weeks after that good day came its opposite. It involved belligerence, agitation, and guttural moaning as if she were in pain deep and unrelenting. Her nurse, Angie, called to get my permission for a second dose of Ativan, designed to relieve anxiety. She said that Cheryl the day before had resisted the medicine delivered through a G-tube. "She pinched off the line," Angie said, to which I said, "She can figure that out?" Angie said, "Then she slapped me."

September 26, six months later, was the first time I felt Cheryl did not know I was with her. With her eyes open, she never looked at me. She never responded to my voice. Her hand was limp in mine. I kissed her, though not really. My lips touched hers without a response. She was a blank. She had fallen into a void and taken me with her.

And yet, on December 4, two days short of a year after the stroke, I had her laughing at lunch. I winked at her, and she thought that was funny. The more she laughed, the faster I winked. "You're so silly," she said. I asked her to wink at me, and she did, causing us both to laugh out loud. Then we went for our walk, me pushing her Broda chair as she drank chocolate milk. I said, "Hey, we're drinking and driving." Her voice airy but clear, I heard her say, "Better not get arrested!"

My journal entries, rendered into a graph, would resemble a saw-toothed mountain range, its peaks separated by wide valleys, every good day followed by a dozen bad days. So it went that first year. Hope, hopelessness, hope, lost, found, lost.

One more mountain peak. After the Potters state championship season, I had produced a fans' book, *True Grit*. I showed her a page that carried a portrait of her, that left eyebrow raised. Another picture showed Jeannie Peabody and Dr. Appleby. She touched the picture. When I thought to show her a different page, she held the book so tightly I could not move it. As I left the room, she pressed the book close to her heart.

I LIVED IN THREE PLACES, AT HOME, RESTMOR, AND THE POTTERDOME. Home was Cheryl's, the colors, the light, family pictures, her chair— I wanted to be there to know she had been there and had made it hers, to feel the strength of her life. At Restmor, I could touch her with more pleasure than I will ever feel in any "moment of lucidity." In the Potterdome, relief. A basketball game gave me reason to pay attention, take notes, go home, and write, hidden away in my office the way I had done it all the years when Cheryl was in the other room, waiting for me. It almost felt normal.

But a basketball game? Is a kids' game worth writing about? Absolutely. Writing was my life. Writing anything gave me reason to stay alive. These girls had played harp music for me, and they had prayed for Cheryl. I damn sure would write something on their basketball games.

THE FIRST NIGHT OF THE POTTERS' 2016–2017 SEASON, I SAW A MYSTERY girl. At halftime of the jayvee game, the varsity players left the bleachers to shoot around. I did not recognize a brown-haired girl. Moved smoothly, confidently. But I had not seen her face. The mystery ended when the brown-haired girl shot a 3 from the corner. I knew that girl. She had been a blonde, a shimmering blonde, her blonde hair so shiny canaries sang in envy. Brandi Bisping.

When she returned to the bleachers, I said, "Uh, Brandi, the hair . . ."

"Too expensive," she said.

No more cut-and-colors at ninety dollars apiece.

"I'd have recognized you," I said, "when the game started."

"I hope I show up," she said.

Four minutes in, Bisping had two offensive rebounds, a steal leading to a fast-break layup, and another layup off a nifty in-the-paint pass from Josi Becker. The Lady Potters had an 8–0 lead that became 17–5 at quarter's end. And so on, until Morton 51, Chatham-Glenwood 24.

By the end of December, the Potters were winners of fourteen straight, twenty-seven in a row reaching into the previous season. They won three times in the State Farm Holiday Classic before losing the championship game to Rock Island, 60–40. Morton, a Class 3A school, had its chances before being worn out by a big, strong, quick, once-beaten team ranked No. 1 in the Illinois top class, 4A.

Bob Becker was upbeat. Eleven of his thirteen players were underclassmen. Some played under big-game pressure for the first time. December is important to him, but he cares more about late February and early March, when state champions are made.

"At fourteen and one we're a really, really good team," Becker said. "Our goal is to get back and win the big one."

The best Becker quote came the day before, after Morton defeated its fiercest rival, Normal U High. He told his players what he thought of them. They had come from behind five times against a previously undefeated team. They had won three Holiday Classic games by three points each time. They threw themselves after every loose ball. But before I tell you what he thought of those girls, I should tell you those girls loved every word of it. You could tell by their sudden burst of laughter.

The coach said, "You are the toughest little shits in the entire state of Illinois."

What a fun season it would be, even on Senior Night in February. Becker wanted Bisping and Jacey Wharram to get one more standing ovation with a thousand people in the bleachers. When he sent Bisping and Wharram into the game with three minutes and one second to play, he said, "You'll come out in thirty seconds." Becker also told them, "Do something sensational."

Bisping and Wharram would make their final appearance forever memorable. Here came Bisping toward the bench in a high-stepping lope. Then she was slowing down . . . and she turned sideways . . . and she tilted her body . . . and she threw herself down to the court and . . .

Wharram came right behind her and . . .

They became little kids doing happy, laughing . . .

CARTWHEELS!!

Also, the Lady Potters defeated Washington, 56–22. They would be 27–2 entering the regional. However good the Potters had been a season ago in winning a second straight state championship, this team was better. A year ago, one starter was over five foot nine. Now three were five eleven. They started two seniors, Bisping and Wharram, juniors Josi Becker and Kassidy Shurman, and sophomore Tenley Dowell. Off the bench: freshman Lindsey Dullard (a six-one shooter), junior Caylie Jones, and freshman Courtney Jones. All of them had played on state championship teams in high school and/or grade school.

I HAD NEVER HEARD OF US ARMY GENERAL ISAIAH STILLMAN.

The Lady Potters first won two regional games, 62–31 and 66–46. They then waxed Galesburg 54–24 and won the sectional championship game by 16 to arrange a super-sectional game against Stillman Valley High School.

During the Black Hawk War that moved across northern Illinois in the early nineteenth century, Gen. Isaiah Stillman led 275 federal soldiers into a battle with Sauk and Fox warriors. The general decided his troops were outnumbered by thousands of Indians when, in fact, there were fifty. The general fled the battlefield, a retreat that history books now call "Stillman's Run."

Morton 48, the Stillman Valley runners 31.

That made the Potters' record 32–2, two victories away from a third straight state championship. Assistant coach Bill Davis went to the locker room chalkboard. There he wrote notes about the two previous seasons and a suggestion for the current one:

"33–3 was good."

"33–3 was good again."

"34 and 2 is the new goal."

"Ain't nothin' to it, just do it."

The day before Redbird, as usual, the Lady Potters ate breakfast at the Bispings'. Then they ate some more. "I got two plates, one in each hand, and they both were full," said Olivia Remmert, a freshman new to the Potters' tradition of breakfast at the Bispings' before winning state again. "Mrs. Bisping is such a good cook. Biscuits with gravy, sausage, eggs, fruit, chocolate-chip pancakes, chocolate-chip scones . . ."

In a semifinal at eleven o'clock the next day, the well-fed Potters defeated a Chicago power, Simeon, 56–41.

"Unbelievable," Bob Becker said, which is a thing a coach says when he does not want to say out loud that he believed it all along. Over three seasons, his team had won twenty straight win-or-go-home games.

There was no reason to disbelieve. The little point guard, Josi Becker, threw in four 3-pointers to keep the Potters alive in the first half. Tenley Dowell scored inside and out. Brandi Bisping, with 1 point at halftime, scored 19 of the Potters' last 34. For the umpteenth time, the Potters ran an opponent into physical and psychic exhaustion. It was 22–all at halftime; with five minutes to play, 48–32, I scribbled a note about Simeon's deflated defenders: "They've quit." Becker said, "That's how basketball should be played."

The morning of the championship game, the Potters gathered for a shoot-around in the Potterdome before the bus ride to Redbird. It was 9:30 a.m. The only sounds were the bouncings of basketballs and the squeaks of sneakers against the hardwood. Then came a voice booming through the gym's public address system.

I've been told it's a good idea to start a speech with a joke. Well, don't get your hopes up. I'm not here to tell jokes.

The Potters worked out casually. They ran fundamental dribbling drills.
Fundamentals on the last day of the season. Of course.
The voice took on a growl, loudly, bouncing off the gym walls.

I'm here to pick a fight. I'm here to pick a fight with second place. I have as much patience for second place as I do for flies in my soup.

Assistant coach Megan Hasler had put together a pep-talk audiotape.

But maybe you like flies in your soup. Maybe you like second place. Maybe you like that "you gave it your best, better luck next" malarkey they spoon-feed runner-ups. Let me put it another way. If you think second place ain't such a bad deal, why don't you ask Napoleon how he felt coming in second at Waterloo. Not so good, not so good.

The Potters went about their shooting. From deep in a corner, Brandi Bisping shot 3s.

And you can spare me the "it's not whether you win or lose, it's how you play the game" bullshit. I guarantee you whoever said that lost the game. Moral of the story, come in first.

Bisping made her first two 3s.

Still wanna hear a joke? Fine, here's one for you. "Knock, knock." "Who's there?" "The guy that finished second." "The guy-that-finished-second who?" Exactly.

HOW BOLD THAT GOAL, A THREE-PEAT, AND THE POTTERS ROSE TO IT. Rochester was strong, quick, and experienced, the best 3A team the Potters played all season. Morton led at halftime, 16–15, but had been unimpressive. Rochester took a 25–21 lead.

I scribbled a sentence on the Potters' side of my notebook and put an asterisk by it as reminder of a moment that can turn a game. *How tough are they?*

I had heard Becker proclaim their heart and resiliency and "burning desire to succeed," and I had seen his whiteboard reminder: "TOUGHNESS." But that was against bad teams. This was against a good team with the state championship at stake.

The answer came quickly. The toughest little shits in Illinois scored the game's next 12 points.

They dared to shoot 3s. Bisping moved outside and put up her first long one. She made it. "Nobody came out on me, so I shot," she said. Thirty-two seconds later, she did it again. Bold now and running hot, the Potters dared to be physical. Bisping pumped both fists in celebration while flat on the floor after drawing a charge. In a trapping 1-3-1 zone press ordered up by Becker at halftime, the Potters stole the ball, forced bad passes, and drove Rochester to distraction. By the time another Dowell 3 opened the fourth quarter and gave the Potters a 33–25 lead, the Morton students recognized what was happening. They chanted, "I BELIEVE WE WILL WIN . . . I BELIEVE WE WILL WIN."

The Potters finished first that afternoon. Hundreds of Morton students chanted, "THREE-PEAT . . . THREE-PEAT." Becker walked in small circles, head down, as if searching for proof on the court that it had happened. He whispered, "You dream of just making it here. . . ."

Here, he was a master. Morton 43–37. Becker hugged each of his thirteen players. Then he walked in small circles on the Redbird court, no one with him, whispering, "Unbelievable." He found his wife, reprising an embrace they shared in March 2015.

Fathers who had coached their daughters wept with those daughters. Benchwarmers danced with stars. Thirteen small-town girls held a big trophy with their names engraved: Brandi Bisping, Jacey Wharram, Josi Becker, Kassidy Shurman, Tenley Dowell, Caylie Jones, Lindsey Dullard, Courtney Jones, Olivia Remmert, Megan Gold, Bridget Wood, Clarie Kraft, Maddy Becker.

THE NEXT WEEK, MARCH 11, 2017, I SAW CHERYL AT RESTMOR. FROM MY journal:

> At lunch, C rubbed my right hand and arm. I looked at her because it was so sweet, her touch. She leaned toward me and I moved closer. She said, out of the blue, "You were running away." She meant y'day when I left early. "No, no, I'm here with you. Every day. I'm not running away. I'm here all the time." She said, "Good."
>
> We moved to the Prairie Room. Big windows. Farmland out back. We were alone there. Good mood. I asked if she remembered the

night I sneaked upstairs to see her. She smiled, and I told her I had written about it, did she want to hear it? "Uh-oh," she said. She knew what was coming.

I read the little story.

It was midnight. It was winter. I remember her bedroom being cold. It was upstairs in her family's little farmhouse by the railroad tracks south of Atlanta. There were two ways to get up to her. I could go through the living room to the big staircase. To go that way meant passing her parents' bedroom. It had no door. I chose the other way up. It was through the kitchen. Maybe all little farmhouses had a hidden staircase behind a narrow door in the kitchen. Hers did.

The doorway was so narrow I had to turn sideways to go through it. I walked up the steps slowly and softly, lest they creak. My shoulders touched the walls on both sides. I didn't know what would happen when I got to her bedroom. I knew only that I wanted it to happen. The staircase opened into the attic. It was dark and cold. What heat the house had was downstairs. I felt my way to a door on the far side.

Behind that door, her bedroom. Maybe I'd been there, maybe she'd told me. I remember only that she was in bed when I whispered, "You there?" "Yes," she said, and then she said, "What are you doing here?" *Yes.* The sweetest, scariest word I had ever heard. What I was doing, I didn't know. I remember her warm against me and I remember a sheet cold against my back. . . .

I stopped there. She said, "Naughty boy."

15

• •

IMAGINE A LIGHTNING BOLT. IN THE DARKNESS, A FLASH OF LIGHT IS here and gone, jagged, scary as hell. My journal was a lightning bolt.

April 20, 2017.

A down day for me. Watching a rug she loved burning in burn pile. Mice had eaten away much of it. My life going up in flames. Self-pity, a year, four months, two weeks after stroke. I feel not dead but without life. Cheryl awake today but not responsive. Smiling and saying hi to passersby but not responding to me. We walked around some after lunch, then I took her to her room and left quickly. Down. No progress. This as good as it will be? Maybe better tomorrow.

Three days later.

Took C to the Oaks lobby, by the grandfather clock that chimes every 15 minutes. In essence, we made out. I rubbed her cheeks, her neck, her hands. "Can I kiss you?" the question I first asked 59 years ago. She puckered up. She rubbed my forearm, took my hand, and kissed it, looked at me sweetly. More I caressed her, the more she let her eyes fall closed, so contented, such peace. We sat thru two playings of the grandfather chimes. "I love you," and she whispered, "I love you." I rubbed her hair, too. I had her laughing again with my winks. I put an arm around her neck. "I love you a bushel and a peck and a hug around the neck." Hugs, my cheek against hers. Kissed. Nibbled her earlobe. Kids!

Three months later, August 6.

At 10:34, at the Evergreen end, she said, "Why am I dying?" Sounded like it. I asked, "Why are you what?" "Why am I . . ." and she couldn't say it again. I left her at nurse's station, asleep, w/ request that they call me when/if she wakes to eat. I was home, 5:15, mowing in front + wishing I'd said something. Then, riding the John Deere, I knew what I should have said. I drove to Restmor. She was in bed, clutching white sheet in her left hand against her face. When I sat on edge of bed, she looked at me. I said, "Today you asked me why you are dying." She nodded, yes. I told her, "You're not dying. God's taking care of you." She lifted her head to kiss me! "You're getting better every day. You're talking better. You're eating. God's taking care of you + I'm taking care of you + I'll take care of you forever. I love you." I put a hand on her cheek. She closed her eyes, she raised up, said, "Bye now." I said, "I'll see you in the morning."

Brian Newman, the Potterdome's public address announcer, hit the words with a sledgehammer: "And now . . . your . . . BACKKK! to BACKKKK!! to BACKKKKKK!!! . . . State Champion Morton Lady Potters!"

It was a November intrasquad scrimmage on Red-White Night a week before the 2017–2018 season began. I liked the energy, and I also liked the small, subtle message at the neckline on the back of the Potters' jerseys. Under "State Champions," these numbers . . . 2015 2016 2017.

Now, four in a row?

The Potters lost Brandi Bisping, the team's combative heart. They also lost Jacey Wharram, a formidable force. They could expect Tenley Dowell, a junior, to be sensational again. Lindsey Dullard, a six-foot-one sophomore, grew in confidence weekly. Four of the starting five—Dowell, Dullard, Josi Becker, Kassidy Shurman—would be 3-point threats.

Also, Becker liked Katie Krupa. Remember that name? One of the little girls with her Heat teammates four years before, now she was a six-foot freshman, strong, quick, and agile. She could score inside, had a nice touch from outside, and was aggressive defensively and on the boards.

Why not four in a row?

That would not happen if a good Richwoods team had anything to say about it, and the Peorians spoke up in that first week.

Richwoods 53, Potters 45.

Sometimes I made a note just to appear sportswriterly. Most often the notes were early observations later rendered meaningless. But sometimes a guy is prophetic. I made five notes after a quarter of that Thanksgiving tournament championship game in the Potterdome. . . .

Fast pace . . . R forcing action . . . R dominating physically . . .
R attacking at both ends . . . Hell-bent

To match Richwoods, each Potter had to be six inches taller, twenty pounds stronger, and they had to learn to jump over people for offensive rebounds. The best the Potters could hope for was a second chance. They could play Richwoods in the postseason when both would be contenders for a state championship.

ON FEBRUARY 22, FOR A SECTIONAL CHAMPIONSHIP, THERE CAME THE second chance. An hour before tip-off, the little senior guard Kassidy Shurman twirled the edges of her Rubik's Cube. The puzzle had become a thing for the Potters. "Maybe eight of us do it," she said. She sat on the Potters' bench, waiting to suit up in the locker room.

"How long does it take you to solve it?" I asked.

"Two minutes," Shurman said. "My goal is under one."

The Potters had won thirty-one games, most of them laughers built on relentless excellence. Four minutes into this one, Shurman made a 3-pointer that gave Morton a 3–2 lead. There came a great roar from the standing-room-only crowd at Dunlap High, maybe 2,500 people there to see Morton, ranked No. 1 in the state, against Richwoods, No. 2, both teams with 31–1 records, both convinced the winner would go on to become state champions. Shurman's shot set off a chant in the Morton student section, "I BELIEVE THAT WE WILL WIN . . . I BELIEVE THAT WE WILL WIN."

Too early, kids.

Forty-five seconds later, Richwoods scored on an offensive rebound. Of Richwoods' 19 field goals, 16 came at the rim. The Peorians were bigger, stronger, faster, and more aggressive. Their 2-3 zone's outside people pushed Morton's offense so far out, the Potters seldom earned a decent look at a 3. Inside, Richwoods' star, six-foot-one Cam Taylor, swatted away three layups and dared anyone to drive into the paint.

At the end of the first quarter, his team down 11–3 and having put up only four shots, Bob Becker looked at his players on the bench and shouted, "WHAT IS THE PROBLEM?"

Momentarily, the Potters rallied. They gained a tie at 13 with 2:57 left in the half. But that was it. Richwoods scored the game's next 22 points. It did to Morton what Morton had done to so many teams. It led at halftime, 20–13, and crushed the Potters in the third quarter. At the end of three, 33–13. Final: 49–29.

For Richwoods' coach, Todd Hursey, the victory was sweet. "This team is on a mission to win the program's thousandth game," he said. "We're two away now." He was thrilled, too, that the victory came against Morton. "Bob's teams have set the bar, not only in the last three years winning the state, but for a decade." Hursey, who had four starters returning the next season, said, "Now maybe it's our turn."

In the game's last minute, Becker took out his seniors, Jones, Shurman, and his daughter, Josi. As each came to the bench, they stopped for a long hug with the coach.

At game's end, I stood with Shurman in the paint at the Potters' end of the court. She wept. "This isn't anything I've ever felt," she said. "This sucks." I had been around many athletes sad in defeat. Kassidy Shurman was the first I put an arm around and drew close, her head resting on my shoulder.

She could not know it, but I needed her more than she needed me.

A MONTH EARLIER, FROM THE JOURNAL . . .

In Prairie Room Cheryl says, "Help me, help me, I can't do anything." Like a whisper, airy, plaintive. I ask what did you say? She
goes silent. I ask again. She's crying. What could I do? Nothing. Two
years here. "Help me, help me, I can't do anything." I can't help her.
Oh, God. My heart goes empty. I'll never not hear those words. I'll
hear them the rest of my life. The pain she is in. I can leave. I can
think of other things. She is trapped and helpless. Please, God.

Nights in bed, to quote Kassidy, sucked. Cheryl was not there. I
could not reach over and touch a bare shoulder. I could not feel her
breathe. I could not go to sleep. It helped counting backward from
a hundred by threes—ninety-seven, ninety-four, ninety-one—until
I remembered an afternoon with our country doctor in Virginia.
Twenty years before, after Cheryl's "minor" stroke, he had asked her
to count down by threes. She laughed. "I couldn't do that," she said,
"when I was in math class."

I wrote a note to my friend Pomerantz: "I'm as near as I want to
get to being a widower, and I believe the greatest loss is a loss of
intimacy—not only physical, which is real, but emotional in that I
could say anything in any way at any time to Cheryl and know it
would be OK—and the same from her side. But now there's just an
empty chair beside me. That's why I reach over for her in bed and
she's not there and I pull a pillow against me wishing it was her.
That's why I'm at Restmor every day, talking to her, hoping she hears
me. I'm trying to keep alive the shared intimacy that kept us alive
and together for so long."

There is a piece of sculpture in a Switzerland park. It was done by
a Romanian, Albert György. It is a copper outline of a man's body.
The man is sitting on a bench, slumped over, his head hanging low

over a giant hole where his torso should be. György called the piece *Melancholy.* I would call it *Emptiness.*

I had lost jobs, lost a grandson, lost my mother, and Cheryl was lost in a stroke. I had twice saved my sweet dog KO with spinal surgeries that cost five grand each and then he, too, was gone. I was empty. As always in these moments of self-pity, I called Dr. Sue, who patched me up and assured me I was OK. "You call me anytime you want," she said.

I called her often, though never again so down. I even told her a story that illustrates a writer's ability to imagine despair on call. James Joyce, famously slow at work, was morose. "Only seven words today," he said, and a friend thought to buck him up. "But, James, for you seven words is good." Joyce said, "But I don't know what order they go in."

ONE NIGHT, NOT KNOWING OR MUCH CARING WHAT ORDER THEY should go in, doing free association, I typed sentences that may or may not have made sense. They did make me feel better. These . . .

My world was disappearing. Mom, 96, and it was time. Jared, the alcohol. Cheryl, the stroke. Newspapers died under me, maybe not the literal newspaper. Many still printed every day. But the idea was gone. These were zombie newspapers. The walking dead. They had given me life and ambition, then they deserted me. I did a nice column on that Tibet protest in Lafayette Park, but the newspaper paying my salary would not print it. Give us no columns with anything a reasoning person thought. Give us color, not thought. No one cared, Dave, what the folks in Tibet thought of your experience in their oppressor's country, China. My newspaper had quit being a newspaper that mattered. It was dead to me. So I quit. All I had ever wanted was to be a newspaperman, and now that was impossible because newspapers no longer existed. The Washington Post maybe, the Times. But not the newspaper paying me to be a columnist. It had gone from hiring the Times' Washington bureau chief as executive editor to firing him and bringing in a man from USA Today who thought a guy doing columns out of Washington ought not have a brain in his head. So I by damn quit. And that was another loss of who I was. I was disappearing. My mother, my wife, my grandson, my idea of journalism. Everything and everyone that had animated my life, dead.

So the girls basketball was more than just a night out. I told people that. I told them it was fun, it was pure. And it was light in the darkness. But it was more, more than even I knew. I loved all the obvious stuff that games give us, the athletic beauty, the competition, and Lord knows I kept telling myself that was why I did it and kept doing it when my big-time friends thought it was beneath me. Truth was, nothing was beneath me. As they say in countries where political enemies are here today and gone tomorrow, I had been disappeared. The girls began as a lark, yes, and I said it was all about the fun and the girls in motion reminding me of the wonder of life, its possibilities. And that is true. It was a good reason to do it. The great American financier J. P. Morgan once said there are two reasons people do anything: a good reason, and the real reason. A couple years in, maybe three or four even, I understood my real reason for writing about the Lady Potters. They kept me alive. Not in the sense of giving me a reason to live. But they made it possible for me to believe I existed. People I loved were gone. The newspaper work I loved was gone. I refused to be gone, to be disappeared. I wrote golf for *Golf Digest*, I wrote a dual biography of Ali and Cosell, and I was deep into a book on the *Washington Post*. I refused to go gentle into that good night. Damned right, I would write about girls basketball. It was fun, and grandmas stayed up late to read that stuff, and a buddy with a master's degree in education said, "Man, are you ever helping these young ladies lay foundations of high self-esteem that are so going to be important. I'm in awe." All good. Not my purpose, but good. My purpose was unbecoming. The writing was proof I existed.

16

FROM THE JOURNAL, A DAY IN OCTOBER 2018.

As alert today as she's been since the "help me, help me" day. As I went into room at 10:15, Debbie & Jasmine putting her on lift blanket and C was laughing. Why, I asked Debbie. I don't know, Debbie said. C said, "Let's go." Walked. Reached out to people, smiled at all, looked at rain outdoors, was "talking" all the time, couldn't understand most of it, but got a word now & then. Hooray! Fell asleep at lunch. 5 mins later snapped awake! Ritalin? Smiling, laughing, playful, teasing me w/offered food. Looking around, looked AT me, eye contact 1st in long time. Pulled me in for kiss. Happy!

MORTON MET RICHWOODS, AGAIN, THIS TIME IN THE CHAMPIONSHIP game of the Potters' Thanksgiving tournament opening the

2018–2019 season. My notes on the game were scribbles, scrawls, and other illegibles. Either it was a three-year-old's homework or a doddering geezer did it after four whiskeys.

On the way home, I stopped at Subway for a foot-long turkey with provolone, lettuce, tomato, and honey mustard. Add chips and a drink, ten dollars. Home, I let the dogs out, let the dogs in, fed the dogs. Ate half the Subway, put the rest in the fridge for breakfast. Turned on the Christmas tree lights. Charged up the iPhone, which had gone dead.

I was stalling against the time to write because then I would be forced to decipher those trembling-hand notes. Good grief, trembling in November? Richwoods did not take prisoners, and Morton refused to go gently. Opening week, with both teams unbeaten and a thousand Potterdome spectators raising a ruckus, the game became an Instant Classic.

After ending the Potters' three-year run the season before, Richwoods went on to win the Class 3A state championship. Now the Richwoods coach, Todd Hursey, said his team intended to go undefeated. He had good reason. He still had those big, strong, aggressive people.

Richwoods won, 64–61, in double overtime.

"Two best teams in the state," Hursey said. Becker said, "Great for November, I love it!"

In defeat, Morton made the case that the sectional loss eight months earlier was an aberration. The Potters led from early in the first quarter until the end of the third. They led by as many as 6 points. Down by 9 points with three minutes to play, they forced overtime. Twice, at the end of regulation and at the horn in the first overtime, Morton had a last shot to win.

Again, Becker wished for another chance at Richwoods. Again, he would get it in late February.

BIG-TIME PRESS BOXES SEPARATE SPORTSWRITERS FROM REAL PEOPLE. THOSE
of us on the girls high school beat are among the real people, cheek to
cheek in the bleachers, sometimes even among the opponent's people,
as when I drove to Monroe, Wisconsin, in early December.

I have no idea how I got to Monroe. It was 189 miles. I had dra-
gooned my trusty ace copilot John Bumgarner into riding north with
me so I would have company if (ha-ha) I got lost. We exited off I-39
near Rockford, drove through fog and rain and the gloom of night
descending at three thirty in the afternoon. We did a couple U-turns
in answer to that familiar I'm-lost feeling. I thought unkind things of
Google Maps, inquired at two gas stations, and delivered my sorry
wandering soul (and poor John) to Monroe High School in time to
see the Potters defeat the Cheesemakers, 57–40.

Best part was the Cheesemaker fan sitting by me. The old fella
said he liked to sit with the opposing team's crowd to learn about
their team. He came to love the Potters. "They're just out-hustlin'
our girls. We got size on 'em, but your girls are qui-eek." When it
takes two syllables to say how quick you are, you are double-quick.

"Your team is good," he said. "You see 'em play a lot?"

"Every game."

"You take notes all the time?"

"Yes, sir."

"How long since we scored."

"It was 24–23, Morton. Now it's 39–23. That's 15–0 in seven minutes and sixteen seconds."

"Over," he said.

How, you may ask, did I find my way home? I long ago learned
you do not need to know everything, but you do need to know how
to find out everything. I asked people to teach me Google Maps. I

asked: (1) Bob Becker's mother; (2) Tenley Dowell's mother; (3) the old man in the bleachers; (4) Bob Becker's daughter, Josi; and (5) my trusty ace copilot John Bumgarner, who said, "Don't ask me, I'm not smart enough to have a smartphone."

NOT ALL FOLKS IN THE BLEACHERS ARE AS KIND AS CHEESEMAKERS. AT the end of December, when a good Kentucky team beat the Potters, 62–51, I used my typing machine to propose a new high school rule. Any fan who believes he is a coach and shouts instructions from the bleachers must be removed, and soon.

I sat five feet in front of a Kentuckian who never shut up. His voice was its own thunderstorm. His primary genius advice to the Union Ryle High players was "BOX OUT!!!" Always delivered with three exclamation points.

He also specialized in "SHOOTER!" And "CORNERS!" And "TWO SHOTS! SHE WAS SHOOTING!!," at which point I turned to the fan/coach/referee across the aisle and said, "She was thinking of shooting, but she wasn't shooting, and thinking doesn't get you two shots," but by then the fan/coach/referee was back to roaring, "BOX OUT!!!"

I was too grumpy. I long ago decided I should never criticize sports fans. They made my job possible. Sportswriting got me cars and houses and all the golf balls I could hit into all the world's oceans. But now? Now I was being paid in Milk Duds. I was free to say these fan/coach/referee people are obnoxious. They should be voted off the island and invited back only as prey for venomous creatures.

Union Ryle, then 14–1, would go on to win the Kentucky state championship. Morton, at 14–2, still had Richwoods out there somewhere.

A WEEK BEFORE CHRISTMAS, I SAW SOMETHING IN BOB BECKER THAT I had never seen in Krzyzewski, Pitino, and Auriemma. Becker wore a tie that played Christmas music.

He had rummaged through a closet to choose a tie for the Potter-dome game against Limestone. He found a red tie with a snowflake pattern. "There's stuff in there," he said, "that's been there a long, long time."

The tie was dullish and wrinkly. It was older than any of Becker's players and perhaps two of his assistant coaches. It was the kind of tie sportswriters wear because its look will be improved by mustard stains.

Evelyn Becker cited her husband's history of wardrobe failures: (1) the time he turned a coat inside out because he could not get it fully off in protest of a referee's utter blindness, and (2) the two pairs of pants ripped in the backside area by vigorous sideline maneuvers. As for the night's tie, she took the Fifth. "I don't know anything about it."

Early in the game, assistant coach Megan Hasler was laughing. She heard music coming from that tie. The coach said, "Huh?" He held the tie to the ear of the nearest player, Peyton Dearing, who later reported, "Music, Christmas carols."

As Becker paced in front of the bench, he had brushed the tie against his shirt and somehow pressed a button in it. Each time he pressed the button, the tie played a different Christmas carol. At his postgame press conference (me with a notebook), Becker held the tie against my ear. I heard a story about a reindeer with a red nose.

CAME FEBRUARY 22, IT WAS RICHWOODS AGAIN. ANOTHER SECTIONAL championship game, three minutes to play, and I said, "Be still, my heart," and my heart said, "But how?"

Fate had this one in her hands. Anything could happen. Three minutes might have been three hours. Young people could grow old, old people could grow young. Tides could turn, the moon could fall from the sky. "Be still, my heart," I said again, and my heart said, "I get it. Shut up, already."

Nearly two thousand people filled the Illinois Valley Central High School gymnasium. We had waited in a long, cold line to get into the building. Then we waited in a long, hot corridor to get into the gym. I had walked into forty-three Super Bowls easier than I got into this sectional championship game. The wait was worth it.

Security had roped off the row of seats directly behind the Potters' bench. Becker saw us too far away, lifted the rope, and said, "Grandmas, down here!" Becky, Chris, Martha, and Joyce scooted down to spots where their knees bumped against the players. I did not hesitate. I scooted with them. If that made me a grandma, I was fine with that.

The Potters were down by eight to Richwoods until, suddenly, they were up by three with a minute and change to go. That minute and change might as well have been time without end. Hurry, Fate. Hurry, tell us whatever will be.

A minute and twenty-nine seconds to play and the Potters were up by three, which was nothing in that moment, for Fate is fickle. She could erase 3 points with the flick of a finger.

A minute twenty-nine to play.

Time-out, Richwoods.

At the Morton bench, Bob Becker was crouched before his five starters. He was coaching like a man with his hair on fire. Early on, upset with a referee's judgment, he did a Houdini trick to get out of his suit jacket and throw the thing down. Later, he had been so rambunctious that his tie hung sideways and his shirttail hung out the back. Now, he was crouched before his team, 1:29 to play, up by 3 points. At the top of his voice to players a foot from him, in all-capital letters with an exclamation point, he told Fate what she damn well could do with her fickle finger.

"THIS IS OUR FRICKIN' GAME!" he told his players.

In Grandma Row, we all felt better.

Richwoods did not score again. The defending state Class 3A champions, ranked No. 1 going into this game, winners thirty times in thirty-two games—the Peorians managed only one shot in that minute and twenty-nine. It was not so much that they failed. It was more that the Potters' Lindsey Dullard succeeded grandly. She made two extraordinary plays. In fewer than six seconds, at 0:23.2 and 0:17.7, the six-foot-one junior got offensive rebounds on free throws to keep the ball in Morton's hands. Then she made a free throw at 0:16.1 to give Morton a 4-point lead.

Final: Morton 46, Richwoods 39.

We saw two of the state's absolute best teams. Both had marquee players headed for Division I. Both played scrambling, unforgiving defense. Neither asked quarter nor gave quarter. More than once a Morton player stepped over a Richwoods girl at her feet, and more than once a Richwoods player stepped over a Potter at her feet.

The difference came on offense. Morton was good from outside (six 3s), Richwoods was good inside (only two of its seventeen buckets came from more than point-blank range). But the Potters were also good in close. Their freshman star, Katie Krupa, led all scorers with 21 points, 7 on free throws, the other 14 on power moves to the rim, scoring with either hand. Her opposite number, Richwoods' All-State senior Cam Taylor, scored 17 points (a good night, considering that Becker chose to double-team her all night).

Morton led at the quarter, 9–4, and at the half, 22–17. Richwoods' only sustained move came in the first five minutes of the second half. A 13–2 run in which Taylor scored 6 points jump-started a Richwoods move that gave it a 34–26 lead with seven seconds left in the quarter.

Seven seconds.

Not much time.

But enough time.

Enough time for Courtney Jones to get the ball to Dullard near midcourt.

Enough time for Dullard to put up a shot.

A shot that was in the air when the buzzer sounded.

And in the net a heartbeat later.

It had been thirteen minutes of game time since Dullard had last scored. She had been tentative shooting. She had fumbled away possessions. She had made passes that Richwoods intercepted. Then she banked it in from forty feet. Instead of being 8 down, Morton was 5 down.

"That shot got me going on the inside," Dullard said.

Still, Richwoods led, 36–29, with under seven minutes to play.

Then Tenley Dowell made a 3 and Dullard followed thirty seconds later with another 3 and it had become Fate's game, hers to decide.

After a Richwoods free throw, Dullard found Krupa inside to tie it at 37–all. Twenty-seven seconds later—you may notice a trend here—Dullard made her third 3-pointer in four minutes. Morton led, 40–37, with 3:50 to play. At 3:32, Richwoods made it 40–39 and never scored again, largely because of Dullard's two offensive rebounds that denied Richwoods two critical possessions in the last minute.

Those were big-time rebounds. As she stood in the middle slot on the left of the lane, Dullard saw that the Richwoods player to her left did not intend to box her out. Dullard circled around that girl and into the lane. And—thank you, Fate—the missed free throw bounced high and to the right. Its flight gave Dullard time to cross the lane and beat everyone to the ball. And fewer than six seconds later, she did it again.

"Oh, I wanted that ball," she said. "I wanted it so bad."

Krupa was thrilled, too. "Everything we had to do all season, the running, the conditioning, the practices—it's so worth it," she said. The freshman's 21 points came on the heels of a 26-point performance in the sectional semifinal. Becker said, "The sky's the limit for Katie Krupa."

The Potters were 30–3 for the season. The year before, you may remember, Richwoods won this game and went on to win it all. No reason to expect less from the Potters, who won their super-sectional game 70–43.

That gave them a chance to win a fourth state championship in five years. I saw their champs in 2015, 2016, and 2017. This team, now 31–3, was better. It could score in transition and out of sets, from down low or from out high. It could suffocate you with a full-court, zone-trapping press they call "mayhem." It could go man-to-man against your best people, and it could throw in a triangle-and-two if Becker decided to confuse you into submission.

"They're playing at a very high level now, at both ends," the coach said. "There's just a belief in each other, a trust, a connectedness. All fourteen players are in it as one. I just love it."

At Redbird in a semifinal, Morton 65, La Grange Park Nazareth Academy 51.

Most everybody in Morton had come to Redbird. Certainly, every high school kid, give or take a few advanced chemistry nerds, was at

Redbird. They came wearing red, the famous Red Sea of Morton. They came with posters and signs and big-head portraits of their heroines. They filled a third of the ten-thousand-seat arena and came to be rock 'n' rollin' fans.

And then the game started. And it got quiet. Nazareth Academy led after a quarter 11–4. Morton had 4 points, Morton averaging 65 a game. I made a note: "As bad as they can play. Scared. Hurried. Needs life."

Along came Tenley Dowell, at her best when it meant the most. Without her, Morton loses. With her—a game-high 23 points, game-high eight rebounds—with Tenley Dowell breathing life into every one of her teammates, they won going away.

At the end of the first quarter, Dowell said, "We have to score." So the six-foot senior attacked. She moved with long strides and great body control. Through traffic, she finished with either hand. Given a glimpse of an opening, she was gone. Fouled on that drive, she made a free throw. One point. Not much. But enough to suggest life. Then came some points. Two by Lindsey Dullard, 2 by Katie Krupa, 2 by Courtney Jones—and it was tied, 11–all, and the Red Sea came to life, roaring.

With 3:54 left in the half, Dowell put up a 3-point shot. "We have to score," she said, and she decided to do it on the season's biggest stage. She shot it and let her wrist fall loose, a shooter's pose, as the ball fell through the net, a shooter's reward. Dowell's only 3-point attempt, it was the climactic moment of a 10–0 run that put the Potters in front 14–11. They stayed there.

One more: Morton 35, Glenbard South 21.

It is so hard to be humble. Bob Becker wants it for his basketball teams. He calls it "humble swagger." It is a Midwest thing. As long as you are good at what you do—Becker calls it "consistent excellence"—just do it, no need to brag it up. The coach had preached humility for twenty years. But when a team wins a state championship and wins it the next year and the next and then, after a year away, wins it for a fourth time, they earn maybe a one-day exemption from humility. Here were the records in their last five seasons: 33–3, 33–3, 34–2, 31–2, and 33–3. That is 164 and 13, a .927 winning percentage. I cannot find my shoes that often. I called them "the Golden State Warriors, only with ponytails."

Katie Krupa stayed in character. She said, "It's surreal, so surreal, and I haven't really processed it yet. It was what we wanted from the first day on. I'm so proud of this team, my teammates, how hard we've worked all season. It's the Potter way."

The Potters won running against running teams, won physically against physical teams, and won shooting against shooting teams. Against Glenbard South in the championship game, they won walking. Save for its historic significance in the pumpkin patches of central Illinois, I would call the game a crushing bore.

Glenbard South ran a man-to-man defense and an offense designed to kill time for its defenders to catch a breath. The result was Xylocaine-ish. Morton's 35 points were the most Glenbard South had given up in its last eleven games.

Those 35 were the fewest Morton could have scored today. The Potters led after a quarter 17–3, and there was no reason to think anything would change. At halftime, it was 24–5. After that, I needed a snooze alarm on my notebook.

Besides the trophy presentation, the day did have one thrilling moment.

It came before the game when Bob Becker first walked onto the court.

He wore a bow tie, a red bow tie.

He had asked a fellow coach about Glenbard South. That coach ended his scouting report by saying, "Wear something good for the championship picture."

After all these years of blacks, browns, and beiges, Becker first looked at a red sports coat.

"I couldn't go there," he said. Humble swagger does not wear a red sports coat.

"But the salesman was really good."

Thus, the bow tie.

17

. . . .

A s 2019 turned to 2020, Cheryl was in decline. From my journal in November, a day at Restmor.

Cheryl strange at lunch, like seeing something at edge of table. Put spoon out there, then tapped on table with fingernails, screaming/ moaning, "NOOOO." Took her out as they brought sandwich and coconut pie. She took spoon and tried to scoop big piece of pie. I took spoon, she kept screaming, "NOOOO." Down to Evergreen lobby. Elese, an activities aide, tried to help, C shoved her with foot. She asked C if she hurt, in pain? No answer. Took her to her room. Outburst there. Looked at me with evil-as-hell look, "SHUT UP!" Closed her eyes, worn out. Five minutes of silence. Now did she want her sandwich? "Yes." Told her the nurses would help her, but she had to help them. She said, "OK." Told her take a nap, I'd see her later. "OK." Three stages of behavior now. Asleep, belligerent, sweet.

A night at the Potterdome, the night of Bob Becker's five-hundredth victory in his twenty-first season, the little guard Peyton Dearing held a huge portrait of the coach and signaled to the Potterdome's faithful that they should cheer. "Bobby B . . . Bobby B . . . Bobby B." As Robert Cantley Becker III sat on the bench, everyone in the building rose in applause.

"It's about the administrators and coaches and players," he said later. He called his wife, Evelyn, "the humbler and the motivator . . . the backbone . . . I love her to death," and he said winning all those games was a testament to "all the great parents and high-character kids."

In the locker room, the Potters were ready. They had gone shopping. "For two bucks each," Courtney Jones said, "we got six confetti poppers." BOOM! . . . BOOM! . . . BOOM! Six times, the poppers exploded confetti of many colors to the ceiling. As the confetti floated down on Becker's head, he went around the room to hug each player.

A night in Canton, Jones and Katie Krupa showed up with a whoopee cushion, two bucks at Cracker Barrel. "Coach, show us some dance steps," Jones said. Becker left the bench at halftime of the jayvee game to do it, and video shows him sitting down only to bounce up and look to see what the hell. "It was really loud," Jones said. "Like, *pfflurt.*" "You, Courtney Jones, I'm going to get you," Becker said, and Jones hurried out of the gym, headed for the safety of the popcorn stand.

Becker had his best team that winter. He had two Division I prospects, Katie Krupa and Lindsey Dullard, and six more who could play: Jones, Dearing, Maddy Becker, Olivia Remmert, Raquel Frakes, and Makenna Baughman. In December, at 10–0, I wrote that an undefeated season was possible. That would be thirty-eight victories and a fifth state championship in six seasons. Becker said, "Thanks for *that,*" meaning no-thanks for the reminder of pressures to come.

Here, Olivia Remmert! Of all things, she reminded me of a Larry Bird shot I had seen. After a running, stumbling, left-handed grenade toss of a shot that went in, Bird betrayed no emotion. He might have been a French Lick roofer who had hammered in the 1,765th nail of a 3,000-nail day. "I expect to score," he said. Not so much with Olivia Remmert. She was a five-foot-six senior who came off the Potters' bench, mostly for defense. But she made a Larry Bird–ish bucket in a super-sectional game. The left-hander moved with the ball from the right side of the lane across the paint. But she had such momentum on the drive that she found herself flying past the basket. What was a girl to do?

She threw up a get-rid-of-the-thing shot. "I saw it go over the rim, and I thought, 'Airball.'" She heard the crowd's roaring. "It was like they're saying, 'How did THAT go in?'" Remmert's prayer floated over the rim only far enough to fall into the net.

I tried to take notes on a night Jones scored 16. When Jones talked, she talked fast. Like . . .

"Itsallthoseyearsplayinginpractice . . ."

She went on.

". . . playingagainstgreatplayerslikeBrandiBispingJosiBeckerTenleyDowell . . ."

And on.

". . . andifIhadntplayedagainstgreatplayerslikethatIwouldntbetheplayerIam . . ."

Here a smile. Jones stopped talking to talk about what she had just talked about.

"Hey, that's a good quote," she said. "I should say that slower."

Please.

"If I hadn't played against great players like that," she said, "I wouldn't be the player I am."

THAT WINTER OF 2019 BECOMING 2020, HERE IS HOW BOB BECKER coached.

As if he had not already won five hundred games. As if he might never win another game. As if he might soon be reassigned to Potters football as a fifth assistant defensive secondary coach also in charge of lining the field on game days.

On a night in January, from Grandma Row, I heard . . .

"MOVE IT!"

"WHAAAATTT?"

"HELP SIDE! HELP SIDE, MOVE!"

"SHE'S HOOKING US! COME ON, HOOKING!!"

"WE'RE STANDING!"

(THE BOOMING LEATHERY SOUND OF A FOOT STOMPING ON HARDWOOD)

"GET THAT PASS!"

"LET'S GO, LET'S GO, GO, GO!"

"C'MON, MAN, SHE GOT HAMMERED!"

That last line in defense of the little guard Dearing led to a monologue that burned a zebra's ears and earned the coach a technical foul, after which he told the press (me), "Peyton just got HAMMERED on a drive and he didn't call it, just HAMMERED. I don't even care about the technical. She got HAMMERED."

THE LADY POTTERS OF THAT WINTER WOULD BEAT YOU ANY WAY YOU wanted to be beaten. Want to run? They will outscore you. Think you have a chance if you slow it down? They will not let you score at all. Bring big people and bang on the boards? Please, try it. The Potters only look angelic. They had one star out waiting to pass kidney stones, another out with a concussion, two out with ACL tears. And they kept winning. From Thanksgiving to the first week in March, this was the best of Becker's teams, ever.

Normal Community coach Marcus Mann said, "Morton's a great team, they're big, they're strong, they're unselfish with the ball, they can light it up with threes."

Geneseo's Scott Hardison said, "You've got the two D1 players [Dullard, Krupa] who can score inside and out. Courtney Jones is the glue that holds them all together. They've got the little left-handed guard who beats you [Dearing], and you've got Bob's daughter, Maddy, who'll make threes all day. And you've got the kid from Lewistown [transfer Raquel Frakes] who can jump out of the building. And if you somehow stop them inside, they get it out to one of their seven shooters. Defensively, they're great. I saw them play Bloomington here the other night, and I saw video of their Sycamore game last week. They played different defenses in both those games—and tonight they played another defense against us. We couldn't run anything we normally run. And they never stop. Late in the second quarter, we were winded and so were they. But Bob came out on the floor and shouted at his kids, 'They're tired—and we're NOT.' And his kids believed it."

Becker: "We can be scary, scary good."

Let us count the ways the Potters scared the bejabbers out of people.

Here is Peyton Dearing running . . .

ZOOOOOOOM!

In sunny months, Dearing was a big-time soccer star. One night in the winter, she took an inbounds pass maybe sixty feet from the Potters' basket. "I was open," she said. Of course. No one defends a little guard at the far end. And she said, "I'm fast."

She did that soccer ZOOOOOOOM thing.

"I'm fast and I'm open and I'm going to the goal."

In the winter, she had the ball on her left hand instead of her feet, and although the poor defenders were in the gym, it was as if they were running in combat boots, while Peyton Dearing, who was fast and open, saw the goal, flew hell-bent for leather across the midcourt line, past the 3-point arc at the left edge of the free throw circle, where she tilted right and bent down the lane and toward the hoop. In six seconds, from catching the pass to curling the ball off the board and into the hoop, Peyton Dearing had won a basketball game.

One night that winter, as long had been Lindsey Dullard's habit, she made three 3s, all from the left side. . . . And after a summer's work adding a powerful weapon to her offense, she showed it off by weaving her way through crowds for driving layups finished with either hand. . . . And she stole passes she had no business reaching and helped shut down the losers' inside offense. . . . And, the team's leading rebounder all season, she ripped them down with a strongman's authority. . . . And she made those passes that no one else imagined, one to Krupa a beauty and the best pass to a sliver of daylight with Dearing waiting to finish a fast break. . . . "We want to attack," Dullard said, "and we want to get into the paint. If we don't score in there, we kick it out and we ALL can shoot."

Everywhere you looked, everywhere the ball went, there was Courtney Jones doing Courtney Jones things. "She was all over the entire eighty-four feet by fifty feet," Becker said. On defense, the Potters' five-foot-seven senior point guard deflected passes and forced bad passes. Offensively, it was Jones's job, and she did it well, to control her team's pace and movement.

How many ways did I love Katie Krupa with the ball? Low on the left side, a step outside the paint. Three steps later, she was across the paint and going up for what was an impossible shot that only a precocious sophomore would think might be a good idea. Her back was to the basket. The rim was somewhere behind and above her.

But she went up and moved the ball from her right hand to the left. And with her left put the ball backward over her head where it kissed the glass tenderly and fell in.

Same night. Olivia Remmert! An opponent held the ball overhead. "Coach always says," Remmert said, "'Don't hold the ball over your head.'"

Remmert walked up behind that girl. Sneaky, soft afoot, she snapped her hands closed around the ball. Before the victim felt a thing, Remmert might have said, "Ah, so kind of you. Thank you very much. Yes, I will take the basketball." The pickpocketry changed that game.

Me at 10–0: They could go undefeated.

Becker at 16–0: "Our kids have got that champion's DNA."

Becker at 32–0: "We're striving for perfection." A smile. "That's not too much to ask, is it?"

BUT WAIT. BACK UP. AT 27–0, IN METAMORA, A MOMENT OF ROMANCE.

Brooke Bisping, a decade after her Potter days, now an assistant coach, alongside Bob Becker, casually, leaning toward him, as if to better hear him. She let her left hand dangle across her right wrist. Occasionally, she lifted that left hand toward the coach. One time she made a fist with that left hand and punched the air in front of the coach's face.

As Bisping moved her left hand, a light seemed to flash from that hand. A glint. A sparkle. You might even call it a diamond's twinkle.

From two rows behind Bisping and Becker, I recognized the source of that light. I violated all the journalistic stay-out-of-the-story rules by suggesting to Bisping, with a gesture, that she stand in front of Becker and use her left hand to scratch her nose with the ring finger.

She did that. Her face was alight with joy. Such fun.

Becker scratched his own nose to brush away whatever Bisping had seen there.

She did it again, the scratching thing. Only she moved from scratching to waving the ring finger in the light, and now Becker, finally yanked out of his basketball bubble, saw Bisping's fingers moving and he saw the twinkle and he understood what it meant and he laughed out loud. Then, more loudly yet, and in agreement with every woman who has ever considered men clueless, the coach said, "I'M AN IDIOT!"

He embraced Bisping, sixteen years after the freshman Brooke Bisping became a rising star on the first of Becker's dominant Lady Potters' teams, ultimately the leading scorer in Potters history and now Becker's assistant on four state championship teams.

Her fiancé, Tommy Rush, said of his proposal, "Nothing real dramatic. We'd been watching *Star Wars* on TV." He was a resident physician in radiology at OSF Hospital in Peoria. "I took the ring out and said, 'Will you marry me?' She said, 'Are you proposing?' I said, 'Yes,' and she said, 'Yes, yes, yes.'"

After the game, as Becker spoke in the locker room, senior forward Makenna Baughman noticed a glint, a sparkle, a flash of diamond's light on Bisping's left hand. A young woman and not a clueless man, Baughman whispered to Olivia Remmert, "Is that an engagement ring on Brooke's hand?"

Remmert shouted, "OH, MY GOODNESS!" and bounded over to Bisping, raised that left hand high, and all hullabaloo broke out.

AT 36–0 THE POTTERS REACHED REDBIRD FOR THE FIFTH TIME IN SIX seasons. In a semifinal, they defeated Springfield Lanphier 48–36.

They needed one more for a state championship. No team in their class had ever won it all five times. Only one had ever been 38–0.

Simeon was 33–3. They were big and strong up front, six foot one, six two, six three. Their defense was a widespread 2-3 zone covering sideline to sideline. Simeon's offense revolved around All-Stater Aneesah Morrow, a six-foot-one shooter who scored 27 a game, inside and out. Mostly, it relied on full-frontal attack. They ran at the rim, threw up a brick if they must, chased it down, and threw it at the glass again. They reached the championship game by beating four-time state champion Lombard Montini 48–40. They had twenty offensive rebounds and won in the paint 28–16.

Of Simeon, Becker said, "Daunting."

At nine in the morning, they were teenagers laughing. They had come to the Potterdome for a shoot-around before going to Redbird. They heard that voice.

I'm here to pick a fight. I'm here to pick a fight with second place. I have as much patience for second place as I do for flies in my soup.

But maybe you like flies in your soup. Maybe you like second place. Maybe you like that "you gave it your best, better luck next" malarkey they spoon-feed runner-ups. . . .

And you can spare me the "it's not whether you win or lose, it's how you play the game" bullshit. I guarantee you whoever said that lost the game. Moral of the story, come in first.

At 9:25, Becker said they needed to lock down the other team's star. He did not name Morrow. He used a number, "Number 24." He said Olivia Remmert would play 24 man-to-man. Remmert was a small, quick, persistent, earnest defender. Number 24 was a big, relentless, efficient scoring machine.

Remmert, a senior and a team captain, became a starter only late in her high school career, moving in when Raquel Frakes went down with a knee injury. She was now asked to do the Potters' most important individual job in the season's most important game. Stop Number 24, who all season had been unstoppable.

"I want you in her face every minute," Becker said to Remmert. "I want her to *hate* you."

He said, "Our three bigs will be here." He meant six-one Dullard, six-two Krupa, and not-that-big five-seven Jones. The coach wanted those three lined up across the paint, no more than a step in front of the basket, always with a foot in the paint. The idea was to keep Simeon's three bigs off the offensive board. Coaches call that a gimmick defense, a "triangle and two," the bigs at the base of the triangle, Remmert glued to 24 with the five-five Dearing flying wherever she was needed.

"We're going to let Number 2 and Number 4 shoot," Becker said. "If Number 2 makes four in a row, yeah, then we'll adjust."

At Redbird that afternoon, shortly before one o'clock, a writer at the press table asked me, "So, what do you think?"

"We'll know in ten minutes of real time," I said.

Soon enough, the Becker plan worked so well—Remmert breathing into 24's neck, the bigs keeping Simeon off the board—that the Chicagoans missed their first thirteen shots and got one offensive rebound in that time.

Morton led 16–0 with 1:54 left in the first quarter. The Potters had been beautiful in every way a basketball team can be beautiful. Ball movement, inside and out. Bodies slamming against rebounders to move them out. They had made three 3s in a minute, bang, bang, bang. Simeon finally scored with 1:41 left in the quarter.

It was 21–12 when Morton brought the ball upcourt in the last seconds of the first half. Simeon watched as Dullard stood with the ball three or four steps past midcourt, thirty feet out. Then, well, why not? Flat-footed, Dullard put up a shot.

With the ball in the air, the buzzer sounded, the red lights on the backboard lit up, and Dullard's shot fell through, nothing but net.

About two o'clock, the Potters ran smiling into the locker room, up 24–12.

By two thirty, Simeon was alive and well. "Maybe we ran out of gas," Becker said. The Potters were playing short-handed, without three of their top six players. Two season-long starters, Frakes and Maddy Becker, were on the bench with ACL tears, and Maggie Hobson, a starter the week before, played a minute on a twisted ankle. Slowly, but with a seeming inevitability, Simeon, bigger and stronger, used a full-court press to close the margin. (The box score would show Simeon with fourteen steals and Morton with twenty-one turnovers to Simeon's five.)

Simeon scored nine straight points early in the fourth quarter and led 38–37. Morton went up 42–38 and led again 44–43 with fifty seconds to play only to give up the game's last basket to one of the bigs they had kept off the boards all day. The girl had scored once in the game's first thirty-one minutes and fifty-seven seconds.

Simeon 45, Morton 44.

At 2:58 on a Saturday afternoon in March, they had lost the state championship on a bucket with three seconds to go.

Remmert sobbed under a towel. Krupa tugged the top of her jersey to her eyes. She moved toward a line of Potters, all crying. She stopped to embrace Dullard. Sports does that. It breaks your heart. Sometimes, not often but often enough that it happens to everybody, the other team goes ahead by a point with three seconds to play.

Dearing's eyes were lost in tears, her face red in the places it was not pale, the spotted colors of sadness and exhaustion. She was bent double on the team's bench.

At 3:35 that afternoon, Olivia Remmert walked out of the Potters' locker room. I touched her shoulder and said, "You were fabulous." The big-timer, Number 24, did not score in the first half and wound up with 8 points. Remmert said only, "I really thought we had it," and walked on.

I looked for Courtney Jones. With the Potters up by a point, she had missed two free throws with thirteen seconds to play, giving Simeon one last chance. Then, with three seconds to play, from the far end of the Redbird Arena court, Krupa threw a pass to Jones. She drove the ball downcourt. If there was a shot, she was to take it. I found her crying, and all I saw was the top of her head. She leaned into Becker's shoulder, the coach who had his arms around her and later said, "My heart aches for her." She did what he asked her to do. Take the shot, win or lose on that shot. Three seconds to do it, the clock ticking, two seconds, one, and Jones got to the free throw circle. She put up a shot, a "runner," "a floater," sometimes called a "teardrop." The ball was in the air and Jones's runner/floater/teardrop could have won the game. There would be hoorays through the night.

Since grade school, Jones had dreamed of being a Potter. She had played on two state championship teams. She put up a shot to win another, a shot in the air, the buzzer sounding, the board's lights red, all time gone, and Jones said, "I was just hoping it would go in."

It was four o'clock.

Outside, the team bus waited.

THE NEXT MORNING, AT A RECEPTION FOR THE TEAM IN THE POTTER-dome, Olivia Remmert stood at center court behind her team-mates and coaches. She was an honor roll student who once said she wanted to be a "biotech patent attorney," which sounded like a job not yet invented. Now she was a basketball player speaking to a couple hundred friends, family, and fans. Early in the quotation here, you will see that she said, "One second." She had stopped for a breath. So happy, she had to cry.

"I just want to start out with a thank-you to the community. You guys have supported us so much through everything. And I'm so happy that we're going to bring a sense of pride every day. From my freshman year through now, my senior year, you guys have been amazing.

"I just want to thank Coach for giving me the opportunity to be a captain . . . One second . . . I spent three years on the bench. I would've never changed that. I loved the bench. I'm sure all the *benchees* agree. It's the best time. We have so much fun. But my senior year, I was given the opportunity to become a leader on the scene, and I am forever thankful for that. I hope I was a good role model for all my other classmates.

"I learned so much from this program, and I will have memories and friendships that will never go away, that will be with me forever, and I am so thankful for that. And I think, last night, right when we were on the bus after the game, we spent a lot of time thinking, 'What if? What if we would've made that shot? What if we would've not checked them all over that time? What if we would've knocked down those three throws?'

"But it's so not about that. We had an amazing four years here. We did so much good in the community, on the court, off the court, everywhere. Our record, 135 and 9, is something I am so proud of, and something I am so thankful to be a part of. So, thank you guys for that. I love you guys. And thank you for letting me be a Potter for four years."

18

. . . .

IN THE FALL OF 2020, SEVEN MONTHS AFTER REMMERT'S STAR TURN, I got a phone call from Michael Karzis, a producer for CBS's news show *60 Minutes*. I had not run Ponzi schemes on my rich friends, nor had I thought to subvert democracy. What did *60 Minutes* want from me? Karzis said he worked with Jon Wertheim, a *60 Minutes* correspondent and long-time writer at *Sports Illustrated*. I figured they wanted guidance on a sports story.

No, no, Karzis said. They knew I had been places and done things, and after all that, I had gone home to write about a girls high school basketball team. "We were wondering," he said, "if you would agree to be a subject for one of our pieces."

Other years, it would make sense for *60 Minutes* to take a break from real-world travails and do a piece on a veteran sportswriter. They could use him as a way into a discussion of, say, how sports had gone global and become the playgrounds of millionaire athletes and billionaire moguls, some of them buddy-buddy with Vladimir Putin. Back in the day, I could have talked for hours. Now, off the grid, I knew nothing about nothing.

Also, I was in a bad place. The Jared book was about to be published. The title, *Leave Out the Tragic Parts*, was an ironic, optimistic quote picked from a story dark with tragedy. His death and the reporting of his life's descent into an addict's hell left me in sorrow. Cheryl, helpless, was in her fifth year at Restmor, her spirit gone, her body smaller and smaller, life disappearing. And now, of all times, *60 Minutes* calls.

A newspaperman from the start, I had never thought of working in radio or television. I did the occasional talking-head moments for local TV or an ESPN documentary. Generally, I begged off even those. The camera that never blinks made me nervous. Given ten seconds to produce a brilliant sound bite, I was a dim bulb. My inclination was to tell Karzis no thanks. But he said Wertheim sold the idea to the big bosses with one line: "Where you said, 'The Lady Potters are the Golden State Warriors, only with ponytails.'"

I knew about ponytails.

This was *60 Minutes*. OK. This could be fun. Suck it up, Kindred. Sure, Michael Karzis, let's have at it.

The *Los Angeles Times* sports columnist Jim Murray once said if he won a Pulitzer Prize, he would put it on the roof and turn a spotlight on it. Yes. Damn right. There is a time, even in darkness or maybe especially then, to yield to a moment of pleasure. Submit yourself to the tender mercies of a makeup artist named Krystyn, down from Chicago to make you presentable on network TV. (She used tiny scissors to clear underbrush from my eyebrows.)

The *60 Minutes* crew was nine deep. There were three producers, the on-camera talent, the talent behind the cameras, and the talent running the lights and sound. They gathered at the Palms Grill in Atlanta. They brought in lunch from Chubby's, a local tavern. They did hours of video in two trips to Atlanta and Morton. I sat with Wertheim for a two-hour interview in the restaurant where, a lifetime before, my little sister and I waited for a Greyhound to take us down 66 to Grandma Lena's tavern.

"Kindred in the Bleachers" was good stuff. The Karzis-Wertheim crew transformed my three ounces of charisma into thirteen minutes of storytelling about the somebody I used to be and the somebody I had become. That 60 *Minutes* program was No. 1 in the prime-time ratings with an audience of 9.2 million people. I watched it through my fingers. I saw glimmerings in my eyes that were tears when Wertheim said I had written that the Lady Potters had "saved" me. "My life had turned dark," I said. "They were light."

Then you hear from kind people. You hear from childhood friends Nancy, Tom, and Joe, who sat with you in grades 1 through 12. They chime in from Florida, California, and Mexico. Red Smith's son—Red, your hero—his son, Terry, asks for your email address. Hazel Porter's daughter—sweet, sweet Hazel, a Kentucky basketball fan who promised to hit you in the face with a pie if you didn't do better by the Wildcats, causing you to type, "Make it chocolate cream!"—Hazel's daughter, Patti, wishes her mother had seen the show. You hear from Scott Beard, the son of Ralph Beard, one of Kentucky's basketball greats, so often the subject of your columns.

You hear from Grantland Rice's great-niece, Elizabeth Champion, of Albany, Georgia. "Honey," she said, that honeyed voice taking me back to sweet Georgia, "I saw you on that television show, and I must say, your exuberance! It so reminded me of Uncle Grannie," and she invited me to Albany to speak to her book club, and she said we could go to Andersonville, down there near Albany, and see the Civil War prison, and she had so much of Uncle Grannie that she wanted to share, and we talked for an hour that day and the next day, too. What a thing, a kid from Atlanta, Illinois, on the phone with Grantland Rice's sweet-talking great-niece.

You hear from old pals in the business. To John Feinstein the news of your appearance is frightening: "The apocalypse is upon us." David Israel feels for you choking up in front of 9.2 million people and quotes Tom Hanks, almost: "There is crying in sportswriting." One of your editors, Glenn Hannigan, now a preacher, quotes you from the pulpit and you go, Oh, God, Feinstein's right.

People ask how you wound up doing this girls basketball thing. It would take a book to explain it. (This one, I hope.) You invoke the name of your generation's greatest sports broadcaster, Bob Costas. He once said he would like to return to his future and do Minor League Baseball. He sends along a message and says he still might work out of the Carolinas in *Bull Durham* territory.

A two-time Pulitzer winner at the *Washington Post*, Dana Priest, signs a note, "Dana, the German Shepherd." You had interviewed her for a book on the *Post*. You asked, "If you couldn't be a reporter, what would you be?" She was a CIA-intelligence-spymaster reporter with a reporter's DNA so dominant that she could think of no alternative to reporting. What on earth could she be? Finally, desperately, she said, "A German Shepherd?" And you think: me, too.

WHAT DOES A DISHEVELED OLD GUY DO AFTER HE HAS BEEN ON *60 Minutes*? First, he allows his eyebrows to return to their natural state. Then he moves on to recording Katie Krupa's winter, also known as the Lady Potters season of 2021–2022. We had seen her coming. As a sixth grader, she watched Brandi Bisping's teams. Now it was Katie Krupa's team and, for the fun of it, Katie Krupa's TikTok.

Krupa gathered her teammates early in the season to do a TikTok in which they lip-synched "What a Drag." That is a song with indecipherable lyrics (Sinatra man here) taken from a cartoon made in (maybe?) Japan. The TikTok was meant to be a onetime thing. But each time the Potters won this and that and another thing, Krupa enlisted her giddy teammates to do another laughing locker-room video.

The Potters won a regional, a sectional, a super-sectional and were headed to Redbird with a TikTok that had reached hundreds of thousands of viewers (and one confused/delighted old man).

The best part of all this was that Krupa could play. One example from an otherwise unmemorable game. Trapped with the ball under her own basket, her back to the baseline, she tight-roped across the paint, and with her left hand—her off hand—she put the ball high and soft off the glass. It fell through the net. Beautiful.

Better yet was a night a year earlier in Galesburg that caused me to shout-type "Katie Krupa! Katie Krupa!" I had been in Galesburg when Brandi Bisping scored 56 in two games. Krupa, in her junior season, nearly duplicated that performance; she had 52 points, 24 in the first game and 28 in the second on 18 of 32 field goals and 16 of 17 at the line.

Already busy as a senior, an All-Stater headed for Harvard, and a TikTok producer, Krupa moonlighted as my interview assistant. I often failed to get a word from Tatym Lamprecht, a five-foot-seven guard who had transferred to Morton from East Peoria High and quickly became an integral part of the Potters, as a strong defender and 3-point shooter. I once asked her, "How did that third quarter feel, making those threes?" Krupa, standing beside Lamprecht, interjected, "ELECTRIC!" That praise caused the shy Ms. Lamprecht to duck and hide. She then whispered two words. She said, "Yes, electric."

(For the record. Covid had shortened the Lady Potters' 2020–2021 season to conference games only with a first-ever conference tournament. The Potters won that tournament. Their season record was 14–3. Enough about that.)

No one expected much from the '21–'22 Potters. Krupa was the team's only scorer, its only rebounder, its only experience. Bob Becker had struggled through the Covid-interrupted season, unsure if he even wanted to coach anymore. With neighborhood rival Peoria High ranked as high as No. 1 in the state, it seemed the Potters would be sent home early, probably dispatched by Peoria High in the first round of postseason play.

And that is why they play the games.

In the regional final matching Peoria and Morton, it was 27–all with 18.5 seconds to play. Lamprecht had the ball, waiting to shoot a free throw. "I knew I'd make them," she said. "I KNEW." How did she know? "I imagined I was at practice." Swish the first, swish the second, and seven seconds later, eleven seconds to play, there she was again. Swish one, swish two.

Morton 31, Peoria High 27.

Jubilation, celebration, and other teenage frenzies ensued, so much so, and I promise you I had not seen this before—not even the four times his team won state championships—Bob Becker took hold of the regional championship plaque, raised it high over his players' heads, and then he, a Hall of Fame coach in his twenty-third season, began bouncing up and down as if suddenly seventeen and at Sycamore High again.

"Incredible," Krupa said. "Funnest game ever," Maggie Hobson said. "Ugliest, prettiest game ever," Becker said. "Fifteen turnovers the first half and we were up by ten. These kids have been so resilient all season, through injuries, finding a way, making a way. Tonight, going from ten up to four down and coming back at the end. Beating the number three team in the state that had been number one, that had beaten us here six weeks ago."

Suddenly, the Potters were making TikToks every week on a march to Redbird Arena that surprised most observers, including

Becker. On March 4, he said, "If you had told me we would get to the Final Four and we would win third place . . ."

Third in the state? With only one starter back from that depressing Covid season? Becker had started one of those sentences that usually ends by suggesting you would be crazy to think such a thing.

Instead, he said, "It would take a lot of work."

The Potters shared the Mid-Illini Conference championship. They won two of the state's most difficult regionals and sectionals. They defeated a No. 1 seed in a super-sectional to get to Redbird for the fifth time in six seasons.

Krupa was the team's best scorer, rebounder, defender, passer, motivator, cheerleader, and, probably, its best dancer in high heels. Without her, these Potters, who finished with a 29–6 record, might have been—oh, why go there? More fun to listen to Becker.

"This was Katie's team," the coach said. "She took ownership. As great a season as she had personally, she knew she couldn't do it alone. She had to make her teammates better, and she did that all season."

Because Lamprecht had played two seasons at East Peoria, where her teams seldom won, before becoming the Potters' second-leading scorer, I asked what the season had been like for her.

"A dream," she said.

In Morton's 55–41 victory over Bethalto in the third-place game, Krupa scored 23 points. In Morton's thirty-five games, she led the team in scoring twenty-six times. In her four seasons, the Potters went 113–13.

Here is as much information as a reasonable person needs on how the Potters did in the semifinals: La Grange Park Nazareth Academy 55, Morton 24.

19

· ·

F ROM OUR HOUSE IN THE COUNTRY, IT WAS 18.3 MILES TO RESTMOR. I
made the drive a thousand times. On the morning of the ninetieth
day of the coronavirus shutdown, a sign on the front door said ALL VIS-
ITORS RESTRICTED. I went to the parking lot just to be near the place.

I had walked with Cheryl everywhere in that building, rolling her
chair from the Woodland wing to Oaks to Evergreen, down all the
corridors, Almond, Hickory, and Chestnut. On the best days, we sat
in the courtyard, by the flowers, and felt the sun on our faces. The
Restmor people were good to us. John, Mike and Jeremiah, Elese,
Kalvin and Hope, Natalia, Kim, Lydia and Naomi, Katie and Bar-
bara, Jodi and Jamie and Lorrinda, Sally, Billie and Amanda, Chrys
and Chery, Diana, Angie, Caitlin, Mary and Maggie, Karen, Kelly
and Kelly, Amy and Nicole, Rhonda, Felicia and Margie.

Throughout that hellish year, Restmor was open and shut and
open again only to be shut again. I could not be with Cheryl for 101
days in one stretch and 68 days another time.

My mother had been a resident three years before dying there.
Cheryl arrived on December 18, 2015, and I became an ex officio

resident. I knew the nurses and CNAs, the cooks, the lunch crew, mechanics, and activities people. Covid had interrupted my lunch-time with Cheryl. Sheila, or Kelly, or Annette, or Chrys, or Lydia would call with how it went.

Elese sent a note. "I just have to share this. Cheryl made me late clocking out of work tonight. She was wide awake, WATCHING TV! I walked in front of her, BIG grin, reached up, grabbed my hand, started talking, a whisper, don't know what she was saying, but OMG. After spending some time, I had to leave. Cheryl put her lips together like to blow me a kiss."

Paulette asked, "Do you want to FaceTime Cheryl?" Ages before, we had written love letters by hand on paper that we put in envelopes with a stamp. Now, FaceTime? I wanted to sit with her and touch her and tell her Kim did a good thing with her hair this time. Still, FaceTime was better than no time.

That ninetieth day, I left the parking lot at one o'clock and headed home. Sheila, a CNA, called to say, "Cheryl had a full bed bath this morning, she got her hair washed, and she enjoyed it all. At lunch, she ate 100 percent. Her weight is 124.2. Today was a really good day. She's a happy camper."

MAKE OF THIS WHAT YOU WILL. I DID.

On a day in April 2020, I watched birds at our feeder. There was a cardinal, bright red, fluffed up against a breeze. On a line of sight under the cardinal, I saw the goose. A big guy. He was alone.

I had seen him often but always with his mate. Now he stood on a bare spot above the pond they shared. He seemed to be wondering where she was. He stretched his neck up and looked around. Five minutes, maybe ten. Just standing there. I had binoculars. I turned them toward the goose nest that a man had placed in our pond to encourage breeding. The nest was empty.

A goose separated from its partner may become so disoriented it never finds its way home. I worried about that lone goose. When at last he moved, it was to walk into weeds and down the embankment toward the pond. There he disappeared.

A few minutes later, in a windbreaker and boots, I walked out there. The goose's trail ended at the pond's edge. I was afraid there would be a sign—scattered feathers, maybe—that a coyote had been around. I saw nothing. I walked across the dam at the north end of the pond. There were tiny footprints in the mud, a fox's?

Then, on the bank by a rotted-out rowboat, I saw the lone goose. He heard me walking and he slid away into the pond. Then his mate came from the dark, weedy shallows at the dam's edge. She slid into the water beside him. They floated off together.

SEPTEMBER 24. CHERYL DID NOT FEEL GOOD. WE HAD NOT BEEN together since Restmor closed outdoor visits at the end of June. Such a beautiful day it was in the heartland. We sat under a flawless blue sky. Six or seven thin clouds moved east to west. They moved so slowly it seemed that we, not they, did the moving.

Odd, maybe, for a man who has been married to a woman forever, but at our appointed time that afternoon, 12:45 p.m., I was nervous. Not like first-date nervous. Just nervous. Maybe anxious is a better word. It had been sixty-eight days since I was last with the girl I saw outside Mrs. Brak's classroom, sixty-one years earlier.

I wanted to see her happy. Four times Cheryl had tested negative for the coronavirus, which in those scary times were a month's worth of happy news. Everyone at the nursing home, staff and residents, had tested negative for two weeks in a row. That run of happy news allowed Restmor to resume the family-and-friends visits done just outside the building's main entrance.

It was 1:19 p.m. when I put my hand on Cheryl's and felt hers close on mine. An aide apologized for being late. No need for that. In four years, ten months, and six days at Restmor, I had come to know the uneasy rhythms of Cheryl's life. It was enough, on this day, to be with her.

Two months later, on Thanksgiving Day, Cheryl tested positive for Covid-19. She never had a fever, never had a serious cough or breathing problem. But for five days, she refused to eat. She once spit out food she had taken in. Was it a loss of taste, of smell? She could not tell us. She spent twelve days in quarantine.

Her nurse, Cora, called. "Her appetite is still poor. But today she drank two health shakes, one at nine this morning and another at lunch. And she had ice cream. She does better drinking right now." The nurse also said, "Her eyes were wide open all the time. She had the best look I have seen."

Because she had not eaten well since she contracted Covid, and because I had been with her at lunch for four years, the nursing-home bosses thought my presence might get her back on track. As an "essential caregiver," each morning I dressed in a surgical gown, gloves, mask, and face shield. I would be in the same room with her for the first time in nine months.

Two thousand times, first for my mother and now for Cheryl, I had walked from the lobby desk to the Woodland wing, this time to Hickory's Room 406. I stopped before turning into the room, not sure if Cheryl would be out of bed. There she was, in her chair, asleep. She wore a sparkly blue top. Her hair was a dark gray moving into silver streaks.

I talked to her and held her hand. A CNA, Sheila, said, "She knows you're here." I wanted to believe her.

Lunch was a patty melt, mashed potatoes, green beans, a health shake, and strawberry pie. I sat on a corner of Cheryl's bed, my knees against her chair. I put a straw in the health shake and held it to her lips. When she first drew on the straw, I was happy. Maybe I could help. I put mashed potatoes on a fork. She took the potatoes and gravy quickly. Green beans, too. Maybe, a month after her Covid-19 infection, her appetite was coming back. She did OK at lunch but refused the patty melt. She needed to do better.

February 24, 2021, was our fifty-ninth wedding anniversary. I moved a spoon toward her lips. It carried a touch of vanilla ice cream. Maybe the cold would wake her up. With her eyes closed, she somehow knew it was coming. She did not wait. She opened her mouth, like a baby bird, and closed it on the ice cream.

Months had passed without that happening. Now she took that ice cream and another bite and a third. I said, "Sherri, we're doing good." I asked the Restmor dining room for half a chicken salad sandwich. I held out a bit of the sandwich so Cheryl might see it. She took over. She wrapped her left hand around my wrist and pulled my arm toward her until the piece of sandwich was at her lips. She took the bread out of my hand and fed herself. A minute later, she scrunched a second bit into her baby-bird mouth.

Maybe she had fed herself sometime in that lost year, but probably not. She was losing weight daily, was awake only for minutes at a time. I knew the end was near, and I chose not to think of that on that very good day, our wedding day.

THE LONG CHILL OF WINTER GAVE WAY TO SUMMER. CHERYL HAD stopped eating. Covid had robbed her of whatever vitality the stroke had allowed her to keep. She had become small under the bed covers. She was so fragile she no longer could be lifted from the bed and placed in her Broda chair. The risk of hurting her was too great. I had ordered hospice care to relieve her of any pain she might know.

The morning of June 24, I sat on the edge of her bed, watching her sleep, hearing her breathe. I kissed her forehead and said, "I loved you from the start, I love you now, and I will love you forever." I left for home.

Two hours later, Cora, the nurse on Hickory, called. "Cheryl passed at 2:05," she said. "Do you want to come in and see her?"

"Thanks, Cora, no. I said my goodbyes."

The funeral home in Atlanta was two blocks from where I had first seen Cheryl Ann Liesman standing in the light outside the Palace movie house. I had been in that funeral home for my father and my mother, and now I was there for my friend, my lover, my wife, who had been bright, strong and resourceful, kind, thoughtful, generous, loving, and more beautiful every day.

One of those days, we were in Springfield, Massachusetts. A limousine picked us up at the hotel. From the limousine, we walked on a red carpet into the Naismith Basketball Hall of Fame. We stood at the top of a long staircase to be introduced to the crowd below. Cheryl held my hand and said, "I feel like Cinderella."

ACT THREE

20

● ●

AFTER CHERYL'S DEATH, GRIEF BECAME MY SILENT COMPANION. I was sad. I missed her. The years in the nursing home, I saw her every day. I could sit with her, talk to her, touch her, and every day I hoped for a better day than the day before. But now she was gone. I could never again be in her presence. Now there was an absence, dispiriting and always there. I called it the presence of her absence.

I told my psychologist Dr. Sue about the daily sadness.

"I don't cry," I said. "But I feel empty."

"Talk to Cheryl," she said.

"Talk to her?"

"Yes, really," Dr. Sue said. "Go ahead. Talk to her. It's good. It's healthy."

Let's call this Scene One of Act Three. I drove to Atlanta. I drove forty miles south through cornfields and bean fields before I saw the smiley-face painted on the canary-yellow water tower at the south edge of town. Past the old high school. Stopping at the ball diamond to say hey to rocks that caused all those bad hops in Act One. I sat at the kitchen table where I had typed *Stanley Frank Musial.* I said,

"Remember our first dance here, Sherri?" One soft summer night, we danced around that kitchen table with Johnny Mathis singing (on a 45 rpm record, 'twas the fifties). *Until the twelfth of never, I'll still be loving you. Hold me close, never let me go.*

Every summer and Christmas, wherever we lived, we returned to Illinois. We would drive to land that Cheryl's father had farmed in a community called Straight Row, just north of Lincoln. She called out the names of her childhood friends, Rita, Bonnie, and Sarah, and showed me where they had lived. "And right here," she said, pointing to a lone oak tree along a gravel road, "our one-room schoolhouse was right here."

Along old US Route 66, we stopped by the sandy remains of a dirt road that disappeared into underbrush covering a drainage ditch. We had been on that road hundreds of times. It took us through a tunnel under railroad tracks. Now the tunnel was backfilled with dirt; only its arch of concrete proved it had existed. We knew her farmhouse was gone, left empty for years, finally destroyed by fire. I went to those places after the funeral, to be with her again, talking in the moonlight. I remembered those nights, of course I did. We did what boys and girls do in cars late on winter nights when they are seventeen.

I read letters we had written in the sixties, mine from Illinois Wesleyan, Cheryl's from Memorial Hospital. I framed a picture of her posing by a fountain outside Buckingham Palace, sometime in the seventies, a wife and mother and my forever-girl Sherri, sure of herself, sexy as hell. When Broadway did a 2022 revival of *Funny Girl*, I heard Lea Michele sing . . . *People who need people are the luckiest people in the world* . . . and I remembered summer nights in 1962 putting quarters in Babe & Jim's jukebox to hear Barbra Streisand sing that song for us . . . *A feeling deep in your soul says you were half now you're whole.* . . . (Babe & Jim's, a dimly lit roadhouse, great steaks, long gone.)

Happy memories began to fill the hollowed-out parts. Act One put us in the Eiffel Tower for dinner. We saw *The Phantom of the Opera* in London, New York, and Los Angeles. We walked up the steps of the Lincoln Memorial. We drank tea in London, wine in San Francisco, and beer in Munich. We slept in Rome, Zurich, Madrid, and Stockholm. We stood under Michelangelo's ceiling, we smiled at Mona Lisa, and we watched Secretariat fly. In Act Two, being old kids, we sat in Grandma Row to watch the Lady Potters be real kids.

Soon enough, Cheryl appeared in a dream. I did not see her and did not hear her. But she was there. I felt her presence. She was with me, no longer absent.

At the local Walmart one day, I went looking for birdseed. A man in the gardening section, Jim Carius, asked about Cheryl and we talked long enough for him to tell me he had been a basketball and baseball coach at Deer Creek, a village near Morton. Back then, he said, the school had no money for chalk on the baseball baselines. "The principal told me to use buttermilk, it'd do." Jim laughed. "Don't you know, before we could play the game, birds ate up the baselines." An old, disheveled guy himself, Jim said he was sorry about Cheryl and said he had read my Lady Potters stuff. "You gonna keep doing that? Should. Keeps you young."

Then came the best part. Let's call this Scene Two of Act Three. A year and a half after the funeral, I went to Carly Crocker's wedding, Carly the daughter we never had.

Such a wedding . . . outdoors an hour north of Minneapolis on December 16, 2022 . . . under pine trees a hundred feet tall . . . with snow floating down.

Tiny snowflakes with icy centers, brilliant as diamonds, gathered on the train of Carly's wedding gown and rolled around on the brim of Ed McGinty's black cowboy hat. In this snow globe made real,

I sat with my sister, Sandra, in the second row of guests, Sandy an unofficial grandmother of the bride, her babysitter from six weeks on.

It had been fifteen years since Carly had announced in Sandy's kitchen that she would not be a cheerleader. "No," she'd said that day, "I'm going to be the one they cheer for." Cheryl and I moved to Illinois in time for Carly's junior season as a Lady Potter. An undersized forward, she was the first girl off the bench for Bob Becker's team that went 31–3 her senior year. After graduation from the University of Iowa in 2016, she applied for entrance to an Emergency Medical Treatment training program. I wrote a letter of reference attesting to her strength, resourcefulness, and courage, adding: "She is not my daughter, nor is she my granddaughter, but the full measure of my respect and admiration for Carly is such that she, and she alone, could get away with saying to me, a young, strong, vital man, 'Gramps, time for your milk and cookies.'"

Carly sailed through that EMT program and became a paramedic in the Hennepin Emergency Medical Services department serving over one million residents in Minneapolis. She wore a bullet-proof vest to work, and one day she ran into the tall, dark, and handsome Ed McGinty. I did a reporter's work on this. It is a paramedics-meet-cute story.

"I was trying to stay under the radar, being a new medic in a major metropolitan area, especially a young, blonde female," Carly said. "But that's even harder when your cheeks are shining bright red from just being in the same room with the guy. Words were hard and I could barely think straight; after one shift, I was so flustered by Ed standing at the time clock that I went home with narcotics in my pocket. I had to drive back, only to find him standing next to the drug cabinet. I can only imagine how embarrassed I looked."

Ed: "Our first date went off without a hitch. Who wouldn't love a nice Applebee's meal followed by a University of Minnesota hockey game?! Gophers won in overtime, and I knew right away that I had found someone special."

Two or three years of adventures. Beaches. Mountains. In the summer of 2021 on a twelve-mile hike in Glacier National Park, Carly thought Ed might propose. . . .

Carly: "He was soooo grumpy because of all the people on the trail and how hot it was. A proposal went way off my radar. Since we had been hiking alone, we used self-timer for photos on my phone, and I had no reason to be suspicious when he said we should do another self-timer in this beautiful location by a glacier. I put ten seconds on the timer and sprinted back to pose.

"He began kneeling and I started to scold him, 'What are you doing?' And then it clicked. He said, 'Will you marry me?' I asked, 'Are you serious? Are you kidding me? Are you joking? Is this real?!!' Ed just smiled and laughed and patiently knelt until I finally registered that it was a yes or no question. One big YES and I was SO SHAKY I had to sit down. A moment and feeling I will never forget! A stunning ring! I'd have been happy with a ring of twine!"

At the wedding ceremony, Carly promised Ed, "I vow to keep you wild, even when you have every urge to play it safe." Ed's vows included a quote from his beloved on how to handle the injuries and stress that are part of a paramedic's life. "Drink some water and suck it up," Carly said. "You'll be fine."

I laughed on hearing Ed repeat that so-Carly line, and so did she. No bride with diamond snowflakes on her wedding gown ever looked happier. Whatever else might happen, and God only knows the joy and pain to come, Act Three was off to a beautiful start.

I talked to Cheryl . . .

Sandy and I drove up from Morton, around four hundred miles, seven or eight hours, through Iowa and straight north and past Minneapolis. We stayed three nights in an Airbnb in a suburb called

Excelsior. It looked like an upscale place you'd find along a beach in California. Great little lunch place, the 318 Café, where half the customers seemed ready to go ice-skating; the rest might have been university professors on Christmas break.

Bob Becker and his wife, Evelyn, left Morton immediately after a Thursday night game and got here Friday noon. "I've had lots of players," he said, "but Carly was one of those kids you're going to remember forever. A good player, and a good person, a fun kid to be around, lots of antics, a fun kid to coach. It was awesome to see her so genuinely happy. This was storybook."

It was thirty degrees today, but there was no wind at all and no one thought it was cold at the wedding. Sandy and I are worn out and will go home tomorrow morning. We'll miss seeing Carly and Ed open gifts, but it's supposed to really snow tonight and get to four below. I want to get ahead of that if we can. So we'll be on the road by seven in the morning. We'll be careful.

Sherri, you'd have just loved this. It was beyond beautiful. Carly was gorgeous, of course, and the wedding site was a dream, Carly and Ed standing in front of perfect rows of pine trees a hundred feet tall with snow on the branches from top to bottom. A writer guy might call it a cathedral of pines. The preacher came with marital advice. "Be quick to forgive, be quick to ask for forgiveness." (That, we did!) Then it began to snow. Not the fluffy stuff you like, but falling straight down, tiny bits, icy. I wanted to hold your hand.

I love you, Sherri. See you soon.

ACKNOWLEDGMENTS

LOVE AND THANKS TO MY BEAUTIFUL SISTER DEAR, SANDRA, WHO
remembered everything about our childhoods in Atlanta, Illinois,
and loved Mom, Cheryl, and me when we most needed it.

Thanks to every young woman who played for the Morton Lady
Potters in my time, every one beautiful, and thanks to their parents
and grandparents.

Thanks to Bob Becker for his humble swagger, his cooperation in
all things, and for creating basketball teams a joy to watch. Thanks
to Evelyn, Bob's girl on the stadium steps and the mother of two
great Potters, Josie and Maddy.

Thanks to Becker's assistant coaches over the years, Bill Davis,
Megan Hasler, Brooke (Bisping) Rush, Rodney Knuppel, Erin
(Chan) Kay, Claire Schmitt, and Dakota Neisen.

Thanks to Dave Byrne, the original webmaster at Mortonlady
potters.com, who gave me the sweetest Milk Duds deal in sportswriter history, and thanks to his successor at the website, Matt Jones.

Thanks to my buddies on Grandma Row: Becky, Chris, Martha,
and Joyce.

Thanks to John and Karin Bumgarner, always there at midcourt,
always there for me.

Thanks to everyone at Apostolic Christian Restmor nursing home, angels all.

Thanks to media types who saw a story in this adventure. Jim Mattson. Kurt Pegler. Ed Sherman. Tony Rehagen. Seth Davis. Jeff Pearlman. Todd Jones. The 60 *Minutes* men, Jon Wertheim and Michael Karzis.

Thanks to bosses who paid me when I would have paid them. Jim Barnhart. Earl Cox. George Solomon. Van McKenzie. Frank Deford. John Rawlings. Jerry Tarde. Mike O'Malley. Sam Weinman.

Thanks to friends who pulled me off the ledge. Gary Pomerantz, every day of every week of every month for years. Verenda Smith. Tom Callahan. Jane Leavy. John Feinstein. Juliet Macur. Jeff Findley. Jim Knecht. Stew Salowitz. At Illinois Wesleyan University, the archivist who knew where to find everything, Meg Miner. My IT guru, Chad Engel. My agent, David Black, who could sell stoves at a shipwreck.

Thanks to Clive Priddle and Ben Adams of PublicAffairs, who bought *Leave Out the Tragic Parts*, on my grandson, Jared, and this one also from the heart. Also at PA, a bow to Kaitlin Carruthers-Busser, Lindsay Fradkoff, and Brooke Parsons.

Thanks to the Geezers for being the Geezers. Dan Jenkins, Blackie Sherrod, Furman Bisher, Edwin Pope, Dan Foster, Bill Millsaps, Frank Luksa. And every old sportswriter who showed a kid how to do it. Red Smith. Jimmy Cannon. Jim Murray. Dave Anderson.

I am a reporter trying to write better than I can. I needed help on this one. I leaned on the woman I met outside Mrs. Brak's English class when we were seventeen. She is beside me now. I love you, Sherri.

Credit: Vicki Raider

Dave Kindred has been a columnist for the Louisville *Courier-Journal*, the *Washington Post*, the *Atlanta Journal-Constitution*, the *National Sports Daily*, *Sporting News*, and *Golf Digest*. Kindred is the author of several books, including *Heroes, Fools and Other Dreamers: A Sportswriter's Gallery of Extraordinary People*, *Around the World in 18 Holes*, *Morning Miracle: Inside the* Washington Post; *The Fight to Keep a Great Newspaper Alive*, and *Sound and Fury: Two Powerful Lives, One Fateful Friendship*.

Kindred is one of only two writers who have earned sportswriting's three highest honors: the Red Smith Award, the PEN America ESPN Lifetime Achievement Award for Literary Sports Writing, and the Dan Jenkins Medal for Excellence in Sportswriting. He also has won the Naismith Memorial Basketball Hall of Fame's Curt Gowdy Award (for outstanding media contributions) as well as a National Headliner Award for general-interest columns. He is a member of the National Sports Media Hall of Fame. He lives in Illinois.

PublicAffairs is a publishing house founded in 1997. It is a tribute to the standards, values, and flair of three persons who have served as mentors to countless reporters, writers, editors, and book people of all kinds, including me.

I. F. STONE, proprietor of *I. F. Stone's Weekly*, combined a commitment to the First Amendment with entrepreneurial zeal and reporting skill and became one of the great independent journalists in American history. At the age of eighty, Izzy published *The Trial of Socrates*, which was a national bestseller. He wrote the book after he taught himself ancient Greek.

BENJAMIN C. BRADLEE was for nearly thirty years the charismatic editorial leader of *The Washington Post*. It was Ben who gave the *Post* the range and courage to pursue such historic issues as Watergate. He supported his reporters with a tenacity that made them fearless and it is no accident that so many became authors of influential, best-selling books.

ROBERT L. BERNSTEIN, the chief executive of Random House for more than a quarter century, guided one of the nation's premier publishing houses. Bob was personally responsible for many books of political dissent and argument that challenged tyranny around the globe. He is also the founder and longtime chair of Human Rights Watch, one of the most respected human rights organizations in the world.

•　　•　　•

For fifty years, the banner of Public Affairs Press was carried by its owner Morris B. Schnapper, who published Gandhi, Nasser, Toynbee, Truman, and about 1,500 other authors. In 1983, Schnapper was described by *The Washington Post* as "a redoubtable gadfly." His legacy will endure in the books to come.

Peter Osnos, *Founder*